Tourism, Aviation and Hospitality Development During the COVID-19 Pandemic

Yuhua Luo · Hongmei Zhang · Jinbo Jiang ·
Doubou Bi · Yujing Chu
Editors

Tourism, Aviation and Hospitality Development During the COVID-19 Pandemic

Editors
Yuhua Luo
University of the Balearic Islands
Palma, Spain

Jinbo Jiang
South China University of Technology
Guangzhou, China

Yujing Chu
Shanghai Normal University
Shanghai, China

Hongmei Zhang
Shanghai Institute of Tourism
Shanghai Normal University
Shanghai, China

Doubou Bi
South China University of Technology
Guangzhou, China

ISBN 978-981-19-1660-1   ISBN 978-981-19-1661-8 (eBook)
https://doi.org/10.1007/978-981-19-1661-8

© The Editor(s) (if applicable) and The Author(s), under exclusive license to Springer Nature Singapore Pte Ltd. 2022
This work is subject to copyright. All rights are solely and exclusively licensed by the Publisher, whether the whole or part of the material is concerned, specifically the rights of translation, reprinting, reuse of illustrations, recitation, broadcasting, reproduction on microfilms or in any other physical way, and transmission or information storage and retrieval, electronic adaptation, computer software, or by similar or dissimilar methodology now known or hereafter developed.
The use of general descriptive names, registered names, trademarks, service marks, etc. in this publication does not imply, even in the absence of a specific statement, that such names are exempt from the relevant protective laws and regulations and therefore free for general use.
The publisher, the authors and the editors are safe to assume that the advice and information in this book are believed to be true and accurate at the date of publication. Neither the publisher nor the authors or the editors give a warranty, expressed or implied, with respect to the material contained herein or for any errors or omissions that may have been made. The publisher remains neutral with regard to jurisdictional claims in published maps and institutional affiliations.

This Springer imprint is published by the registered company Springer Nature Singapore Pte Ltd.
The registered company address is: 152 Beach Road, #21-01/04 Gateway East, Singapore 189721, Singapore

Preface

This proceedings book is a collection of the selected papers of the 10th International Conference on Tourism and Hospitality between China and Spain (www.china-spain.org) held in Shanghai both online and on-site, November 6–7, 2020.

Starting from early 2020, a pandemic of COVID-19 spread to all the countries over the world. Human society experienced an unprecedented disaster that has never been in the history. The pandemic changed every aspect of social life and all the areas of the economy. The tourism industry together with the air transport industry may be the most severely hit. The two industries have been facing a dramatic crisis. The tourism sector in China, where the outbreak occurred, was hit first and recovered first. The experience of China is no doubt a successful path for the tourism industry recovery in other areas in the world.

The first part of this book consists of papers that address the impact of COVID-19 pandemic on Chinese tourism and air transport industry. The strategy and measures for recovery are reported. Instead of being pessimistic, some sectors within the Chinese tourism industry see the opportunity from the crisis. For example, the heritage tourism, especially regional heritage tourism, has become a new trend of tourism consumption because of its relative niche, rural characteristics with security. On the other hand, air transport is affected severely worldwide. Border closures, travel bans, lockdowns and quarantine for incoming passengers have affected the air transport to reach a temporary standstill. One of the papers describes the historical development of air connectivity between China and Spain and the change under the COVID-19 pandemic.

Papers in the second part of the book concentrate on how destination image affects tourism motivation and the new way of marketing under the pandemic atmosphere. One of the papers examines the image of Spain as a tourist destination for the Chinese market before and after the pandemic outbreak. It suggests improving the security and attractiveness of the destination image during the pandemic, thereby emphasizing the special concern over health issues. In another paper, language proficiency is treated as an important factor that affects the perception of the destination image. Spanish language proficiency is becoming one of the most requested professional skills due to its relevance in the labour market. As a result, Spain has become an ideal tourist destination for Chinese students to improve their Spanish skills and cultural knowledge. The paper gives recommendations for improving the attractiveness of Spain as a destination to prepare a future wave of Chinese tourists once the COVID-19 pandemic ends.

The tourism development under both the normal situation and the COVID-19 pandemic is the focus of a couple of papers in the book. The marine tourism development in the Zhoushan island shows how the marine tourism industry can be developed in the context of a free trade zone. The resident perception about the tourism development in the minority area and a scenic spot are studied, respectively, in two papers. The authors conclude that the perception of the residents towards tourism activities can deeply affect tourism development. The factors that affect the residents' perception are analyzed and identified. These can undoubtedly help the further development of the tourism industry.

In this book, there are also a few papers dedicated to hospitality sector development such as hotel human resource management, overcoming the staff job burnout etc. The job burnout issue is even more severe during the pandemic. Strategies for dealing with these problems and reducing the turnover rate of employees in the hotel industry are suggested.

Analysis of the tourism research situation among the academic researchers is a great concern of some of the authors in the book. What are the hot topics in the research on tourism development, what methodologies do they use for research. All these can be a good reflection of the tourism development itself. Up-to-date visualization technology has been applied in these studies to show the research trends and the hot spots in tourism development research.

International tourism is experiencing a total cessation situation in many countries, because of the closure of national and international borders and airports since the outbreak of COVID-19 pandemic. Up to today, the pandemic has not been showing its termination. We have to face many factors in tourism development that are difficult to predict due to the great uncertainty caused by the pandemic. The analysis of the situation in the tourism, air transport and other related industries will help to define new strategies and countermeasures to answer the challenges from this completely new situation. We hope that the publication of this book can contribute to the joining effort of human battle to fight this terrible virus in this special moment of human history. It may serve as a "snap-shot" record of this special moment for our future generations in many years to come.

The series of our conferences (www.china-spain.org) is aiming at facilitating the exchange of research and development experience in tourism and its related industries. We will continue our efforts together with the researchers and practitioners in the world.

Seattle, USA	Yuhua Luo
Shanghai, China	Hongmei Zhang
Guangzhou, China	Jinbo Jiang
Guangzhou, China	Doubou Bi
Shanghai, China	Yujing Chu
January 2022	

Contents

The Influence of the COVID-19 Pandemic on Tourism and the Countermeasures for Recovery in China 1
Qiuyue Pan and Yingying Chen

The Air Transport Network Between China and Spain During the Covid-19 Pandemic 15
Marta Guerrero Socas

COVID-19 Pandemic Impacts on Chinese Outbound Tourism and Survival Strategy 35
Dongmei Ren and Dolores Sánchez-Aguilera

New Opportunities of Heritage Tourism Under the COVID-19 Pandemic: A Case Study of Zayton Port 51
Chengyuan Wei, Xia Cheng, Xinru Liu, and Jianzhong Li

Effects of Destination-Language Proficiency on Tourists' Motivation 67
Yinan Li, Raúl Hernández-Martín, and Pablo Rodríguez-González

Destination Image of Spain Perceived by the Chinese Tourists During the Pandemic 85
Dongmei Ren and Dolores Sánchez-Aguilera

Exploration and Innovation of Zhoushan Marine Tourism Industry in the Context of Free Trade Zone 101
Xu Guo and Park Jaepil

Minority Women's Willingness to Participate in Tourism Poverty Alleviation—A Case Study 119
Yujing Chu, Songmao Wang, Yang Yang, and Tong Ding

Residents' Perception and Its Impact on Community Participation of Tourism Development 139
Lihua Cui, Xinze Song, and Minhui Song

Communication Patterns for Traditional Chinese Culture in Tourism 153
Liping Ren

Relationship Between Emotional Intelligence, Job Burnout and Turnover Intention of Hotel Staff 173
Xueying Lu, Jiajue Wang, and Limin Zhao

Informal Tourism Employment for Poverty Alleviation Under the Covid-19 Pandemic: Research Advances and Novel Challenges 191
Muchun Li and Xingnan Wu

Predicting Green Hotel Visit Intention of College Students Using the Adjusted Theory of Planned Behavior 205
Yiwei Zhang, Aiping Xu, and Lin Gu

Tourism Research on National Parks and Protected Areas 219
Donghui Lu, Xiaoyu Wang, and Hongxi Zhang

Research Hotspots on Inbound Tourism from the Perspective of Globalization 245
Wei Wei, Kehanfei Li, Sandy Chen, and Xin Xu

The Influence of the COVID-19 Pandemic on Tourism and the Countermeasures for Recovery in China

Qiuyue Pan and Yingying Chen

Abstract The scale of the COVID-19 pandemic is unprecedented in the human history. Due to the impact of the COVID-19 pandemic, the tourism industry is facing a very severe crisis. Change in consumer behavior indicates a new transition point of the tourism industry. At the same time, new opportunities for further development are emerging. By our macro data analysis and the questionnaire investigation, this paper aims to discuss the impact of the pandemic on the tourism industry, the countermeasures of the tourism recovery and the new ways for development. The paper expounds the strategies to deal with the crisis by both governments and the tourism enterprises. In particular, the paper shows the importance of recovering the tourist confidence. New tourism formats are suggested together with other measures such as developing new tourist routes and products etc. These could meet the needs of tourists seeking safety, health and reliability. Online travel, as a new tourism format, can meet the need of other groups of traveling consumers who need to stay home.

Keywords Tourism crisis · Strategies for recovery · New tourism format · Online travel

1 Introduction

COVID-19 (Novel Coronavirus), named by the World Health Organization (WHO) on January 12, 2020, causes highly contagious infections. Confirmed cases have been reported around 128 million worldwide up to date as of March 31, 2021. Severe cases can lead to death due to severe complications such as acute respiratory distress syndrome (ARDS) sepsis. In the case of Wuhan, in response to the rapid spread of the virus, long-distance bus and subway passenger transportation were suspended from 10:00 am on January 23, 2020. The airport and railway stations were all closed

Q. Pan · Y. Chen (✉)
College of Culture and Tourism, Xiamen University of Technology, Fujian, Xiamen, China
e-mail: 515615950@qq.com

Q. Pan
e-mail: qiuyuepan@sina.com

at the same time. Subsequently, 31 provinces (autonomous regions and municipalities directly under the Central Government) in China announced that they entered the state of the first level of emergency response. All localities have taken relevant measures such as closing down urban residential areas, tourist attractions and entertainment locations, shopping malls, and the majority of public areas. Tourism related hotels, exhibitions, catering, retail and other industries have been hit hard and suffered a major economic loss. At the same time, some overseas media also took the opportunity to hype, greatly damaged the image of the country's tourist destinations.

It was well known that tourist industry has been affected severely by the pandemic. What changes will the pandemic bring to tourism and how to adopt measures to face the challenge are urgent questions to be answered. The paper aims at discussing the impact of the pandemic on tourism, tourism enterprises and the tourists. It tries to expound the strategies to deal with the crisis from the role of the government and the tourism enterprises respectively. The result of analysis of the macro data and the questionnaire investigation presented in the paper may help to build new tourism formats.

2 Literature Review

According to International Health Regulations (IHR, 2005), "public health emergency of international concern" means an extraordinary event which is determined, as provided in these regulations: to constitute a public health risk to other states through the international spread of disease and to potentially require a coordinated international response. On January 30, 2020, WHO Director-General Tedros Adhanom Ghebreyesus declared in Geneva the novel coronavirus outbreak as a "public health emergency of international concern (PHEIC)."

Richter discussed the crisis of international tourism and public health events and pointed out that with the rapid development of tourism and the increase in the number of tourists, the global tourism industry would face an increasing public health crisis, which not only threatens tourists, but also threatens the countries where tourists enter and stay [1]. This forward-looking prediction has gradually become a reality. Among the major domestic and foreign public health events of concern in recent years was SARS in China in 2003, the first influenza A H1N1 epidemic in Mexico and the United States in 2009, the Middle East respiratory syndrome in the Middle East in 2012, the Ebola outbreak in West Africa in 2014, the wild-type polio epidemic in 2014, the Zika virus epidemic in Brazil in 2016, the Ebola outbreak in Congo in 2019, and the COVID-19 pandemic in 2020.

According to the World Tourism Organization (WTO), tourism crisis is an unexpected event that affects tourists' confidence in the tourism destination and interferes with the normal operation of tourism industry. Arbel Avner proposed the planning mode of tourism crisis management [2]. Hou concluded that crisis management is a scientific management method for tourist destinations to take preventive or elimination measures against the risk that may arise in the course of tourism development and operation. The scientific management method of taking remedial measures after the occurrence of danger includes the identification, evaluation, prevention and disposal of tourism crisis. By establishing tourism crisis management organization, formulating tourism emergency plan, implementing crisis management, making overall arrangements, and establishing crisis early warning mechanism, crisis management mechanism and crisis assessment mechanism. In different crisis stages, corresponding crisis management measures should be taken to minimize crisis losses [3]. For this reason, Xu analyzed the risks of the tourism industry [4]. Enea Constanta elaborated the impact of crisis management on tourism service industry and its impact on sustainable development of tourism [5]. Chen Bin pointed out that the core intermediary variable in tourism is the confidence of international tourists. Public health emergencies restrict the development of international tourism by influencing the confidence of international tourists. Regardless of the direct loss of tourism economy, public emergencies have a long-term negative impact on tourists' travel confidence, which has a great impact on consumers' travel decision-making and consumption behavior [6]. Li analyzed the safety theory system of tourism industry [7]. Bao Fuyuan summarized the single and comprehensive factors that affect the tourism market [8].

After the outbreak of the pandemic, the government should not only quickly respond to the pandemic and take appropriate measures to control the spreading of the disease but should also make efforts to overcome negative effects in public opinions. The rapid response and treatment of public opinions is helpful to intervene the seriously affected tourism network public opinions in time, to restore the image of the tourist destination, and to reshape the tourists' perception of the tourist destination. Sifeng Nian mainly studied the conversion of negative aspects of terrible disasters into development opportunities, with special emphasis on the initiative and active participation of the tourism sector in the above-mentioned transformation [9]. Marina Novelli elaborated the management mode from the immediate response stage to the recovery [10]. It also studied the importance of the consequences of management failure to affect tourism in developing countries.

In addition to causing direct economic losses of tourism, serious public health events also have a negative impact on the psychology of tourists and affect tourism decisions [11]. The core intermediary variable in tourism is the confidence of tourists. In other words, the reason the public health emergencies can affect the tourism development is through the variables that affect the confidence of the tourists. The traditional crisis loss was mostly measured by casualties and property losses, and the loss of public confidence crisis is more reflected in the impact on the image reputation of the relevant subjects and places of occurrence [12]. Some researchers have also found a strong negative relationship between the perceived risks of travelling and visit/revisit intentions [13, 14]. Yang pointed out that the crisis of public opinion had an impact on tourists' psychological expectations and cognitive patterns, which made tourists a negative perception of the image of tourist destinations [15]. To a certain extent, it changed the intention to travel and posed a threat to the sustainable development of tourism [15].

3 Methodology

3.1 Literature Analysis

In this study, we analyze the impact on tourism mainly through the network resources including the UNWTO data, China National Bureau of Statistics official websites, local bureau of statistics official websites and the financial statements of listed by tourism companies. We aimed at discussing the impact of the pandemic on global tourism industry, China's tourism industry and China's tourism enterprises from macro to micro dimensions.

3.2 Questionnaire Survey

We investigate and analyze the psychological impact of the pandemic on tourists using questionnaire surveys. The questionnaires raise questions for tourism consumers' choices for tourist destination, travel modes and travel focus before and after the pandemic. The study also analyzed the impact of the pandemic on tourists' travel intention and travel requirements. We believe that the results could provide references for tourism enterprises to develop, change and adjust their business methods, tourism routes and tourism products in time to better meet the needs of consumers. The questionnaires were mainly collected online. After the pre-survey reliability test, formal questionnaires were issued. Forty-two questionnaires answers were excluded because there was no intention to travel before the pandemic. A total of 119 valid questionnaires were obtained.

4 Findings and Discussions

4.1 The Impact on Tourism Industries, and Enterprises

Out of all 217 destinations worldwide, 156 (72%) have placed a complete stop on international tourism according to the data collected as of 27 April 2020 (Fig. 1). In 25% of destinations, restrictions have been in place for at least three months, while in 40% of destinations, restrictions were introduced at least two months before. Most importantly, the study also found that none of the destinations has so far lifted or eased travel restrictions. International tourist arrival declined sharply because of 100% of destinations worldwide still have COVID-19 related travel restrictions for international tourists in place, as shown in Fig. 2. The crisis could lead to an annual decline between 60 and 80% when compared with 2019 figures [16].

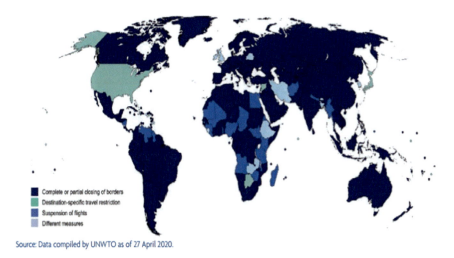

Fig. 1 Destinations with complete closure of borders to international tourism as of 27 April 2020

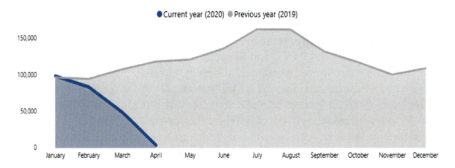

Fig. 2 International tourist arrivals (Thousands). *Source* Data from UNWTO

Data of China's economic operation in the first half of 2020 from the National Bureau of Statistics showed that education, culture and entertainment have been seriously affected by the pandemic. In the first half of 2020, per capita spending on education, culture and entertainment decreased by 35.7%, but the decline was slower than that in the first quarter of the year (Fig. 3).

According to a reminder from the China Immigration Administration on February 8, 2020, 102 countries and regions took control measures against passengers from China and even refused for the transit. During the Golden Week of the Spring Festival, from January 24 to January 30, the number of trips nationwide was only 152 million, 63.9 percent decrease from the previous year. Tourism and related hotels, exhibitions, catering, retail and other industries have suffered huge economic losses. Taking the survey data of Hunan Provincial Tourism Association (2.19.2020) as an example, the direct loss caused by the scheduled withdrawal because of the pandemic was about 924.9642 million yuan to 554 tourism enterprises. The loss of 94 scenic spots (points)

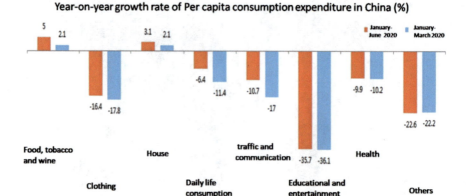

Fig. 3 Year-on-year growth rate of per capita consumption expenditure in China

included in the statistics was 345.843 million yuan with an average loss amount of 3.6792 million yuan. The loss of 221 travel agencies was 175.8722 million yuan, with an average reached 795.8 thousand yuan. The hotel industry had also been severely affected. The total loss amount of 177 hotels in this provincial association was 234.92 million, with an average of 1.3272 million yuan. The total loss of 32 Bed and Breakfast (B&B) was 7.6935 million yuan with an average of 240,400 yuan in loss. The transportation industry was also heavily affected. 6 travel transportation enterprises lost a total amount of 14.4 million yuan, with an average loss of 2.4 million yuan. Other 24 tourism related enterprises lost 146.2355 million yuan in the same period, with an average loss of 6.0931 million yuan.

For a more intuitive representation of the impact of the pandemic on tourism companies, we collated data from the financial statements of listed tourism companies in the first quarter. The financial report data of listed tourism companies and online travel agencies in the first quarter of 2020 (Table 1) show that the revenue of listed tourism companies declined by an average of approximately 200% compared with the same period.

4.2 The Impact on Consumers

The change of consumers' travel decisions and consumption behaviors will have a great impact on the timely adjustment of tourism enterprises' products and marketing strategies. Thus, this study also made a questionnaire survey and interviews about the impact of covid-19 pandemic on consumers' tourism inclination. The results showed that tourists' attention to tourism network opinions were more inclined to the attraction of tourism destination itself, price, discount promotion, transportation information, etc. before the pandemic. After the pandemic, tourists paid great

Table 1 Net Profit Q1 in 2020 tourism companies and online travel agencies in the first quarter of 2020

Company	Net profit Q1 in 2020 (million)	YoY growth (%)
Ctrip (OTA)	−5353	−216.04
Tuniu (OTA)	−205	−34.25
Songcheng performance development Co., Ltd	49.96	−86.5
Xi 'An tourism Co., Ltd	−11.83	−233.07
Hainan dadonghai tourism centre (holdings) Co.,Ltd	−2.49	−258.39
BTG hotels (group) Co., Ltd	−526	−811.25
Jinling hotel corporation, Ltd	−18.90	−246.23

attention to the tourism network opinions information such as public health control, the restriction of the number of people and guidance in scenic area, hotel daily sterilization, protecting measures and so on (Tables 2, 4).

Data in Table 2 are analyzed by multiple response analysis combined with crosstab chi-square test. A significant difference in the score of questionnaire survey about the tourists' attention was found between the two groups ($p < 0.05$), as shown in Table 3. After the pandemic, tourism consumers began to pay close attention to public health opinions, generally choose the near-range natural landscape as a tourist destination,

Table 2 Factors that tourists pay more attention in their travel plan—before the pandemic and during the pandemic

Option	Proportional selection before the pandemic (%)	Proportional selection during the pandemic (%)
A. Economic capability	(79) 66.39	(75) 63.03
B. Travel time	(81) 68.07	(76) 63.87
C. Physical condition	(31) 26.05	(51) 42.86
D. Favorite travel destination	(86) 72.27	(63) 52.94
E. Health and safety conditions during the journey	(54) 45.38	(78) 65.55

Table 3 Results of multiple response analysis combined with crosstab chi-square test

Chi-Square Tests			
	Value	df	Asymp. Sig. (2-sided)
Pearson chi-square	12.846[a]	4	0.012
Likelihood ratio	12.930	4	0.012
Number of valid cases	674		

Note 0 cells (0.0%) have expected count less than 5. The minimum expected count is 40.27

as shown in Table 4, which meet the opinion in other report [17]. The changes in consumer tourism behavior can bring more opportunities for travel companies to adjust their travel products and service.

According to the statistics of the Ministry of Culture and Tourism in China, the "May Day" holiday 2020 received a total of 115 million domestic tourists, with realizing the domestic tourism income of 47.56 billion yuan. To traveling consumers, their attitude to travel changed from staying at home to short distance trips. It was obvious that the consumer confidence was recovering gradually. Protective measures during the pandemic are taken by tourism scenic areas, hotels, restaurants and other hospitality industry widely. Easy access to public opinion about the pandemic, the government's effective rapid response mechanism … all these play key roles in

Table 4 Information tourists pay more attention before a journey—comparison between the situation before and during the pandemic

Option	Strongly disagree	Disagree	Neutral	Agree	Strongly agree	Score
Health conditions and infrastructure in the cities in tourist destinations	1(0.84%)	0(0%)	13(10.92%)	55(46.22%)	50(42.02%)	4.29
Local government tourism policy in tourist destination	1(0.84%)	0(0%)	27(22.69%)	59(49.58%)	32(26.89%)	4.02
Promotion and tourism new products in tourism destination	1(0.84%)	5(4.2%)	40(33.61%)	51(42.86%)	22(18.49%)	3.74
Tourism network opinions information released by relevant departments	1(0.84%)	2(1.68%)	22(18.49%)	61(51.26%)	33(27.73%)	4.03
Pandemic prevention measures in scenic spots and hotels	1(0.84%)	1(0.84%)	11(9.24%)	62(52.1%)	44(36.97%)	4.24
Travel policies for different regions	1(0.84%)	1(0.84%)	18(15.13%)	63(52.94%)	36(30.25%)	4.11

the restoration of tourism consumer confidence. At the same time, the restoration of tourism consumer's confidence also brought the tourism network opinions more positive impact.

5 The Recovery Strategy

5.1 National Policy and Local Support

Luan pointed out that the development of tourism is highly vulnerable to external factors, and appropriate recovery strategies are very important after the crisis. Tourism resource is a non-renewable resource with time, and the loss of time cannot be compensated. Only by adopting active, prudent and flexible policies can the loss be reduced to the minimum [18]. Li believes that when external factors such as social and economic natural disasters reduced the demand of tourist market to a large extent and seriously affected the survival and development of tourism, the government should implement policy assistance [7]. In order to further improve the pandemic prevention and control in tourism and support travel agencies to actively cope with the current difficulties, the Ministry of Culture and Tourism decided to temporarily refund the quality deposit of the travel agency. The maximum refundable amount is fixed at 80% of the amount of charge. As of February 25, 2020, 3.462 billion yuan had been returned to the agencies. This measure provided a considerable amount of working capital for the travel agency industry, overcome the temporal operating difficulties, and created the conditions for recovery and development. In addition, the tourism management department is making appropriate adjustments in fiscal policies, tax policies, industrial development policies and other aspects to provide confidence to the industry and help to tide over the difficulties.

5.2 The Countermeasures of Enterprises

The countermeasures of tourism enterprises mainly include perfecting the system internally, improving the brand reputation externally, developing new business channels and developing alliance of interest. Local tourism industry associations said they would arrange online training for tour guides, dormitory administrators, and other professionals to improve their professional skills during vacations. As an example, in order to reduce the economic losses and establish a good corporate image, BTG Homeinns Hotels (Group) Co. Ltd. has launched enterprise-specific home isolation rooms in seven cities in combination with the home isolation needs of enterprise workers after the holiday. Under the guidance of the epidemic prevention department, strict disinfection and disease prevention measures are taken for isolation rooms. The first batch of pilot hotels involved 60 hotels in 7 cities, including Beijing,

Shanghai, Guangzhou, Tianjin, Shunde, Jiangmen and Zhongshan. Primus Hotel Wuhan Hannan and MOQI Wuhan, which belong to Greenland Hotel and Tourism Group also responded quickly and decided to provide free service to front-line clinical staff. Through these measures, these enterprises not only responded to the call of the country to participate in the actual action against the pandemic, but also gained a good corporate brand image. In order to help tourism enterprises to broaden their business channels and reduce the economic losses, the Ministry of Culture and Tourism encouraged the development of online tourism in qualified tourism enterprise, cultural venues and scenic spots. By means of pictures, videos, VR, 360 holograms and so on. The tourists can "travel" through the client side, which not only recoups part of the revenue of tourism products, but also creates an online promotion platform for tourism enterprises. For example, the Palace Museum, National Museum of China, Shanghai Museum, Nanjing Museum and others all have opened online exhibitions. The Shenyang Museum attracted 1.07 million visitors in just half a day.

In addition, tourism companies have flocked together to confront the difficult. For example, in order to support all partners to tide over the difficulties, the Grand Skylight Hotel Management Company has announced that it will waive its management fee, franchise fee and consultant management fee from 26 January to 25 March 2020. Tourism enterprises in some regions also have begun to develop pre-purchase or low-price promotion programs after the pandemic, to better control costs and attract tourists.

5.3 Guiding the Tourism Social Network Discussion

Liu pointed out that with increasing globalization and information, the government must timely disclosed crisis information and crisis administrative information when facing the serious sudden crisis events [19]. Through the authoritative channels of government administration, the society and the public could understand the truth of crisis events and the administrative dynamics of the government in the process of crisis handling. In this way, the crisis and its destructive impact could be cured in a timely and effective manner, and the unnecessary panic and agitation caused by the uninformed could be alleviated, so as to prevent the further expansion and deterioration of the crisis [19]. Fu Yeqin pointed out that after the occurrence of tourism network opinions, the response to public opinions should adhere to the four principles of rapid response, active response, standardized response and scientific response, and did a good job in the observation, classification and research of media, internet users and other subjects [20].

After the outbreak of COVID-19 in China, especially after the closure of Wuhan, in order to prevent the public from excessive panic and psychological agitation caused by the influence of negative public opinion, authoritative central and local official media broadcast the epidemic news continuously and in a timely manner. The news introduced the prevention measures against the spread of the virus and many positive events. There is a massive amount of live broadcasting online about all the actions taken to fight the COVID 19 virus such as the treatment of the patients in the hospital; medical workers from other provinces arriving to rescue the people in Wuhan; Community workers stayed to their posts without returning home for a long time etc. At the same time, the authorities and administration opened many channels for different voices, and quickly investigated and handled the problems reflected. Timely news release and proper handling of public opinions not only won the public's understanding and support, but also set up a good national image in the world. The Chinese government's rapid responding to the pandemic and the achievements were highly appraised by the World Health Organization.

Under the influence of positive public opinions, tourism social network opinions also recovered from a negative mood. Some tourism enterprises started to receive a large number of consumer's inquiries, showing that the intention of domestic consumers to travel in the second half of the year was very promising. This is a signal that tourists' psychological feeling was being repaired and the tourists' confidence in tourist destinations were also recovering.

As the pandemic began to spread in other countries around the world, inbound and outbound tours were greatly affected. However, it should also be noted that due to China has established a "highly responsible" national image, supported by the tight epidemic control and strong medical capability, the number of inbound tourists from the neighboring countries has increased significantly. These show that it is very important to deal with many psychological problems such as social anxiety and panic, the spread of rumors and the psychological adjustment of the public during the crisis. Positive guide of public discussion includes telling the truth, stopping the spread of rumors and report positive successful examples etc. All these in tourism social network discussion successfully helped China's tourism industry recovered from the dilemma.

5.4 Developing New sales Platforms and Tourism Products

Due to the impact of the pandemic, there will be some changes in tourists' psychology. The sensitivity to crowd gathering and personal space will also be increased. We predict that the number of tourists who choose to travel with groups will be greatly reduced after the pandemic. Instead, tourists will be more inclined to travel with family or friends. Free tours with high flexibility and high-end customized tours will be favored. Facing this reality, tourism enterprises are promoting ecological tourism of natural scenery, developing new tourist routes and products that can meet the needs of tourists seeking safety, health and reliability. For example, in order to cope with the impact of COVID-19 on the tourism industry, Tongcheng CITS, a branch of Tongcheng Group, announced that it will access the Midian SAAS system and upgrade thousands of its travel consultants to e-commerce experts. Based on the original sales of tourism products, more categories are being added to fully meet the needs of users for travel and entertainment. After cooperating with Midian, the tourism consultants in Tongcheng CITS over the country sold more than 10 million yuan tourism products in one-day. At the same time, the average weekly commission of its tourism consultants reached ten thousand yuan, even exceeded the traditional tourist season.

Major museums and galleries in China have successively issued the notice of closure due to the pandemic. In order to show the exhibition to the public during the closure period and meet the needs of visitors, most of the venues have launched cloud exhibitions relying on online platforms such as their official webpages. Inspired by the same idea, as of March 8, more than 1,000 scenic spots in at least 20 Chinese cities had opened online sightseeing services. Online Travel Agencies, such as Ctrip, Flying Pigs and Hornets' Nest, are among the fastest to update their cloud tourism services. The Chinese online blog website Sina Weibo has been read 730 million times and discussed 236,000 times on the topic of "cloud tourism". In response to the industry's general doubts about "cloud tourism", Wang Xiaoyu, an expert of the World Federation of Tourism Cities, answered the questions about cloud tourism in the industry. He mentioned that in theory, cloud tourism is divorced from the essence of tourism—sense of distance experience. But cloud tourism is by no means a single product. It is a combination of online and offline products. Cloud tourism means that tourists can listen to the professional explanation in the video or live broadcast, so as to get exclusive stories that they can't get to know in the offline free travel or package Tours, or experience some thrilling and exciting projects from the first perspective with the live tour guide. On the one hand, he said, it could break through the limitations of traditional tourism activities such as weather, venues, and brought tourists new experiences and understandings. On the other hand, cloud tourism can provide better marketing channels and service basis for tourism suppliers, from pre-trip preview, enhanced experience in the tour to post-trip review, and improve all the details of tourist services in all directions. From graphics, text and voice to live streaming video, the expression form of "cloud tourism" has been making good progress. In particular, live broadcasting interaction brings refreshing audio-visual experience to the audience.

One of the main problems about cloud tourism is how to make a profit. Taking the sales data after the online live broadcast of Suzhou Museum on March 1 as an example, the live broadcast attracted more than 330,000 people to watch, equivalent to the number of offline visitors in the past two months. After the live broadcast, the income of top three items of cultural and creative products in Taobao store of Suzhou Museum reached over 20,000 yuan. The sale-model-based pattern of live broadcast with goods could be regarded as a reference in Cloud tourism. It was feasible to embed the purchase link of characteristic products in the travel live broadcast. Specifically, the establishment of a network platform, the combination of online tourism and live sales, will meet the needs of tourism consumers who must stay at home. It can make up the lack of remote experience of the cloud tourism tourists. In the process of selling goods of the cloud tourism live broadcasting, higher requirements are necessary for live tour guides. At the same time, we should not ignore the importance of the uniqueness of tourist souvenirs. How to make cloud tourism into a profitable project is a question that tourism enterprises need to put more efforts in the post-pandemic period.

6 Conclusions and Outlook

The outbreak of the COVID-19 pandemic will have a profound impact on all industries. Tourist industry has particularly been affected severely. Under this situation, it is important to recognize the seriousness of the impact and take timely measures to recover the loss. As pointed out in the paper, governments and enterprises are important actors to take efficient measures to limit the losses. At the same time, taking good care of the problems reflected in the social networks about tourism, guiding the tourism network discussion towards a positive direction will contribute to the recovery of the tourist confidence. Creating new tourism formats will be an effective direction to bring new tourism economic growth points. After the outbreak of the pandemic and the tight control of the disease in China, with the change and transformation of the focus of tourism development, tourism industry is welcoming a big boom in the country.

As the data obtained from our questionnaires, Tourists' travel habits and concerns have changed greatly because of the pandemic. The tourists are paying more attention to the sanitary conditions, transparency of disease prevention measures and the information availability. However, it must be pointed out that the protection by the government and self-help by enterprises are still insufficient. These should be improved as soon as possible to meet the growing needs of the consumers.

The topics for our research in the near future may include timely policies adjustment, marketing replanning, tourism route replanning, destination image improvement, tourism innovation service improvement etc.

Acknowledgements This research was funded by the Fujian Provincial Philosophy, Social Science Research Project (Grant No. JAS20320) and the Talent Support Program (Grant No. XPDST20001; No.XPDST19013).

References

1. Richter, L.K.: International tourism and its global public health consequences. J. Travel Res. 4l(4). 340–347 (2003)
2. Avner, A., Jona, B.: A planning model for crisis management in the tourism sector. Eur. J. Oper. Res. **5**(2), 77–85 (1980)
3. 侯国林.SARS型旅游业危机及危机后旅游业发展新思维[J].南京师大学报(自然科学版) (03), 97–100 (2004)

4. 许武成,徐邓耀.SARS疫情与中国旅游业的可持续发展创新机制[J].西华师范大学学报(自然科学版), (02), 219–222 (2005)
5. Constanta, E., Constantin, E.: Crisis management effects on tourism services firms and its impact on development sustainable cities. Ann. Const. Brancui **1**(1), 159–170 (2009)
6. Chen, B.: A reflection on tourism health and safety[J]. Econ. Forum **14**, 138–139 (2005)
7. 李海建,谢五届.现代旅游产业安全理论体系与研究框架构建[J].全国商情(理论研究), (20), 83–85 (2013)
8. 鲍富元,杨玉英, 海南入境旅游影响因素的实证研究——基于1993—2017年数据[J].江苏商论 (11), 44–49+53 (2019)
9. Nian, S., Zhang, J., Zhang, H., et al.: Two sides of a coin: a crisis response perspective on tourist community participation in a post-disaster environment. Int. J. Environ. Res. Public Health **16**(12), 2073 (2019)
10. Novelli, M., Burgess, L.G., Jones, A.: 'No Ebola…still doomed'—The Ebola-induced tourism crisis. Ann. Tour. Res. **70**, 76–87 (2018)
11. Wong, J.Y., Yeh, C.: Tourist hesitation in destination decision making. Ann. Tourism Res. **36**, 6–23 (2018)
12. Tapachai, N., Waryszak, R.: An examination of the role of beneficial image in tourist destination selection. J Travel Res **39**, 37–44 (2000)
13. Chew, E.Y., Jahari, S.A.: Destination image as a mediator between perceived risks and revisit intention: a case of post disaster Japan. Tour Manag. **40**, 382–393 (2014)
14. Chen, C.F., Tsai, D.C.: How destination image and evaluative factors affect behavioral intentions? Tour Manag. **28**, 1115–1122 (2007)
15. Yang, Q.Q., Xie ChW., You, K.W.: The interactive effect of tourist's micro-macroscale security perception and travel intention—a case study based on Paris fear. Travel J. **33**(05), 68–78 (2018).
16. https://www.unwto.org/news
17. Khan, M.J., Chelliah, S., Haron, M.S., et al.: Role of travel motivations, perceived risks and travel constraints on destination image and visit intention in medical tourism: theoretical model. Sultan Qaboos Univ. Med. J. **17**(1), e11–e17 (2017)
18. 栾惠德, 外部冲击与旅游业的发展:以"非典"为例[J], 统计与信息论坛 **24**(01), 66–69 (2009)
19. 刘珊, 论信息化时代的公共危机管理[J], 四川大学学报(哲学社会科学版) (4), 29–34 (2004)
20. 付业勤,新媒体环境下旅游舆情危机的形态,传播与标本兼治[J],旅游研究 **10**(05), 12–15 (2018)

The Air Transport Network Between China and Spain During the Covid-19 Pandemic

Marta Guerrero Socas

Abstract The air transport network between China and Spain constitutes a market with a high strategic value and an extraordinary capacity of growth. In 2019, more than half a million Chinese tourists visited Spain, fact that demonstrates the strengthening of Chinese tourism. However, as the world is facing an unprecedented global health, social and economic crisis with COVID-19 pandemic, travel and tourism is one of the most affected sectors. The introduction of measures ranging from border closures and travel bans, including internal mobility restrictions such as lockdowns and quarantine for income passengers, has affected air transport between China and Spain and tourism between both countries has come to a temporary standstill. This paper describes the historical development of air connectivity between China and Spain based on passenger and air traffic flow evolution with source of data until tourism was paralyzed as a result of the worldwide pandemic. Moreover, it provides an outline of the impact of COVID-19 on the Spanish and Chinese aviation industry, emphasizing in the loss of airline capacity due to travel restrictions.

Keywords Liberalisation · International aviation · Air transport · Passenger flow · Evolution · Travel restrictions · COVID-19

1 A Brief Overview on the Role of Aviation in the Tourism Industry

Air transport is key for tourism. Starting with the second half of the twentieth century, air transport has had a major influence on tourism development, considering that the introduction of commercial jet aircrafts in the 1950s was an important driver in the growth of international tourism [1].

In this respect, air transport is a fundamental component of tourism, providing the vital link between the tourist generating areas and destinations. Consequently,

---

M. G. Socas (✉)
JetClub, Palma de Mallorca, Spain
e-mail: marta.guerrero@jetclubgroup.com; mguerrero@monlexabogados.es

there are very close links between air transport and tourism, where a two-way relationship exists. On the one hand, good accessibility, which is determined by the air transport services provided, is essential for the development of any tourist destination. Conversely for the air transport industry, there can be substantial benefits from tourism because of the additional demand which this type of travel can produce. Therefore, it can be affirmed that aviation is an increasingly important mode of transport for tourism markets [2].

However, COVID-19 pandemic has brought a damaging impact to the air transportindustry. Although the aviation industry has emerged stronger from all previous shocks such as the Gulf wars, SARS pandemic, global financial crisis, the magnitudes of global declines in volume and revenue in the current pandemic are unseen in any of the previous crises.

The pandemic has had and still has dramatic consequences for almost all airlines. Globally, flight numbers decreased by almost 80% as of early April 2020. For airlines relying exclusively on the international market such as Cathay Pacific Airways, its operations were almost entirely grounded during that time. In addition to the dramatic demand reduction, severe travel restrictions were imposed in 98% of the markets in terms of passenger revenue [3].

With respect to COVID-19, this study aims to provide a review of the pandemic impact on China and Spain aviation industry as well as the market recovery path.

2 Air Transport Liberalisation Process

During World War 2, civil aviation experienced a major change because of the enormously increased range and reliability of aircraft. This brought renewed international cooperation for civil aviation even before war had ended. On December 7, 1944, at a convention in Chicago, the pattern was set for the regulation of civil aviation. Initially 52 national attended and laid down the foundations of international air transport. The conference resulted in the signing of the Convention on International Civil Aviation, commonly known as the Chicago Convention.

The Chicago Convention of 1944 laid down a basis upon which a system of international bilateral air service agreements (ASAs) was founded. The mentioned ASAs specified which airlines could operate between countries, the routes carriers could operate (e.g., which airports they could fly to), whether carriers could offer beyond services, limits on the frequency and capacity that the carriers could operate, and often placed controls over airline pricing [4].

A restrictive aspect of bilateral ASAs, which has limited the aviation industry globalization, has been the airline ownership and control clauses. Bilateral ASA's require airlines to have substantial ownership and effective control by nationals of its home country or by its home State. For example, the European Union requires that foreign ownership of an EU airline cannot exceed 49% of ownership.

One of the essential market access features of any air services agreement are the freedoms of the air. The freedoms of the air are traffic rights granting an airline of one country the privilege to enter another country's airspace and land in its territory. Negotiating international air services agreements implies determining which freedoms of the air are granted [5].

The freedoms of the air are defined in the following (Table 1).

In the last three decades there has been a trend towards the liberalisation of the international air market. One of the earliest instances of liberalisation was the deregulation of the U.S. domestic air market in 1978. Prior to deregulation, the pricing, routes and capacity operated on air services within the U.S. was tightly controlled by government. Deregulation removed all of these controls and allowed market forces to determine service and price levels. In addition, the U.S. proposed a more flexible model of bilateral air services agreements in the early 1990s, the 'Open Skies' agreements [6].

Table 1 Freedoms of the air

First freedom	The right or privilege, in respect of scheduled international air services, granted by one State to another State or States to fly across its territory without landing
Second freedom	The right or privilege, in respect of scheduled international air services, granted by one State to another State or States to land in its territory for non-traffic purposes
Third freedom	The right or privilege, in respect of scheduled international air services, granted by one State to another State to put down, in the territory of the first State, traffic coming from the home State of the carrier
Fourth freedom	The right or privilege, in respect of scheduled international air services, granted by one State to another State to take on, in the territory of the first State, traffic destined for the home State of the carrier
Fifth freedom	The right or privilege, in respect of scheduled international air services, granted by one State to another State to put down and to take on, in the territory of the first State, traffic coming from or destined to a third State
Sixth freedom	The right or privilege, in respect of scheduled international air services, of transporting, via the home State of the carrier, traffic moving between two other States
Seventh freedom	The right or privilege, in respect of scheduled international air services, granted by one State to another State, of transporting traffic between the territory of the granting State and any third State with no requirement to include on such operation any point in the territory of the recipient State, i.e. the service need not connect to or be an extension of any service to/from the home State of the carrier
Eighth Freedom	The right or privilege, in respect of scheduled international air services, of transporting cabotage traffic between two points in the territory of the granting State on a service which originates or terminates in the home country of the foreign carrier or (in connection with the so-called Seventh Freedom of the Air) outside the territory of the granting State
Ninth freedom	The right or privilege of transporting cabotage traffic of the granting State on a service performed entirely within the territory of the granting State

Source Manual on the regulation of international air transport (Doc 9626, Part 4)

The expression "Open Skies" is based on Order 92–8-13 issued on 5 August 1992 by the then Assistant Secretary of Transportation of the U.S., Jeffrey Shane, establishing an official definition of "Open Skies", which would contain, amongst others, the following elements [7]:

- No limitation on flights or capacity between both contracting states (third and fourth freedoms).
- No limitations on flights or capacity between both contracting states and a third one (fifth freedom).
- Multiple designations of airlines.
- Double disapproval pricing.
- Promotion of liberalisation in the field of charter flights, cargo and computer reservation systems.
- Performance of own support functions at airports located in the territory of the other party.

The liberalisation of the EU's internal aviation market took place later than in the U.S. It was carried out gradually with the adoption of three packages of measures covering air carrier licensing, market access and fares. The first package (1987) covered intra-EU traffic, limited the right of governments to reject the introduction of new fares and gave some flexibility concerning seat capacity-sharing. The second package (1990) further opened up the market, notably allowing greater flexibility over fares and capacity- sharing. It also allowed all EU carriers to carry an unlimited number of passengers or cargo between their home country and another EU country. The third package (1993) completed the process by allowing from April 1997 the freedom to provide 'cabotage', that is, 'the right for an airline of one Member State to operate a route within another Member State [5].

Special reference to China's Liberalisation Process.

China's airline industry was founded during the early 1950s and was controlled by a division of the Air Force, the Civil Aviation Administration of China (CAAC). By then, there were no airlines as we know them today (Air China, China Eastern, etc.) and all flights were run by a division of the CAAC, called CAAC Airlines, which was the monopoly civil airline in the country.

Following the opening-up policies of China in 1978, measures were taken to reform the inefficiencies and conflict of interest. CAAC was separated from military control, and split up the management of airlines, airports and air traffic. Running airlines was turned into a profit-driven business. Airlines were allowed to be set up in partnership with local governments and the private sector (such as Xiamen Airlines in 1984, Shanghai Airlines, Xinjiang Airlines in 1985, and Sichuan Airlines in 1986). The CAAC, however, remained both regulator and operator of the air transport industry (including airports, the majority of airlines and, air transport services) [5].

From the beginning of the 1990s, China's international aviation market embraced the global market with more effort after the deregulation process on market entry and route entry. In 1996, China's airports were registered in the system of the International Civil Aviation Organization (ICAO), and Hainan province was allowed to open the third, fourth, and fifth freedom of the air, while Xiamen and Nanjing expanded the fifth freedom of the air. This signified that China's aviation market started to relax its aviation market entry criteria for foreign countries [8].

A particular remarkable reform was airline consolidation in 2002 where nine CAAC-controlled airlines were consolidated into three airline groups, namely, Air China, China Eastern and China Southern airlines. After the 2002 airline consolidation, the Chinese government gradually deregulated the domestic market; carriers were given greater freedom on route entry and more power to determine their own airfares [9].

Further liberalisation occurred in the mid-2000s when airfare regulations concerning price minimum were further relaxed, a strong incentive for the Low-Cost Carrier model (by 2017 there was an average of five airlines adopting the low-cost business model) and also a way to enable airlines to compete with China's new high-speed rail network.

Deregulation of international routes was also initiated in 2018, relaxing the *"one route, one airline"* policy from 2009. This enabled more competition between Chinese carriers, which were essentially restricted to their home base for international flights (Air China, for example, had priority for international flights in Beijing), as well as enabling new private companies to enter the competition [10].

3 Air Services Agreements Between China and Spain, China and the European Union

China and Spain established diplomatic relations on March 9, 1973. China-Spain aviation links were formally established in 1978 by the signing of the bilateral Air Services Agreement. Two carriers from each side were allowed to operate routes from different points in China and Spain. Based on that simple start, amendments were made in 1993 and 2000.

The key features of China-Spain 1978 agreement and 1993 and 2000 amendments are as following (Table 2).

It should be noted that in the past years several agreements have been reached between China and Spain's civil aviation authorities and its dependant agencies. The mentioned agreements haven't been published in Spain's Official State's Gazette but the agreed rights have been requested in writing in both countries and have entered into force. In 2017, both civil aviation authorities eliminated any geographic restriction between the two countries and allowed any international route between the mentioned countries.

Regarding EU-China Air Services Agreements, the first cooperation initiative between China and the EU in the field of Civil Aviation dates back to 1999. From the beginning both authorities and industries have coordinated with the objective in mind of developing industrial and economic cooperation as well as aviation safety. The success of this initial phase led to the creation of the EU-China Civil Aviation

Table 2 China-Spain ASA's key features

Key features	1978 agreement	1993 amendment	2000 amendment
Airline designation	Unique	Unique	Unique
Ownership	Ownership and control by nationals from designated airlines	No changes	No changes
Tariffs	Double-disapproval	No changes	No changes
Routes	1 point in Spain, via any intermediate point and 1 point in China via any intermediate point (in both directions)	2 points in each country via any intermediate point	Intermediate points can be freely selected by each party but 5th freedom isn't granted
Origin and destination (O&D) points	O&D points must be agreed by civil aviation authorities in both countries	O&D points can be freely chosen by designated airlines	No changes
Traffic rights	5th freedom must be granted by civil aviation authorities in both countries	No changes Additionally, sixth and eighth freedoms are forbidden	No changes

Source Own compilation based on 1978 Agreement and 1993&2000 amendments

Cooperation Project (EUCCAP, 2010–14) to deepen mutual cooperation and understanding. Now the EU-China Aviation Partnership Project (EU-China APP) aims to take this cooperation to the next level through the development of a mutually beneficial partnership [11].

In May 2019, the European Commission and China signed two agreements to develop mutual aviation standards:

- Bilateral civil aviation safety agreement (BASA): mutual recognition of civil aviation safety evaluations and certifications. The BASA will also promote cooperation between the EU and China towards a high level of civil aviation safety and environmental compatibility.
- Horizontal aviation agreement: allows all EU airlines to fly to China from any EU member state with a bilateral air services agreement with China under which unused traffic rights are available. Until now only airlines owned and controlled by a given member state or its nationals were allowed to fly between that member state and China. By signing the horizontal aviation agreement China recognizes the principle of EU designation, which guarantees non-discrimination and equal market access to EU member states for routes to destinations outside the EU. Thus the horizontal agreement will bring bilateral air services agreements between China and EU member states into conformity with EU law. This will be beneficial for European as well as Chinese airlines [12].

According to the European Commission, the above-mentioned agreements will serve to boost the competitiveness of the EU's aeronautical sector and enhance overall EU-China aviation relations. The agreements are in accordance to the Juncker Commission's *Aviation Strategy for Europe*, designed to generate growth for European business, foster innovation and let passengers' profit from safer, cleaner and cheaper flights.

4 Evolution of the Aviation and Tourism Market Between China and Spain

China's international airline markets have experienced tremendous growth in the past two decades and are likely to continue the rapid expansion once the current pandemic is over, thanks to the country's active participation in the global market in terms of a more open economy, international trade, and tourism.

Regarding tourism, the Chinese government has promulgated a series of measures and policies in recent years to further develop tourist resources and boost growth in China's tourism industry.

Selected measures include:

- The National Outline for Tourism and Leisure (2013–2020) aims at the implementation of a national system of paid holidays by 2020 as a way of boosting leisure consumption from both urban and rural residents.
- The 13th Five-Year Plan (2016–2020) highlights tourism as one of the pillars of China's strategic industries. The plan laid out the development goal for the tourism industry, aimed at reaching annual increases of 10% in number of tourists, 11% in tourism revenue, and 14% in tourism investment. According to the plan, the sector will contribute with 12% to GDP and with more than 85% of turnover in sectors such as catering, hospitality, civil aviation, and railway passenger transportation [13].
- In addition to the above-mentioned, on March 11, 2021, the 14th Five-Year Plan (2021–25) was approved. According to the Plan, China will promote the integrated development of the cultural and tourism industries and will develop a number of world-class tourist attractions and resorts with rich cultural connotations, building tourism and leisure cities and urban zones with distinctive cultural traits.

Chinese tourism has mainly remained between the country's borders as China's domestic tourism (Chinese citizens traveling within the country) has experienced a rapid growth in the last years. China's economic growth together with the country' rising in living standards have contributed in making China one of the world's largest domestic tourism market.

Domestic tourism saw a year-on-year growth of 8.4% in the number of trips made by Chinese travellers. More than 6 billion trips were made across the country during 2019, generating a revenue of 5.72 trillion yuan (0.8 trillion U.S dollars).

Despite the domestic travel development, outbound travel has grown strongly in the last 10 years. According to a report released by the National Bureau of Statistics

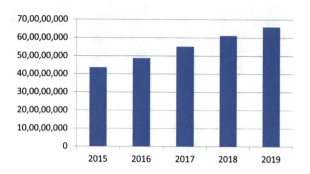

Fig. 1 Passengers transported in China (2015–2019). *Source* Own compilation based on CAAC, 2019

(NBS), a total of 169.21 million outbound trips were made by Chinese tourists in 2019, up 4.5% from the previous year, although rising trends could not continue in 2020 due to the COVID-19 pandemic. From the 169.2 million outbound trips, more than 100 million trips were made to China's special administrative regions of Hong Kong and Macao as well as to Taiwan.

In relation to inbound tourism, in 2019, China received, according to the NBS, a total of 145.31 million tourist arrivals from outside Chinese mainland, a year-on-year increase of 2.9%. The majority of China's foreign tourists came from Hong Kong, Macau, and Taiwan, followed by South Korea, Japan, Russia and U.S (Fig. 1).

The number of air passengers transported in China has increased year on year reaching more than 600 million passengers during 2019. According to the CAAC Annual Report issued in 2020, the contribution of domestic flights were of 585,7 million (+6,9%), Hong-Kong-Macau-Taiwan of 11,7 million (-1,7%), and international flights of 74,3 million (+16,6%).

Beijing Capital International Airport received more than 100 million passengers in 2019, making it the busiest airport on the Chinese mainland, followed by Shanghai Pudong International Airport and Guangzhou Baiyun International Airport.

In terms of international passengers, China's international air networks show an obvious clustering pattern for short- and medium-haul travel in Asia because of the proximity of East and South-East Asia to China. However, the region most connected by China's international airlines changed from East Asia to East and South-East Asia (countries such as Korea, Japan, Thailand, and Singapore). The policy change regarding visas for international travel also stimulated the rapid growth of international air travel. With the implementation of BRI, China's international air networks expanded to the BRI countries in South-East Asia, Europe, and Africa to improve interaction with these countries. After China became actively involved in the global market, foreign trade and foreign tourism between China and other countries increased considerably, which resulted in increased demand for international air travel between China and other countries, thereby contributing to the fast expansion of China's international air networks [8] (Fig. 2).

According to the CAAC, in 2019, China had 62 commercial airlines. These 62 airlines operated a total of 3645 aircraft, an +166 increase (+4,6%) compared to 2018.

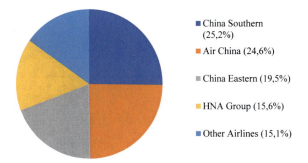

Fig. 2 Share of passengers transported in 2019. *Source* Own compilation based on CAAC, (2019)

As mentioned on CAAC Annual 2019 Report, China Southern Group, Air China Group, China Eastern Group, and HNA dominated the airline industry, with respectively 25,2, 24,6, 19,5 and 15,6% of passengers transported. Other airlines represented 15,1%. Among this group, it is important to mention that Spring Airlines lead Chinese Low-Cost Carriers expansion.

On the other hand, with regard to Spain's aviation and tourism market, in 2019, Spain was the second most visited country in the world, which marked the seventh consecutive year of record-beating numbers. Although tourism plays an important role in the Spanish economy, it still has some weaknesses. For instance, Spain's high seasonality, the underutilization of available resources and the difficulty of attracting more tourists who are in the high spending capacity group. For these reasons, one of the main aims of the Spanish Ministry of Tourism is to increase the spending made by foreign tourists in the country instead of pursuing an increase in the number of tourists. Thus, the Spanish tourism industry needs to understand and adapt to the new high spending international source markets, such as China and Russia, along with other established outbound markets like U.S [14] (Fig. 3).

According to AENA statistics, Spain recorded 275.2 million passengers during 2019, representing a 4.4% increase compared to 2018. Of those passengers, 188.8 million flew internationally, with a 3.5% increase on the previous year. Passengers on domestic flights amounted to over 85.5 million, a 6.4% increase on the previous year.

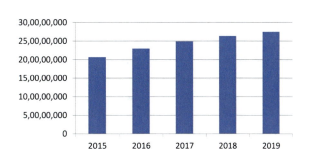

Fig. 3 Passengers transported in Spain (2015–2019). *Source* Own compilation based on AENA statistics

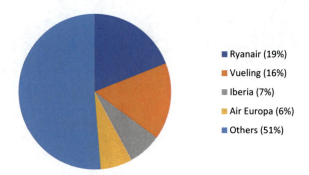

Fig. 4 Share of passengers transported in 2019. *Source* Own compilation based on AENA statistics

Spain has the third largest volume of air traffic in Europe, after the United Kingdom and Germany. Adolfo Suárez Madrid-Barajas Airport ranks 4th in the EU in terms of passengers, while Josep Tarradellas Barcelona airport ranks 5th in passenger traffic.

A further five Spanish airports registered traffic of over 10 million passengers in 2019: Palma de Mallorca, with over 29 million; Málaga-Costa del Sol, with 19.8 million; Alicante-Elche, with 15 million; Gran Canaria, with over 13.2 million; and Tenerife Sur with over 11 million.

69.2% of commercial traffic in all airports in the Spanish airport network is international, and the remaining 30.8% is national. The main source countries of air travel passengers to Spain are the United Kingdom, Germany, Italy, France, the Nordic countries, the Netherlands, Belgium, Switzerland, the U.S., Ireland and Russia (Fig. 4).

More than 130 airlines offered flights in Spain during 2019, with European Low-Cost carrier Ryanair leading with 19% market share, followed by Vueling, Iberia and Air Europa, with respectively 16, 7 and 6% of passengers transported.

5 Air Transport Network Between China and Spain

In 2004, Spain was approved by the Chinese National Tourism Administration (CNTA) as an international destination and the number of Chinese visitors has been increasing year on year. However, an exponential growth of Chinese tourists was experienced between 2017–2019. 896.000 Chinese tourists visited Spain during 2019, an increase of 14% on the previous year and a difference of 124% regarding 2015, when 399.000 Chinese travellers visited Spain.

The contribution of Chinese travellers in Spain's tourism is growing, however it only represents the 7% of Chinese visitors to Europe. Despite this low representation, visits from China are expected to grow at annual rates ranging from 15 to 20% once the pandemic is over. To increase the number of visitors from China, Spain plans to ease visa requirements for Chinese nationals, encourage more direct flights between the two countries and open more tourist offices in China.

Average spending per Chinese visitor was 2.563€ in 2019, the highest of all international visitors (as an example, the average spending per German visitor was 1.052€). In addition, Barcelona is the most popular destination in Spain for Chinese travellers, followed by Madrid and Seville.

In relation to Spanish tourism in China, 150.000 Spanish visited China during 2019, an amount that has increased year by year at annual rates ranging 5–8% until COVID-19 pandemic started. Compared to the millions of tourists that visit China from worldwide, Spanish visitors still represent a low amount.

The low frequency of direct flights between the two countries has characterized the air traffic network between China and Spain. Even in the past decade non-stop flight have increased exponentially, they are still low compared to direct connections between China and other European countries such as United Kingdom, Germany or France.

China's Eastern Airlines launched its direct Shanghai-Madrid flight in June 1992 but cancelled it in November 2003 after years of losses. China and Spain resumed direct flights with Spanish carrier Air Europa, which scheduled flights from Madrid to Beijing and Shanghai in 2005. In order to compete with Air Europa, the also Spanish airline Air Plus Comet, launched flights from Madrid to Beijing in 2005. Both airlines ceased operations to China in 2006 due to the high operational cost and seasonal variation in the passenger flow (80% of passengers flew during summer season). As both airlines suspended its flights, by the end of 2006, Air China entered the market with a non-stop flight between Madrid and Beijing.

Ten years later, Iberia launched non-stop Madrid-Shanghai flight in 2016, becoming Iberia's first Asian destination ahead of its previously announced launch of flights to Tokyo. By then, there were no direct flights between Shanghai and Madrid, so the route was expected to bring an enormous improvement in connection opportunities between the two cities.

In the following tables, the air transport network evolution between China and Spain and its positive trend can be analysed (Tables 3, 4 and 5).

The above tables show positive trends across both number of passengers and operations. The number of passengers and operations of non-stop flights handled by both Chinese and Spanish airlines has increased year by year in the last four years. Since 2016, the total number of passengers has risen steadily, with a difference of

Table 3 Evolution of number of operations (arrivals/departures) between China and Spain (non-stop flights)

	2016	2017	2018	2019
Air China	1.138	1.338	1.525	1.515
China eastern airlines	240	396	370	486
Beijing capital airlines	130	190	200	184
Hainan airlines			164	218

Source Own compilation based on AENA statistics

Table 4 Evolution of number of passengers between China and Spain (non-stop flights)

	2016	2017	2018	2019
Air China	136.664	183.275	249.453	250.132
China Eastern Airlines	41.952	71.472	72.482	102.114
Beijing Capital Airlines	23.006	32.162	43.478	37.758
Hainan Airlines			22.874	36.014
Iberia	33.085	75.408	78.470	81.985

Source Own compilation based on AENA statistics

Table 5 Non-stop routes between China and Spain

Airline	Direct Flights During 2019
Air China	Madrid-Beijing
	Barcelona-Beijing
	Barcelona-Shanghai
China Eastern	Madrid-Shanghai
	Madrid-Xian
Beijing Capital Airlines	Madrid-Chengdu
	Madrid-Hangzhou
Hainan Airlines	Madrid-Shenzhen
Iberia	Madrid-Shanghai

Source Own compilation based on airlines data

116% between 2016 and 2019. It can also be observed a growth in number of flight operations, with an increase of 85% in the mentioned period.

It should be noted that Air China is by far the largest airline operating between China and Spain. In terms of number of passengers, during 2019, Air China transported 114% more passengers than China Eastern Airlines, second leading carrier, and 205% more passengers compared to Iberia.

During the pre-pandemic period, several airlines reinforced their commitment to the Spanish market which could be observed mainly with the increase of both number of flight frequencies and routes by introducing non-stop flights to non-major destinations for travellers such as Chengdu, Xian and Hangzhou.

6 COVID-19 Impact on China and Spain Aviation Industry

Along with other sectors of the economy, air traffic is vulnerable to external factors, such as oil crises, natural disasters, armed conflicts, terrorist attacks, economic recessions and disease outbreaks. These outside influences seem to have a more severe and more rapid impact on air traffic numbers as sudden increases in flight cancellations, aircraft groundings, travel bans and border closures are quickly felt in lower load factors and yields for airlines, while airports lose non- aeronautical revenues One of the characteristics of the COVID-19 outbreak has been the quick geographical spread of the virus, with an initial manifestation in Asia and a lagged response in the rest of the world's regions. Most airlines tried to operate a normal schedule until they were prevented by drastic mobility restrictions. These translated into sudden drops in flight numbers from mid-March 2020, when lockdowns and border closures started to be the dominant policy response across Europe and America. In consequence, the impact has been stronger in international markets than in domestic markets [9].

Due to COVID-19 pandemic, the Chinese government imposed travel restrictions at the end of January. China's total air travel sales volume, including domestic, inbound and outbound travel, registered the greatest loss with a decline of 81% between February 12 and 18, 2020, compared to the equivalent week in the previous year. As the coronavirus crisis was getting worse across the globe since March 2020, the drop of flight ticket transactions continued [15].

In March 2020, the CAAC issued the International Flight Phase Five Plan according to which international air travel was restricted in accordance with the following principle: each Chinese airline could maintain just one weekly scheduled passenger flight on one route to any specific country; each foreign airline could maintain just one weekly scheduled passenger flight on one route to China.

Since June 2020, Chinese and foreign airlines already included in the Phase Five Plan may continue to operate international passenger flights to/from China in accordance with the following principle, namely, each Chinese airline can maintain only one route to any specific country with no more than one flight per week; and each foreign airline can maintain one route to China with no more than one weekly flight. Airlines operating such flights can adjust their domestic and overseas points based on their operating permits. CAAC subsequently released a list of cities with airport(s) capable of accommodating international passenger flights, including Beijing, Changzhou, Chengdu, Dalian and Fuzhou.

During 2020, the CAAC, the Ministry of Foreign Affairs, the National Health Commission, the General Administration of Customs, and the National Immigration Administration established a joint mechanism to implement incentives and circuit breaker measures for flights based on the results of nucleic acid tests of inbound passengers upon arrival. Under the incentive mechanism, if no passenger arriving by flights on a route operated by an airline tests positive for three consecutive weeks, that airline could add one flight to the current weekly quota without exceeding the limit set in the route operating permit and with a cap of two flights a week.

The circuit breaker will be triggered when five passengers traveling by one route operated by an airline test positive. In this case, if less than ten passengers show positive results, the said airline's flights on this route shall be suspended for one week. If ten or more passengers test positive, the suspension will be extended to four weeks. Quota cut by the circuit breaker shall not be transferred to other routes. The airline can only resume its one-flight weekly schedule after the suspension ends [16].

The above-mentioned restrictions have allowed China to prevent the spread of the virus and keep cases as close to zero as possible with the highest number of COVID-19 cases far below that of many other countries.

However, China still maintains strict entry restrictions. Inbound tourism to China is still not feasible. Now there are three ways for foreigners to enter China:

- Holding a valid Chinese residence permit for work, personal matters, or reunion.
- Holding a diplomatic, service, courtesy, or C visa.
- Applying for a new China visa (the previous visa will not be cancelled)—only visas for work or emergency humanitarian needs, such as visiting a seriously ill family member, are possible [17].

The spread of Delta and Omicron variants have led China to take more restrictive measures. In this respect, the CAAC has recently announced that it will reduce the number of international flights in and out of China to 408 per week from the period between October 31, 2021 and March 26, 2022. This is a 21.1% reduction from the same period in 2020.

China expects re-establishing international air travel, from 2023 onwards. For this reason, the already mentioned 2021–2025 Five-year Plan has been divided into two parts:

- For the 2021–2022 period, China will consolidate its efforts in pandemic control and prevention, as well as focusing on reforms and specifying more support measures, so that "developmental momentum" can be unlocked later.
- 2023–2025 would be a period of growth. *"The focus is to expand the domestic market, restore the international market, release the impact from reforms and improve the level of opening up.",* according to the CAAC [18].

Notwithstanding the above, China aviation industry has been recovering faster than most countries emerging from the COVID-19 as Chinese airlines have resumed a quicker pace with domestic passenger travel heading up. In June 2020, average landing and take-off volumes at domestic airports increased 18.8% compared to May, with maximum daily volumes nearing 2016 levels, according CAAC [19].

Chongqing Jiangbei International Airport and Sanya Phoenix International Airport led the recovery, with their numbers of outbound flights bouncing back to over 80% of 2019's volumes.

Good news came in August 2020 when airline bookings in China reached about 98% of 2019's levels in the second week of August, according to ForwardKeys. Domestic arrivals stood at 86% during such period.

However, China's domestic air traffic, once the world's envy after a fast rebound during the pandemic, is faltering due to the zero-Covid policy that has led to tighter travel rules and weaker consumer confidence after repeated small outbreaks. Domestic capacity at the country's three biggest airlines reached around 115% of pre-Covid levels in April 2021 but by October 2021 had fallen to around 77% due to outbreaks. During November 2021, the situation worsened when the city of Beijing announced that travelers from any Chinese city that had reported even a single COVID case within the past 14 days would be restricted from entering the capital, which is being protected ahead of the 2022 Winter Olympics [20].

Regarding COVID-19 affection to the Spanish tourism industry, according to figures published by the National Statistics Institute (INE), 204,926 international visitors arrived in Spain in June 2020, a drop of 97.7% from the same month in 2019. This culminates the worst semester on record for the Spanish tourism industry, with just 10.78 million visitors, a fall of 71.7% from the same period in 2019 [21].

As is well known, Spain is highly dependent on tourism and, for this reason, the tourism sector has been one of the hardest-hit by COVID-19. In March 2020, the Spanish government declared a state of alarm, which limited all non-essential trips to the country. The situation worsened in April and March 2020, with zero tourist arrivals recorded. In mid-June, German tourists visited Spain's Balearic Islands on a pilot program, and on June 21 of the same year, the state of alarm came to an end and Spain reopened its borders to countries within the Schengen Area (with the exception of Portugal, which reopened on July 1).

The markets with the current best performance are Denmark and the Netherlands, with a volume of seats scheduled to Spain during the third quarter of 2021 reaching 96 and 93.2% of the air capacity for the same period in 2019, respectively.

From the UK, volume of seats scheduled to Spain during the third quarter of 2021, reached 66,7% of what was operated in the same months of 2019; from Germany 75% of 2019; from Italy 72% of 2019 and from France 62% of what was operated in the same months of 2019. The markets that are showing a slower recovery are the long-haul markets, whose air capacities are still 58.7% below 2019 levels in the case of the US, 76.8% in the case of Russia [22].

The importance of Spanish domestic tourism in relieving the tourism industry crisis due to COVID-19 cannot be overestimated. Even when mobility between countries begins to return to its previous levels, the fear of travelling, especially by air, will take time to disappear. This is an important limiting factor since the main origin markets are located at considerable distances from Spain, and the most used means of transportation is air travel. The option to arrive by private cars seems to be a viable option only for certain French and Portuguese tourists. Moreover, domestic tourism plays a pivotal role in the most important countries that contribute to Spanish tourism, such as Germany and the UK. This fact suggests that even when international mobility starts to rebound, domestic tourism in these countries will be a strong (and reinforced) competitor for Spain [23].

Air transport network between China and Spain deserves a special mention where air capacity is 92% below 2019 levels. Air transportation demand between China and Spain decreased in late January 2020, Iberia drew down its scheduled China-Spain combination services by the beginning of February 2020. Chinese carriers also suspended some, but not all, of their China-Spain scheduled combination services. By March 2020, all airlines suspended their commercial flights between China and Spain.

The CAAC is responsible for approving direct international flight routes to and from China and the currently approved flight routes between Spain and China for the period from October 31, 2021 to March 26, 2022 are Madrid-Beijing and Madrid-Hangzhou, both operated by Iberia as charter flights.

Finally, it should be pointed out that since the start of the COVID-19 pandemic, just two segments of aviation have managed an extended period back at 2019 levels of traffic: all-cargo and business aviation. Business aviation briefly matched 2019 volumes in summer 2020. Growth as strong as this comes from changes in both supply and demand: operators finding new ways to reach customers, and new services to offer, such as shared flights; plus new passengers turning to business aviation flights, because the connectivity they want isn't currently available with the timing or quality that they want [24].

Globally, midway into January 2022, just over 200,000 business aviation sectors flown globally, 25% more than in January 2021, 16% more than in January 2020. The impetus now appears to be coming from aircraft owners, with private and corporate flight departments flying 21% more than January two years ago.

Companies and wealthy individuals in China have sharply increased their use of private jets during 2021, with total flights almost doubling compared to pre-pandemic levels as the country's economic recovery prompts a shift in business travel. Domestic use of jets either hired privately or flown exclusively for their owners are up 87% in 2021 compared to the same period two years earlier, according to data from WingX Advance GmbH, a data company.

Private jet operators say the rise in demand in China also reflects remaining limitations on commercial airlines, as well as concerns from executives about sharing planes with large numbers of fellow passengers.

In Europe, the Omicron wave and associated lockdowns are discernibly slowing flight activity in some countries, with business jet movements in Germany down by 3%, Italy down by 2%. But these are trends relative to January 2020; compared to January 2021, these two countries' traffic volumes are up respectively by 48% and 63%. Overall, the European region is seeing 13% more activity in January 2022 versus January 2020, with strongest growth in Spain, Russia, Turkey, Sweden. The growth trend for the European region in Q421 compared to Q419 was 24%, so the early January trend has clearly moderated.

7 Analysis

This paper reveals the Chinese market is gaining more importance for Spanish destinations, both in terms of economic contributions and diversification of the market. Air transportation between China and Spain is a crucial factor in the success and efficiency of trade and tourism in the two nations. Given the current economic contribution of tourism to the Chinese and Spanish national economies, tourism innovation in these two countries becomes a vehicle for improving tourism competitiveness and sustainability.

It is also important to better manage the seasonality of both Chinese and Spanish markets. Seasonality issue is mainly caused by large amount of package group tourists who visit the China and Spain in specific periods concentrating on of certain periods of time due to a lack of paid leave but having to travel mostly during public holidays—for example, the Chinese New Year (between January and February) and summer holidays (between July and August).

In addition, a key factor is to improve connectivity and facilitating visa processes, and one of the pending issues is the adaptation of hotel offers for Chinese travellers. Given that almost half of Chinese travellers make their travel decisions based on the opinion of other visitors, and with the growth of the independent traveller segment, hotels are increasingly willing to make changes. Investing in expanding carrying capacity—more qualified Chinese speaking staff and tour guides, suitable hotel rooms and (Chinese) restaurants in order to provide quality services and achieve high traveller satisfactions.

The impact of the pandemic, the behavioral changes of future travelers, and the measures adopted by the sector have led to several emerging trends which represent both challenges and opportunities to relaunch tomorrow's tourism. Short-term consumer trends are: "staycations" (taking holidays closer to home), longer holidays, short booking windows (confirmed by an increase of last-minute bookings), travelers searching for local experiences, special attention to safety and hygiene, and renewed interest in outdoor and nature-based activities. Long-term industry trends are related to achieving greater sustainability and further digitalization. These trends were emerging before the pandemic, but the health emergency has accelerated the speed of change and represented a good moment to reflect on the future of tourism [5].

It should be pointing out how important digitization is to helping Chinese travelers to have better experiences. This includes inspiration and pre-trip planning channels, digital resources at tourist attractions and destinations, and mobile payments not just at businesses catering to tourists but even those that are not specifically part of the tourism industry.

There will certainly be challenges ahead tourism between China and Spain, the most immediate of which is the current uncertainty about the speed of vaccine rollouts and when government regulations will allow for Chinese outbound tourism to resume. Related to this are issues of visas, reciprocity in terms of vaccine recognition, and travel restrictions.

Addressing these challenges depends on governments, local health authorities, and potentially the virus itself. But moving beyond them and making the post-pandemic Chinese travel experience in Spain better than ever is something that can be achieved and planned in advance.

8 Conclusions

First of all, as transport in general is an important component of tourism, air travel represents a significant part of the tourism product. The evolution of air travel over the last years determined changes in the way tourism products are created. Previously, tourism providers were interacting with customers mostly via intermediaries—travel agencies or tour operators—selling their packages pairing contracted room allocations with transport—usually charter flights. Nowadays, as a consequence of the development of low-cost airlines and the rise of internet, more and more providers decide to promote their services on airlines websites. Secondly, there is a strong relationship between air travel and development of destinations, taking into consideration both tourism development and regional economic growth. Low-cost airlines brought international air traffic to regional and secondary airports, contributing this way to the development of new forms of tourism. Moreover, airports became important generators of economic growth and tourism development. In an era defined by globalization and technology, airports became essential and generated a new form of urban development, "aerotropolis". Also, as a consequence of undergoing a process of commercialization and privatization, airports started to develop as businesses and sometimes as tourist attractions, even "quasi-destinations". This contributed to the development of a new form of tourism "stopover tourism", based on a partnership between airlines, airports and tourism organization. The objective of stopover programs is to transform transit passengers into tourists for that destination. Thirdly, air travel has significantly changed the behaviour and the typology of the modern traveller. Living in a globalized world, with family scattered worldwide, with global enterprises having employees on all continents made air travel indispensable for most travellers [25].

Since both China and Spain liberalised their international air transport, traffic has increased at well above regional and world average rates, maintaining year-on-year, increasing market share. Removing restrictions on market access equals a range of consequences. Allowing air carriers to operate on intra-European, intra-Chinese and international routes led to a direct impact on the number of air passenger flow. There is a significant evidence of a positive connection between the degree of market regulation and the volumes of traffic. Emerging new airlines—now under deregulated market conditions—have not only increased traffic volume but also changed route structure. Development of air services market directly impacts aviation business growth and creates spill over effect all over economy. Increased volume of passengers has brought revenue growth and allowed to create additional workplaces at all business entities related with aviation, airlines and airports in particular [26].

In relation to China and Spain's air network relationship, as studied in this paper, besides 1978 Air Services Agreement and its amendments, both countries have established several agreements in the past decade. The aim of these strategic agreements is to promote transport between both countries, provide better service, strengthen bilateral relationships, help Chinese citizens get to know Spain better and make an outstanding contribution to the development of the Spanish economy. The contribution of the mentioned agreements, demonstrate a positive trend in both number of passengers and frequencies between the two countries.

Regarding COVID-19 impact in aviation industry, this paper exposes that even air travel is closely linked to economic growth and business fluctuations; the aviation industry has been badly affected by the pandemic. Restoring consumer confidence while keeping up the necessary health precautions is the key for airlines, as flights are no longer expected to be the same as they were before.

References

1. May, M., Hill, S.B.: Unpacking aviation travel futures and air transport. J. Fut. Stud. **7** (2002)
2. Graham, A.: Aviation and tourism, implications for Leisure travel (2008)
3. Achim, I., Xiaowen, Fu., Zheng, Lei, Tae, H. Oum.: Post pandemic aviation market recovery: experience and lessons from China (2020)
4. Button, K.: The impact of US–EU "Open Skies" agreement on airline market structures and airline networks (2009)
5. Debyser, A.: European parliamentary research service, EU external aviation policy (2019)
6. InterVISTAS-EU Consulting Inc. The Impact of International Air Service Liberalisation (2009)
7. International Transport Forum.: Liberalisation of Air Transport Research Report (2019)
8. Deville, J.: A portrait of the Chinese airline industry in 2019 (2019)
9. Wang, J., Yang, H., Wang, H.: The evolution of China's international aviation markets from a policy perspective on air passenger flows (2019)
10. O'Connell, J.F.: J. Air Trans. Manag. (2011)
11. Deville, J.: A portrait of the Chinese Airline Industry in 2019: a Historical Perspective (2019)
12. EU-China Aviation Partnership Project website
13. European Union. Commission Section website
14. Abato, R.: Tourism in Focus. China Tourism (2018)
15. Lojo, A.: Chinese tourism in Spain: an analysis of the tourism product, attractions and itineraries offered by Chinese travel agencies (2016)
16. Suau-Sanchez, P., Voltes-Dorta, A., Cugueró-Escofet, N.: An early assessment of the impact of COVID-19 on air transport: Just another crisis or the end of aviation as we know it? (2020)
17. Statista Research Department.: COVID-19 coronavirus impact on China's air travel 2020, by transaction type (2020)
18. Ministry of Foreign Affairs of the People's Republic of China website
19. China Travel Restrictions: When Will China Open Its Borders (chinahighlights.com) (2022)
20. China Travel Restrictions 2021/22 - Latest Travel and Entry Requirements (china-briefing.com)
21. http://www.caac.gov.cn/en/
22. Qiu, S., Freed, J.: China's domestic air traffic recovery faltering due to zero-COVID policy (https://cn.reuters.com)
23. www.ine.es
24. www.eurasiareview.com
25. Arbalú, I., Razumova, M., Rey, J., Sastre, F.: Can domestic tourism relieve the COVID-19 tourist industry crisis? The case of Spain (2021)
26. www.eurocontrol.int

COVID-19 Pandemic Impacts on Chinese Outbound Tourism and Survival Strategy

Dongmei Ren and Dolores Sánchez-Aguilera

Abstract This study uses data collection methods from different Sources in order to explore how China's outbound tourism-related economic sectors responded during the pandemic from the perspectives of policy support, corporate self-rescue, new opportunities for tourism demand, etc. This review article identifies that China's outbound tourism industry has suffered a huge setback, but China's domestic short-distance tourism has recovered well. This is inextricably linked to China's stringent anti-pandemic policy and the use of Big Data to control the flow of people in real time. Chinese outbound tourism companies suffered heavy losses at the beginning of the pandemic but were able to adjust their marketing strategies in time and make full use of practices such as virtual tourism, live broadcast, and e-commerce sales to realize their own self-rescue. Finally, the research hypothesis considers China's trends and experience with the recovery of its tourism industry as a reference that may shed light on what other countries should or should not do as they wait for the resumption of normal travel.

Keywords COVID-19 impacts · China's tourism recovery · Innovative short-term solutions · Survival experience

1 Introduction

China had the world's largest outbound travel market when measured by trips and expenditures before the COVID-19 pandemic occurred. As a result of the rise in living standards and the creation of policies that opened the country to the outside world, the Asian giant has become a market of great strategic importance due to its high purchasing power and potential, making it a desired market worldwide. Containment policies against the virus and an international context that discourages mobility have

D. Ren (✉)
University of Barcelona, Barcelona, Spain
e-mail: 18801950203@163.com

D. Sánchez-Aguilera
Department of Geography, University of Barcelona, Barcelona, Spain

© The Author(s), under exclusive license to Springer Nature Singapore Pte Ltd. 2022
Y. Luo et al. (eds.), *Tourism, Aviation and Hospitality Development During the COVID-19 Pandemic*, https://doi.org/10.1007/978-981-19-1661-8_3

led to new strategies in the sector of tourism, which point to new trends in tourism activity that can be consolidated in the still uncertain scenario of a pandemic world. With China's COVID-19 lockdown over, travel began to resume in May 2020. With the advent of the information age, technology has made it possible to collect, compile, and archive vast amounts of data, which are now easily accessible to researchers. The purpose of this paper is to examine the changes that are occurring in the Chinese tourism industry and to analyze the impacts of COVID-19 and new strategies within the industry.

2 Literature Review

According to UNWTO (2020), crisis management has become a hot topic for businesses in the hospitality and tourism sector due to the drastic drop in both tourist numbers and loss of revenue [1]. Thus, strategies for crisis management and recovery from distress are imperative to the recovery of the hospitality and tourism sector [2–4]. Following a review of 142 articles on the subject of crisis and disaster management in tourism, Ritchie and Jiang [5] argue that current studies on crisis management in tourism mainly focus on case studies of the response and recovery phases. In addition, crisis communication, recovery marketing, and stakeholder collaboration are considered three important strategies for successful tourism recovery. In this study, the analysis of more than twenty relevant contributions supports the need for a research agenda that focuses on market recovery and communications, rather than prevention. As Carlsen and Liburd [6] stated, most of the research in the literature tends to focus on tourism crisis prevention and crisis management. However, in comparison, less attention is paid to impact and recovery following involvement in a severe crisis [7]. Crisis management advocates that the key to surviving in an evolving environment is finding solutions from history and past experience [8]. Similarly, according to Faulkner's [9] tourism disaster management framework, gaining knowledge from past experience can provide corresponding solutions for similar crises in the future. In view of the importance of the tourism crisis experience, our research analyzes the response, recovery, and restoration strategies implemented by policymakers, tourism supply and demand during the stages of COVID-19.

The China Tourism Development Report [10] noted that, from the perspective of tourism demand, the pandemic has had a strong impact on the development environment of China's tourism market. Indeed, the domestic tourism market was strongly affected and gradually recovered after the strong shock; the inbound and outbound tourism market has been continuously affected and is estimated to continue to stagnate after the strong shock. In addition, the in-depth integration of tourism and Internet stores, along with the IP (intellectual property) strategies of cultural and creative tourism, provide a positive reference for the recovery of the tourism industry [11]. Dragon Trail Research [12] findings show that Chinese consumers are willing to travel. Although they are concerned about the safety of overseas travel, they express a higher perception of the safety of destinations in Asia than in other regions.

COVID-19 Pandemic Impacts on Chinese … 37

Meanwhile, Chen et al. [13] of McKinsey state that the implications of China's tourism recovery experience can be summarized as follows:

- The national zero-case policy has regained the confidence of tourists.
- It has focused on domestic tourism to revive the tourism sector.
- It is necessary to build digital touchpoints.
- A discount and pre-sales strategy are established to stimulate tourism demand.
- Methods of remote cultural participation are digitally mediated by live broadcast.

In addition, as Chen et al. [13] pointed out, in the face of the unstable pandemic situation abroad and China's long-standing policy of mandatory quarantines, the recovery of international tourism is difficult. Therefore, short-term domestic travel would be the main driver of the recovery of China's tourism industry. Meanwhile, tourism consumption will start to favor the domestic luxury travel sector. Similarly, according to the Global Self-guided Tour Report [14] released by Mafengwo (a social media, travel platform), Chinese tourists turn to domestic tourism exploration, and domestic tourism has rebounded. In particular, the popularity of local tourism and rural tourism is soaring. In light of the Ctrip survey [15], the demand for small, customized themed trips has become more popular. Meanwhile, mid-range and high-end tourists lead the growth. In contrast, low-priced and low-quality tours will die out. Song [16] suggested that offering strong promotions has contributed to the recovery of domestic air travel. The travel industry has shifted its marketing focus to emerging social platforms, such as through livestreams and short videos, to encourage tourism amongst young consumers in particular.

This article focuses on the need to develop a specific research agenda for the recovery of China's tourism market. The assessments provide a number of implications for the recovery of the tourism industry in the context of COVID-19, highlighting the importance of recognizing that China's domestic tourism recovery is based on the government's "Zero-COVID" approach.

3 Research Methodology

For this study, the secondary data has been gotten form official government policy reports and the response strategy for tourism management in pandemic crisis, apart from that, the secondary data also has been collected from China National Knowledge Infrastructure (CNKI). CNKI database provides full-text articles from more than 2000 Chinese journals with a focus on economics and management. We searched for articles with the help of keywords, such as "pandemic" and "tourism", etc. After viewing the abstract, 24 articles have been selected based on the theme of the impact of COVID-19 on the tourism industry in China, the recovery strategies, and the new demand for domestic travel. Besides this, news articles, web pages and conference reports were also considered for the secondary data for the research study (Fig. 1).

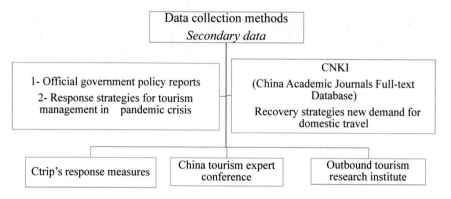

Fig. 1 Research methods

4 Findings and Analysis

In order to evaluate the pandemic's impact and the impact of response strategies on the tourism industry, review articles related to tourism during COVID-19 were studied. The analysis found that the existing results mainly focus on two levels of content: first, the negative impact of the pandemic on China's tourism industry and the rescue measures implemented. Second, the new trend of China's tourism industry under regular pandemic prevention.

4.1 The Four Stages of Recovery

In accordance with the evolution of China's anti-pandemic policy from strict to loosen restrictions, Zhai et al. [17] believed that China's tourism industry has gone through the following four stages during the pandemic:

1. In the first stage from January to March 2020, the whole China tourism industry was temporarily stagnant for the outbreak control closure periods to the specific pandemic.
2. In the second stage from April to June 2020, the sector struggled with the impact of the latest travel restrictions in North and Central China. However, in other Chinese regions where the pandemic had been completely controlled, where gradual resumption of work and production had occurred, where various national favorable policies had been introduced, and where cultural and travel consumer vouchers had been issued, the type of travel was limited to mainly parent–child travel, visiting relatives, self-driving tour, rural travel, etc. According to experts, this stage of the pandemic consisted of road trips and travel occurring near the home.

3. The third stage, from July to September 2020, was the recovery period of the tourism market when travel bans were lifted. Moreover, eliminating uncertainty from the fear of COVID-19 contributed to the increase in the demand and desire for travel. At this stage, health-fitness traveling, wellness tourism, forest-based ecotourism, sports tourism, rural tourism, study tourism, etc. became more and more popular.
4. The fourth stage from October 2020 was regarded as the full-fledged recovery of this economic sector. However, China's tourism recovery is slightly "imbalanced", with domestic tourism outperforming outbound and inbound tourism. This phenomenon occurs because the pandemic control in other countries has not kept up with that within China.

4.2 Government Action

4.2.1 Rigorous, Precise, and Effective Prevention to Ensure Public Safety

Facing this devastating disease, the Chinese government launched a resolute battle to prevent and control its spread and place public health as the top priority. Therefore, China adopted extensive, stringent, and thorough containment measures [18] and had efficient organization and mobilization capabilities to do so. In addition, the citizens have an awareness and habit of abiding by collective norms, which has enabled China to adopt a nationwide, rigorous, and precise prevention and control model for handling the pandemic and implementing closure and isolation measures for regions and individuals. The government has conducted a contact tracer method and a nucleic acid test to determine who has come into contact with the virus. Also, the Chinese government manages the country at all levels by dividing it into three risk categories: high-risk, medium-risk, and low-risk areas. As a result of the government's anti-pandemic policy, tourism has begun to recover (Table 1).

4.2.2 Support and Policy Guidance for Enterprises

In the first stage, the tourism ecosystem has been hit hard by travel restrictions, community-level lockdown, and contact tracing from late January 2020. Specifically, the cancellation of conferences, catering, and accommodation orders, and the termination of travel plans have caused numerous "cancellations waves" that have brought huge losses to the tourism industry [18]. In addition, the health crisis has led to severe difficulties for companies to meet their financial obligations. Many industries and enterprises face bankruptcy. To get the industry back on track, the government proposed a series of measures to support tourism businesses to adapt and survive, including refunding travel agency warranty money, deferred payment of social security, tax exemption for domestic travel, rent subsidy, and issuing guidance

Table 1 Government actions to pave the way for tourism recovery

Government action	Target group	Achievement
A nationwide rigorous-precise prevention and control model	Covid-19	To ensure public safety and pave the way for tourism recovery
Provided economic assistance	Tourism companies	To support tourism businesses to adapt and survive
Launched large-scale free online training	Tourism practitioners	To develop high-quality and high-level tourism service industry
Implemented digital upgrade projects	Cultural and tourism enterprises	To promote the construction of smart tourism
Issued some official statements	Tourist attractions	To prevent mass gatherings, avoid peak times
Promotion of online and offline integrated tourism	Chinese people	To meet the people's travel demand

Source Compilation based on information supplied by the references [19]

on the resumption of work and production in the tourism industry, etc. The government has launched large-scale free online training, implemented digital upgrade projects for cultural and tourism enterprises, vigorously promoted the construction of smart tourism, strengthened tourism market management, and industry rectification [19, 20].

The government issued some statements to strengthen the management of population flow to prevent mass gatherings. Travelers are required to make reservations and are encouraged to visit tourist attractions in different time periods to avoid peak time.

4.2.3 Online and Offline Integrated Tourism to Meet the Travel Demand

During the first stage, the state advocated for the promotion of online and offline integrated development of fitness and tourism. Although tourism activities in various places had been suspended, in order to meet the people's travel demand, museums in various provinces had moved their exhibitions to the Internet, launching online themed exhibitions presenting people with a visual feast, so that people can take a tour around the Internet, exploring the many possibilities of exhibiting online without leaving home.

During the pandemic, the State Administration of Cultural Heritage introduced five batches of 250 online exhibitions, and almost all museums met with the audience on the "cloud". Through the use of VR and AR technologies, people could safely visit the desired destination and expand their cultural knowledge. In the era of the pandemic, online and offline integration has brought new ways to travel.

Table 2 Live streaming ecommerce and Innovative technologies to recover tourism industry

Supply side	Cooperation platform	Innovative marketing mode	Result
Derivative products	e-commerce Taobao	Cloud tourism	Get the e-commerce's original customer base
Scenic resort	social media	KOL (Key Opinion Leader)	Realize a large number of pre-sales
Museums	Douyin Kuaishou Weibo	Local internet influencer	Attract potential consumers Drive sales and boost conversions
Hotels	UGC	Tourism ambassador	Drive sales, Flash sales
Flights	Mafengwo Qunar	Personal IP (Intellectual Property)	High-quality content boost Internet Traffic Monetizing
Vacation packages	OTA	Boss Livestream Tourist coupons	Encouraging consumers to travel more
Tourist destination	Ctrip Fliggy	Hosting interactive Q&A	Revives consumer spending
Catering	Food delivery platforms	In-house restaurants tap into food-delivery	Garner revenue
	Innovative technologies	VR/AR, big data, artificial intelligence, IOT (Internet of Things), cloud technology, 5G	Rides the 'contactless' wave Stimulate to consume online

Source Compilation based on information supplied by the reference [17, 19–27]

On top of that, The OTAs (Online Travel Agencies), travel agencies, tourist locations, and other business entities have actively rescued themselves and found their way out of the crisis through transforming, upgrading, and diversifying their operations in order to turn crisis into opportunities [21]. Below, we reveal the innovative short-term solutions that have been used (Table 2).

4.3 Innovative Short-Term Solutions from Supply Sides

4.3.1 Tourist Attractions Cooperate with Ecommerce Videos to Promote

A number of major domestic and overseas museums and scenic spots, as well as Douyin (TikTok in China), Kuaishou (China's hottest video-sharing and live-streaming apps), and Taobao (China's biggest e-commerce) have invested in cloud tourism, launching the sensational "Earth Live" and "Potala Palace Cloud Live", and other eye-catching exhibits [25] (Table 3).

According to data from the Research Institute Dragon Trail Interactive [12], during the COVID-19 pandemic, China's live broadcast viewers grew to 560 million, accounting for more than 60% of Chinese Internet users. Chinese consumers are accustomed to buying goods, learning about new places, and exploring different lifestyles online via live streams. Live streaming has become an important way to acquire information and make reservations. This is why Fliggy (Travel Platform of Alibaba Group) has continued connecting Chinese audiences with European destinations, most notably via live streams. Since May 2020, Fliggy has broadcast live streams from Serbia, Finland, Germany, and the U.K. as well as from some of the continent's most treasured cultural destinations including the Palace of Versailles, the British Museum, and Madrid's Prado Museum. These platforms have developed live streaming partnerships with European travel organizations during COVID-19, with the purpose of engaging future travelers by giving viewers a sense of what being in a certain place actually feels like, in real-time. The focus of online travel is not just to create a live broadcast that is followed by tens of millions of users. More importantly, live travel broadcasts not only make up for the regret of not being able to travel and enjoy the scenery, but also make a strategy for the next tour in advance. Hosting interactive Q&A (question and answer) sessions on modern platforms is a fantastic way for businesses, broadcasters, and influencers to create high-quality content that is easy to produce that boosts interaction and grows online presence, which not only can attract potential consumers, but also boost and drive sales and Internet Traffic monetizing through an online interaction and live broadcast benefits. Moreover, live travel broadcasts not only increase pre-sales in conjunction with e-commerce platforms, such as reservations for travel packages, tour tickets, etc., but also promote more cultural, creative, and individualized products that leads to increased revenue [20].

Table 3 Tourist attractions cooperates with e-commerce and video-sharing platforms

Date of launch	Name	Platform	Audiences (million)	Garnered likes
20/02/2020	Wandering around the museum at home	Douyin	26.76	/
15/02/2020	The British Museum	Kuaishou	2	500,000
23/02/2020	8 well-known domestic museums	Taobao	20	/
06/03/2020	Danish Andersen Museum	Kuaishou Mafengwo	> 1	/
14/05/2020	Palace of Versailles	Fliggy	> 1	> 50,000
22/07/2020	The Prado Museum	Fliggy Taobao	0.41	100,000
27/08/2020	The Victoria and Albert Museum (V&A)	Kuaishou	3.8	166,000

Source Compilation based on information supplied by online reports in 2020

4.3.2 Boss Livestreaming as a New Major Marketing Channel to Push Sales

With China's coronavirus pandemic winding down, and demand for tourism picking up, Ctrip has been moving to spur the hospitality industry's recovery by Boss's live streaming since March 23rd of 2020. This live-streaming session has been held by Liang, co-founder of Ctrip, who relies on the cosplay style of "dressing into travel scenes" online to pump up sales of many types of travel products, from hotels, flights, and vacation packages to tourist attraction tickets and more. Liang endorses the high-end hotels from his personal experience and has played twenty roles (including opera face-changing, rap, and folk arts), and strongly matches his personal IP with the backdrop of the hotel scenery in his live streams to increase the hotel reservations.

His show was an innovative and effective way to save the company during hard economic times. Behind Ctrip Live, there is a solid team that works on intensive product selection, screening, pricing, and evaluation. Additionally, his images are not entirely determined by his intuition. Rather, it is a role chosen by Ctrip based on the analysis of internet data so that it can attract more consumers.

According to Ctrip data report from 2020, from March 23rd to October 28th, 2020, Ctrip.com group's live stream series had generated more than USD 360 million in GMV (Gross Merchandise Value) and received more than 150 million global views. Based on the current trends in China, Ctrip's international live streams are forecasted to first feature accommodation providers in Asia before moving onto the rest of the world. Furthermore, livestream broadcasts have showcased destination partners and have featured "LIVE for Trip" campaigns viewed by millions of customers. This kind of Cross-border retail has driven offline tourism consumption. Except for the flash sales sessions, Liang's livestream e-commerce has greater symbolic significance. When the tourism industry fell to a freezing point, Liang used his personal efforts or personal IP to inspire many peers of the industry to overcome difficulties. A more important aspect is the goal to try and recover the travel industry by encouraging consumers to travel more.

4.3.3 Using Local Internet Influencer Marketing to Attract Tourists

During the pandemic, the tourist destinations have spared no effort to actively and innovatively make use of new methods, especially through social media with local internet influencers, to promote local tourism and to help local residents sell products.

Due to a short video accidentally shot by a photographer on the road, a Tibetan teenager Ding Zhen from Litang county of Sichuan province went viral overnight because of his charming looks and lifestyle. Just a few days after his first video went viral, the local government invited Dingzhen to be the tourism ambassador of his hometown. In order to promote local tourism, the documentary "The World of Ding Zhen" was published by Timeisland. Several days later, the total amount of video views had reached 150 million, and the number of online searches of #Dingzhen#

Fig. 2 Local internet influencer -Ding Zhen: "Sweet Wild". *Source* Ding Zhen's World—HD Version 《丁真的世界》 from timeisland

had exceeded nine billion. Inspired by documentaries, many netizens were seriously planning to travel to Litang. Thanks to Dingzhen, the number of searches for Litang through China's biggest online travel agency Ctrip skyrocketed by 620% in ten days. Searches for flights and hotels concerning Litang also increased on Ctrip.com. Consequently, a small county of Dingzhen's hometown, became one of the nation's super popular travel destinations in 2020. Similar to how the local government of Sichuan has used the online sensation Dingzhen to boost tourism to its rural region, international brands should utilize local figures to make a brand accessible and communicable to Chinese consumers [24] (Fig. 2).

4.3.4 Using Artificial Intelligence Technology to Provide 'Contactless' Services

The coronavirus has raised global awareness of the potential invisible risks associated with physical touch. For that reason, the goal of a hands-free experience has become a priority for travelers and brands [28]. COVID-19 has accelerated the adoption of contactless technologies in China. Accordingly, contactless has become the new buzzword in consumer-focused businesses due to the contact infection. In the context of the pandemic, products and services ranging from robotic waiters to driverless disinfection and sanitation vehicles, to unmanned smart hotels are proliferating. At unmanned smart hotels, guests can do everything from reserving a room, checking in online using facial recognition, to turning off the lights, drawing the curtains, and adjusting the air conditioner, all without human assistance. That gives peace of mind in a time of concern about infectious diseases. In China, more than 5,700 hotels under

Huazhu Group strengthen the implementation of intelligent contactless services. Moreover, since the outbreak of the pandemic, Meituan, (online-to-offline) local life service platform, has launched services such as contactless delivery, contactless smart meal picking cabinets, and contactless take-out protective covers.

4.3.5 Star Hotels Tap into Food-Delivery to Garner Revenue

For full-service hotels, catering revenue has always been an important part of revenue, and there are a few full-service hotels whose catering revenue even exceeds room revenue. The pandemic has had a large impact on the catering industry, especially on in-house restaurants of star hotels that used to rely on dine-in only. Launching a takeaway platform or a hotel's WeChat, a purchasing social media platform, official account has become the most important self-help method for restaurants. Star hotels across the country are delivering food prepared from their in-house restaurants to homes, in a bid to create an alternative revenue stream. Take-out food options for star hotels cannot completely make up for the losses caused by the pandemic but is a new way to survive in the context of COVID-19 pandemic.

4.3.6 Using Tourist Coupons to Promote the Resumption

In order to promote the resumption of work and production in the tourism industry, various regions have issued tourist coupons and launched free tours to scenic spots, such as Hubei Province's "Huiyou Tour Hubei", Shanxi's "Ten Thousand Welfares, Benefits to Jinzhong". Airlines have launched a series of preferential packages such as "flying as you wish" and "flying happily". These measures have effectively stimulated tourism consumption. The tourist resorts were all reopened in July and August 2020, and the number of visitors has reached 90% of the same period last year.

According to the data of the Ministry of Culture and Tourism of P.R.C, during the National Day and Mid-Autumn Festival of 2020, the country received 637 million domestic tourists, a year-on-year recovery of 79.0% on a comparable basis; domestic tourism revenue was 466.56 billion yuanes, a year-on-year recovery of 69.9% on a comparable basis.

4.4 Radical Changes in Tourism Behavior and Demand

Given the interlinked consequences of the economic and health crises, and the progressive lifting of travel restrictions, the demand side has been more deeply impacted as the longer the pandemic has gone on. Based on this study, tourists' demands, and behaviors have radically changed in the following aspects (Fig. 3).

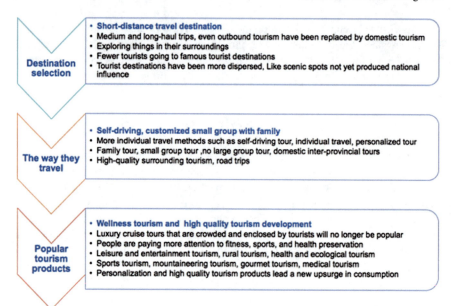

Fig. 3 The four aspects of tourists' demand and behaviors have radically changed. *Source* Compilation based on references

4.4.1 Destination Selection: Shorter Travel Destinations

Before outbound travel resumes, domestic tourism will boost the resumption of the tourism industry in the wake of the pandemic [15, 30]. While Chinese tourists prefer short-haul travel to explore their environment during the COVID-19 pandemic, remote locations and longer trips have not been popular. Medium and long-haul trips and even outbound tourism have been replaced by domestic tourism, in particular short haul trips to a large extent [18]. There have been fewer tourists going to famous tourist destinations, and instead, people have been choosing to visit lesser-known and safer destinations. As a result, tourist destinations are more diverse, and scenic spots within the region that have not yet produced national influence have received a large number of tourists, which will be beneficial to the balanced optimization of the overall layout of the national tourism development space in China.

4.4.2 Ways of Travel: Self-Driving, Customized Small Group with Family

The obvious trend of domestic travel is the shift from large groups to small groups. In order to avoid the sudden and possible outbreak of "communicable disease" risks, some people will choose more individual travel methods such as self-driving tours, individual travel, personalized tours, and family tours [28]. Since the resumption of domestic inter-provincial tours in 2020, the proportion of Ctrip's small groups represented by private and exquisite small groups has exceeded 50% [15]. In fact, self-driving travel and even RV (recreational vehicle) routes offer new opportunities for growth. With the sharp increase in personal space sensitivity brought about by the pandemic, the demand for traditional low price and quality large group tours will shrink. However, mid-to-high-end tourist products lead the growth in the post-outbreak pandemic era. According to projections, personalized small group tours and self-organized expeditions will increase. Apart from this, increasing the demand for high-quality surrounding tourism and road trips have become a trend in China.

4.4.3 Popular Tourism Products: Wellness Tourism Development

Due to the pandemic, road safety, food safety and public health have become the main considerations for tourists. Low density natural, health and ecological tourism products have become the new favorites of tourists. On the contrary, amusement and theme parks with large crowds may be greatly affected. People are paying more attention to fitness, sports, and health preservation. Therefore, wellness tourism products such as sports, mountaineering, gourmet, and medical tourism have become an important trend in market development. Pure health tourism, compensation vacation tourism for the purpose of health, cultural festival tourism, cultural and art tourism for the purpose of "experiencing happiness", outdoor recreation and hot spring tourism for the purpose of therapeutic tourism, and rural tourism, will be more popular [31]. The so-called luxury cruise tours that are enclosed and crowded with tourists will no longer be popular among wealthy travelers. Personalization and high-quality tourism products lead to a new upsurge in consumption. Tourism destinations with sparse personnel, air circulation, and beautiful natural scenery, such as rural tourism [32], ice and snow tourism, and other related scenic spots and resorts will have the opportunity to create new tourist destinations of similar types.

The pressure of pandemic prevention and control and policy changes throughout the year 2020 have caused China's tourism industry to undergo "stress" changes from recovery to tourism models and marketing [33].

5 Discussion

The last year and a half have opened a new phase in tourism activity. The COVID-19 pandemic has marked a turning point with different consequences from a territorial point of view. The pandemic remains serious, and the development of the pandemic remains variable, with different trends in each region. Since the first COVID-19 outbreak discovered in China began in 2020, new cases are mostly imported because of the high efficacy of China's internal travel control laws. This has become one of the main bottlenecks for international travel and tourism into and out of China.

The study of future scenarios for the development of the tourism industry requires, in a context of standardization of pandemic prevention and control, emphasizing the growth of the tourism industry through the integration of the sector with new forms of online tourism and smart tourism [21]. There is an urgent need to seamlessly connect big data, virtual simulation, artificial intelligence, and 5G communication technology to promote the new development of smart tourism [23, 27].

The breakthrough of COVID-19 has very quickly changed the pattern, form, marketing, and experience of tourism industry development [35]. In addition, the participation of more Internet, mobile communications, and artificial intelligence and digital enterprises has strengthened the vitality and boosted the momentum of the tourism industry and offers new possibilities for an industry that has been pushed to change [19].

The experiences through which Chinese tourism has undergone represent a step forward in terms of new strategies for the sector. The transformations that have been detected in Chinese tourism (less mass tourism, closer destinations, and guaranteed safety) are relevant because they could be considered as indicators of the forms of tourism that will gain prominence in the coming years. Also, new travel destinations are emerging, closely related to new consumption patterns that point to trends in new technologies and new habits established by a different tourism model. The promotion methods are also being transformed, and dissemination on social networks is becoming particularly relevant.

6 Conclusion

The pandemic has affected multiple aspects of our daily lives, but tourism is undoubtedly one of the activities where the impact has been greatest.

In addition to changes in demand almost paralyzed for a few months, there have also been transformations in supply. In this context, in which many advocate a rethinking of the productivity model that characterized many of the areas receiving tourists, the Chinese experience is valued as a reference for possible recovery strategies from an unforeseen crisis [13, 35]. In particular, it is worth highlighting the deployment of innovations in the field of technology, sometimes linking tourism, e-commerce, and social networks to recover economic activity and minimize the impact on a very sensitive sector.

On the other hand, the case of China allows us to appreciate how the demand structure has changed: the new context and the perception of security are very relevant in the configuration of a tourist demand that prevents overcrowding. In addition, the pandemic has changed the image of tourist destinations, so that the recovery of a tourist destination is a very important factor after this period.

Finally, the crisis that began with the COVID-19 pandemic contributes to redefining the research agenda in tourism studies, with more emphasis on the mechanisms of recovery and reconversion in a new scenario.

Acknowledgements This research was funded by the project: "Tourism and the city: analysis and evaluation of the synergies, conflicts and challenges generated by tourism development in Spanish cities" (PGC2018-097707-B-100) financed by the European Regional Development Fund (ERDF)/Ministerio de Ciencia, Innovación y Universidades—Agencia Estatal de Investigación (AEI) (Ministry of Science, Innovation and Universities—State Research Agency (AEI).

References

1. Barbara, A.A.: Crisis management in the Australian tourism industry: preparedness. Tour. Manage. **27**(6), 1290–1297 (2006)
2. Yeh, S.S.: Tourism recovery strategy against COVID-19 pandemic. Tour. Recr. Res., 1–7 (2020). https://doi.org/10.1080/02508281.2020.1805933
3. Wut, T.M., Xu, J., Wong, S.-M.: Crisis management research (1985–2020) in the hospitality and tourism industry: a review and research agenda. Tour. Manage. **85**,(2020). https://doi.org/10.1016/j.tourman.2021.104307
4. Anderson, B.A.: Crisis management in the Australian tourism industry: preparedness, personnel and postscript. J. Tour. Manag. **27**(6), 1290–1297 (2006)
5. Ritchie, B., Jiang, Y.: A review of research on tourism risk, crisis and disaster management: launching the annals of tourism research curated collection on tourism risk, crisis and disaster management. Ann. Tour. Res. **79**, 102812 (2019)
6. Carlsen, J.C., Liburd, J.J.: Developing a research agenda for tourism crisis management, market recovery and communications. J. Travel Tour. Mark. **2–4**(265–276), 23 (2008)
7. Beirman, D., Van Walbeek, B.: Bounce back: tourism risk, crisis and recovery management guide. Pacific Asia Travel Association, Bangkok (2011)
8. Cioccio, L., Michael, E.J.: Hazard or disaster: tourism management for the inevitable in Northeast Victoria. Tour. Manage. **28**(1), 1–11 (2007)
9. Faulkner, B.: Towards a framework for tourism disaster management. Tour. Manage. **22**(2), 135–147 (2001)
10. China Tourism Academy: 中国国内旅游发展报告 2020 China Tourism Development Report. Changes in the development of tourism after the pandemic and countermeasures (2020). [Online]. Available: http://news.carnoc.com/list/543/543621.html
11. Ji, P.: 化危为机 开文旅高质量发展新局. 群众 **20**, 37–38 (2020)
12. Dragon Trail. Chinese Consumer Travel Sentiment Report (2021). [Online]. Available: https://dragontrail.com/wp-content/uploads/sites/6/2021/03/Chinese-Consumer-Travel-Sentiment-Report-March-2021.pdf
13. Chen, G., Enger, W., Saxon, S., Yu, J.: What can other countries learn from China's travel recovery path? (2021). [Online]. Available: https://www.mckinsey.com/industries/travel-logistics-and-infrastructure/our-insights/what-can-other-countries-learn-from-chinas-travel-recovery-path
14. BBTNews: Global Self-guided Tour Report (2020). [Online]. Available: https://k.sina.cn/article_1988645095_768850e702000uxip.html?from=travel
15. Ctrip: The New Era of Small and Beautiful: A report on the consumption of new domestic groups in 2020 (2020). [Online]. Available: https://mp.weixin.qq.com/s?__biz=MzU1NDk2MTEwNg==&mid=2247496545&idx=1&sn=2969f336abadeb37ea493e963d9bed89&scene=21&token=940833875&lang=zh_CN#wechat_redirect
16. Song, A.: The recovery of China's travel industry (2020). Available: https://www.gartner.com/en/marketing/insights/daily-insights/the-recovery-of-chinas-travel-industry
17. Zhai, Y., Shi, H.P., Lu, M.: The impact of the new crown pandemic on the tourism industry and the path to revitalization. Open Guide **05**, 93–99 (2020)

18. Dong, L., Li, Q.: 新冠肺炎疫情影响下我国旅游业发展问题及对策. *[J]. 渭南师范学院学报* **35**(12), 16–23 (2020). DOI: https://doi.org/10.15924/j.cnki.1009-5128.2020.12.004
19. Zou, G., Ma, Y.J.: New problems, new opportunities and new directions of Shanghai's cultural and tourism development under normalized pandemic prevention and control. Tour. Tribune **02**, 10–11 (2021)
20. Dang, H.: 重大疫情中旅游危机的演化机理及应对策略. 宏观经济管理 **05**, 43–50 (2020). DOI: https://doi.org/10.19709/j.cnki.11-3199/f.2020.05.007
21. Ma, B., Wang, J.: 常态化疫情防控下的旅游产业新走向. Tour. Tribune **36**(02), 1–3 (2021)
22. Zheng, Q.: Research on the characteristics and countermeasures of my country's tourism market change since the pandemic. China Price **10**, 107–109 (2020)
23. Shen, L.: China tourism group development report in 2020 (2020). https://travel.ifeng.com/c/82Bx5tHhZoA
24. 21st Century Business Herald: 疫情反复旅游业难破冰 网红、直播、线上拓新机 The tourism industry is difficult to upbuilding due to repeated pandemics: Internet celebrities, live broadcasts, and online new chances (2021). [Online]. Available: http://www.cs.com.cn/cj2020/202101/t20210118_6131044.html
25. Jiang, S.:疫情中旅游直播的传播特点及影响. 新闻论坛 **34**(04), 30–32 (2021). DOI: https://doi.org/10.19425/j.cnki.cn15-1019/g2.2020.04.008
26. Zhai, Y., Shi, P.H., Lu, M.: The impact of the new crown pandemic on the tourism industry and the path to revitalization. Open Guide **05**, 93–99 (2020)
27. He, J.: 中国旅游发展笔谈——常态化疫情防控下文化和旅游发展的新问题、新机遇与新方向. Tour. Tribune **36**(02), 1 (2021)
28. Yang, Y.: 常态化疫情防控下旅游经济研究的新问题与新机遇. Tour. Tribune **36**(02), 3–4 (2021)
29. Sina travel:《中国旅游景区发展报告(2021)》(2021). [Online]. Available: https://travel.sina.com.cn/domestic/news/2021-12-09/detail-ikyamrmy7861343.shtml
30. Zhao, L.: Research on the characteristics of domestic tourism development and countermeasures under the new crown pandemic. Econ. Res. Guid. **33**, 125–127 (2020)
31. Li, Z., Zhang, X.X., Yang, K.L., Singer, R., Cui, R.: Urban and rural tourism under COVID-19 in China: research on the recovery measures and tourism development. J. Tour. Rev. (2021)
32. Jiang, L.Y., He, Z.: Research on the impact of tourism crisis on the tourism industry and coping strategies: taking the new coronary pneumonia pandemic as an example. Rural Economy and Technology, pp. 107–108 (2020). Doi: CNKI: SUN: NCJI.0.2020 -19-046
33. Peng, S.S.: China's tourism: research on recovery and revitalization in the post-pandemic Era. J. Yangzhou Univ. **05**, 54–66 (2020)
34. Marianna, S.: Tourism and COVID-19: Impacts and implications for advancing and resetting industry and research. J. Bus. Res. **117**, 312–321 (2020)
35. Chen, G., Enger, W., Saxon, S., Yu, J.: China's travel sector is undergoing a nonlinear recovery: what should companies do? (2020). [Online]. Available: https://www.mckinsey.com/industries/travel-logistics-and-infrastructure/our-insights/chinas-travel-sector-is-undergoing-a-nonlinear-recovery-what-should-companies-do

New Opportunities of Heritage Tourism Under the COVID-19 Pandemic: A Case Study of Zayton Port

Chengyuan Wei, Xia Cheng, Xinru Liu, and Jianzhong Li

Abstract The outbreak of COVID-19 has made the long distance tourism across the Region strictly restricted in China. Heritage tourism, especially in the region, has become a new trend of tourism consumption because of its relative niche, rural character and security. Zayton Port(Ancient Quanzhou)was China's largest trading port in the 12–fourteenth centuries (the Song and Yuan Dynasties). It occupies an extremely important position and far-reaching influence in the history of the Maritime Silk Road and the East–West Communicate History. This paper aims to investigate the current status of the cultural heritage and examine the factors affecting the conservation and utilization of the ancient port. In order to collect first-hand data, the fieldwork method was applied. Six critical factors that affect the heritage conservation and utilization are identified, namely: relics legislation, protection concept, consumer demand, technology, social participation and the financial support. Finally, suggestions and recommendations are given accordingly.

Keywords COVID-19 · Heritage tourism · Maritime silk road · Zayton · The Belt and Road

---

C. Wei (✉) · X. Cheng · J. Li
Xiamen University of Technology, Xiamen, Fujian, China
e-mail: wcyuan@163.com

X. Cheng
e-mail: 13055201068@163.com

J. Li
e-mail: 827997816@qq.com

X. Liu
Wuyi University, Jiangmen, Gongdong, China
e-mail: xinru.liu1011@qq.com

1 Introduction

China tourism sector based on international and national destinations experienced a total cessation of activity, just after the closure of national and international borders and airports since the outbreak of COVID-19 pandemic. Up to today, we have to face some factors in tourism development that are difficult to predict due to the great uncertainty regarding the covid-19 pandemic and the world economic and trade environment.

1.1 New Opportunities

However, it is increasingly clear that COVID-19 has brought three changes in China's tourism industry to bring new opportunities to heritage tourism. (a) The change of tourism destination: mass tourism destination to Minority tourist destination. Considering the safety of epidemic prevention, people have become very cautious in making travel decisions and gradually transfer to remote rural areas and areas with few personnel instead of a crowded place. Heritage tourism is essentially a minority tourism, which is very in line with the attribute requirements of less people and safety. It is one of the alternative destinations for tourists. So the transformation of tourism destination also brings a good opportunity to accelerate the development of heritage tourism. (b) Changes in tourism scope: outbound tourism, inter provincial tourism to intra provincial tourism, peripheral tourism and local tourism. To avoid the risk of infection on the road, people now hold a relatively exclusive attitude towards long distance tourism. People are more and more inclined to choose peripheral tourism and local travel. Based on this, local heritage tourism (especially in rural areas) must be more and more favored by most tourists, and its development will usher in opportunities. (c) Changes in the number of tours: the transformation from one-time tour of sightseeing tourism to multiple tours of peripheral tourism and local tourism. Generally, tourists rarely choose to revisit after visiting a scenic spot, especially in inter provincial tourism and outbound tourism. The advantage of short distance makes tourists mostly repeat game behavior, and they are more likely to choose to revisit especially when people can't go out for leisure for a long time because of COVID-19. On the premise of meeting the needs of local tourists to obtain a good experience, they will choose to patronize many times. So local tourists can provide a continuous driving force for realizing the recovery and development of local heritage tourism.

In short, long distance tourism has been strictly restricted in China due to the restrictions on cross regional mobility. Suburban tourism, short distance travel and rural leisure have become new choices for public tourism and leisure. Among them, cultural heritage tourism (especially in the rural) has become a new trend of tourism consumption because of its niche, rural, safety and cultural connotation. Then, this paper will take Zayton port cultural heritage tourism as a case study as a representative of the cultural heritage of the maritime Silk Road.

1.2 Zayton

Zayton (Ancient Quanzhou) is located in at a junction between the ocean, rivers and inland. Zayton was famous for its four bay and sixteen ports in the twelfth centuries, and developed Meizhou Bay and other deep water ports later. In the sea of Sailing Age, Zayton was seen as a good port in terms of environmental condition. Firstly, there was little fog in Zayton providing a excellent envriement for navigation. Secondly, Zayton was an unfrozen port with excellent hydrological conditions and suitable temperature. Besides,the perennial northeast wind was easy for ships to depart, while the summer southwest wind was convenient for foreign merchant ships to return. Additionally, there were several small islands in the bay providing excellent cover conditions and smooth flow. That's why Zayton Port was very prosperous at the time of Song and Yuan dynasties, which was known as "one of the world's largest port". According to historical records, the customs tariff revenue of Zayton Port was accounted for 18.7% of the state's fiscal revenue at that time and reached 20% at the beginning of the Souhtern Song Dynasty [1].

As the origin of the oriental Maritime Silk Road, and the production base of China's export porcelain in Song-Yuan Dynasty, Zayton Port has rich heritage resources, not only involving "historical sites of navigation and trade" but also including "cultural heritage sites". For example, Zayton is also known as the "World Religious Museum", for its religions sites including Confucianism, Buddhism, Taoism, Islam, Manichaeism, Nestorianism, Hinduism, and local belief systems.

Heritage is seen as the legacy and representation of the tradition and the selective inheritance of the past in contemporary society [2]. It also can be treated as the tool for the state to strengthen national identity. Since the "Silk Road Economic Belt" proposed by President Xi Jinping in Kazakhstan on September 7, 2013 and the "21st Century Maritime Silk Road" announced in Indonesia on October 3 of the same year, different fields at home and abroad, including academic circles, have been paying close attention to the Belt and Road. As the historical and cultural foundation of the Belt and Road Initiative, the ancient Maritime Silk Road has presently become the focus of social attention and academic research.

At the same time, Fujian Province is recognized as the core area of the 21st Century Maritime Silk Road. The Plan for the Construction of the 21st Century Maritime Silk Road Core Area of Fujian Province proposes that Fujian Province should vigorously develop distinctive characteristics and themes for the Maritime Silk Road cultural tourism products and build a Maritime Silk Road cultural tourism destination. Moreover, Zayton tried to declare a World Heritage Site with the "Maritime Silk Route-Quanzhou (Zayton)" in 2018 [3]. Therefore, the protection and utilization of the Zayton Port heritages has become a major theoretical and practical topic.

Currently, the academic studies of the Maritime Silk Road can be classified into several aspects, including the regional cooperation, trade positioning, cooperation mechanisms, development potential and strategies, the value and significance, economic effect, as well as the environmental and climatic consideration of the

Maritime Silk Road development. These studies are mainly focus on trade integration and national strategy. Although, huge progress has been made in the academic field, there is limited research about the heritage protection and tourism development, especially the Zayton Port.

This paper aims to investigate the current status of these Maritime Silk Road world heritages through fieldwork approach. Comparative analysis and the georgraphic system will be applied according to examine the factors affecting the conservation and utilization of these ancient Maritime Silk Road sites.

2 Status Analysis

Based on the literature review, the project team has conducted an extensive and in-depth field research in the Zayton Port heritage sites during 2015.7–2019.10. Through observation and in-depth interviews with the support from the local cultural and tourism authorities. It was found that Zayton preserves the largest number of ancient maritime trade sites and has made the most outstanding achievements in heritage protection and utilization in China.

2.1 Representative Sites Selection

Firstly, Zayton Port has all kind of the Maritime Silk Roads heritage resources. It not only involves those indicating the port and ocean trade: wharves, bridges, navigation facilities, ancient shipwrecks, and commodity production bases, but also includes ancient buildings, ancient sites, ancient tombs, grottoes and stone carvings, murals and so on, which embodies cultural exchanges. 2018, a total of 16 cultural heritage sites in Quanzhou (Zayton) are listed in the World Heritage application text: "Historic Monuments and Sites of Ancient Quanzhou (Zayton)." While now a total of 22 monuments and sites are nominated in the new application text: "Quanzhou (Zayton): Emporium of the World in Song-Yuan China", categorised into "historical sites of navigation and trade" (Shihu Dock, Jiangkou Wharf, Shunji Bridge Site, Wanshou Pagoda, Liusheng Pagoda, Luoyang Bridge, Anping Bridge, Shiposi Site, Jiuri Mountain Wind-Praying Carving, South Waizong Zhengshi), "historical sites and multi-culture"(Tombs of Islamic Saints, Laojunyan Statue, Statue of Mani in the Caoan Temple, Zhenwu Temple, Tianhou Temple, Kaiyuan Temple, Qingjing Mosque, Confucius Temple), and "historical sites of urban construction"(Deji Goat Site, Luoyang Bridge, Anping Bridge, Dehua kiln Site, Jinjiaoyi Hill of Cizao kiln Site, Anxi Iron Smelting Site), representing the prosperity of Zayton in the Song (960–1279 AD) and Yuan (1271–1368 AD) dynasties as an important hub of the Maritime Silk Roads [4].

In addition, it was found that there should be two important representative heritage sites: Xu Dock Site and Nanyin.

New Opportunities of Heritage Tourism Under … 55

(a) According to the specific attributes of the heritage resources, compared with the value orientation of the UNESCO, it was believed that Xu Dock is one other heritage sites provide an important testimony to the trade route and the diverse cultures. Located in Wuli Street Yongchun County, Xu Dock was the most important inland river wharf for transporting Dehua porcelain and the distribution center for foreign goods in Song -Yuan-Qing dynasties. "Yongchun County Annals" states that in the Song Dynasty, "Along the Jinjiang Dongxi River there are commercial boats from Zayton to Shigutan." Due to frequent flooding, the eastern section of Guantian City was washed away. Later, merchant ships went straight to the higher-lying-Xu Dock, and the market gradually moved westward to a place away from the county town (i.e. Wuli Street) to conduct mountain and sea cargo transactions. Then, an alley for merchants gradually was formed: Haike Lane, and some Arab businessmen also began to leave Zayton center and gather there. Now the old dock has been destroyed due to the construction of flood-control channel, but the old Wuli Street is relatively well protected, paved with pebbles with two to three meters wide. In particular, the Haike Lane (for hosting traders) and the descendants of Arabic and the inheritors of spice techniques in the ancient street, become the historical witness of the ancient Maritime Silk Roads.

(b) In the same way, Nanyin is one of important and intangible heritages. It is the most representative achievement of Zayton local folk culture and art, and known as the Living Fossil of Chinese Music. Nanyin is a relatively rich and complete genre of ancient music in China. It gathers the essence of Central China Music since the prosperous Tang Dynasty, and later absorbed the specialties of Yuanqu, Yiyangqiang and Kunqiang, and integrated with the folk music of Southern Fujian. It not only flourishes in Southern Fujian, but also spreads and takes root in all parts of the world with the steps of overseas Chinese from southern Fujian. On September 30, 2009, Nanyin was selected into the UNESCO "representative works list of human intangible cultural heritage".

In other words, it was believed that there are 24 representative heritage sites in Zayton Port. Thus, according to the classification system of Classification, Investigation and Evaluation of Tourism Resources (GB/T18972–2003) of the national standard of the People's Republic of China, the Maritime Silk Road Cultural Heritage in Zayton Port involves three main categories, six subclasses and eleven basic types, which are shown in Table 1.

In addition to the above typical representative sites, there are many other important Maritime Silk Roads sites in Zayton. However, due to technical and other reasons, a large number of underwater heritage around the Zayton Port have not yet been excavated. For example, these is a Song Dynasty shipwrecks near the Jiangkou Wharf having been surveyed but still buried underground. Moreover, a large number of precious heritage have been preserved and displayed in the Quanzhou Maritime Transportation Museum after being excavated or collected in different times. Besides, it is undeniable that there are some heritage ontology and cultural environment destroyed or disappeared with the development of urban construction, such as the

Table 1 Classification of maritime silk road cultural heritage in Zayton port

Main class	Subclass	Basic type	Resource name
(E) Relics	(EB) Social, economic and cultural activities	(EBD) Abandoned production site	Dehua Kiln site Jinjiaoyi Hill of Cizao Kiln site Anxi iron smelting site
		(EBE) Traffic sites	Shunji bridge site Xu dock site
		(EBF) Waste cities and settlements	Deji goat site
(F) Buildings and facilities	(FA) A comprehensive cultural tourism destination	(FAC) Religious and sacrificial sites	Zhenwu temple Tianhou temple Kaiyuan temple Qingjing mosque Confucius temple
	(FC) Landscape architecture and ancillary architecture	(FCG) Cliff calligraphy and painting	Jiuri mountain wind-praying carving Laojunyan statue Statue of Mani in the Cao'an temple
		(FCB) Tower building	Wanshou Pagoda Liusheng Pagoda
	(FE) Burial place	(FDD) Celebrities' former residences and historical monuments	Shiposi Site South Waizong Zhengshi
	(FF) Traffic building	(FEA) Cemetery	Tombs of Islamic Saints
		(FFA) Bridge	Luoyang bridge Anping bridge
		(FFC) Port ferry and wharf	Shihu dock Jiangkou Wharf
(H) Humanistic Activities	(HC) Folk customs	(HCC) Folk performing arts	Nanyin

ancient Zayton Trade Market Sites. Additionally, there are some related important heritages, but they do not mainly serve for the overseas trade. For example, the Kuzhaikeng Kiln Site, one of the China's Top 10 New Archaeological Discoveries in 2016, is not included in the above list because its products are not mainly used for export.

2.2 Overall Status Analysis

Overall, the above 24 Zayton heritage sites almost represent the status of the ancient Maritime Silk Road heritage in China.

(a) Zayton is rich in ancient Maritime Silk Road heritage. Zayton does not only have a large number of ancient sites, but also has a variety of typologies such as abandoned production sites and traffic sites etc. These heritages represent the most significant characteristics of three identified dimensions of Zayton maritime trading prominence in the 10th to fourteenth centuries, namely: the port infrastructure, the religious diversity, and the industrial production of trade products. Compared with other Chinese port cities such as Guangzhou, Ningbo, Yangzhou, Zhangzhou, Fuzhou, or Nanjing, Zayton preserves the largest number of historic buildings with different typologies linked to the ancient maritime trade. That's why these Zayton Port heritages exhibit a unique ocean-river-land transportation system that supported the flourishing of transnational trade and inter-cultural exchanges [5]. This is basically accepted by the world and even the three famous travelers of the Middle Ages, Marco Polo, Odorico da Pordenone and Ibn Battuta, having described the prosperous city of Zayton in their writings.

(b) In general, the Maritime Silk Road heritage of Zayton Port have been well protected and utilized. There is a set of institutional arrangements, technical support, professional talents, and financial guarantees involving the survey, statistics, planning, maintenance, monitoring, and display of the Zayton Port heritages. For examples, the Quanzhou Municipal Administration of Cultural Heritage has designed monitoring systems to address the identified pressures, including disaster prevention and early warning systems. Recently, these heritages are given some protection by constructed levees, and flood control measures are implemented by the Quanzhou Municipal Government, as well as fire control to wooden structures, and lightning protection for the pagodas. Of course, one of the most representative measure is the construction and operation of Quanzhou Maritime Transportation Museum. Founded in 1959, it is one of the first class museums and the earliest Maritime Museum in China reflecting the ancient overseas transportation, Maritime Silk Road and various economic and cultural exchanges. The Museum has several fixed thematic exhibitions, including Zayton Ancient Ship Exhibition, Zayton and Ancient Overseas Transportation History Exhibition, Zayton Religious Stone Carving Exhibition, Chinese Boat World, Arab Persian in Zayton and so on. More than 400 stone carvings of Islam, Ancient Christianity, Hinduism and Manichaeism found in Zayton during the Song-Yuan Dynasties are displayed in the Zayton Religious Stone Carving Exhibition.

(c) A great progress has also been made in the tourism utilization of the Zayton Port Heritages. Tourism service and presentation system has been developed for the Zayton Port sites in the Municipal Heritage Management Plan under the background of the culture and tourism integration advocated by the government.

(cont.) This involves the establishment of visitor centers, museums and exhibition halls, interpretation, and the use of video, internet and virtual technologies. Some of the Zayton Port sites such as Jiuri Mountain Wind-Praying Carving, Laojunyan Statue and Kaiyuan Temple have been developed into tourist attractions, and demanded to carry out the tourism carrying capacity and establish monitoring indicators by the Quanzhou Cultural and Tourism Bureau. For example, tourism has been developed well in Jinjiaoyi Hill Cizao kiln site, where there is an exhibition hall, well-design signage system, and a porcelain-making studio for demonstrating porcelain making skills to residents, students and tourists.

(d) Due to various historical and practical reasons, there are still some weak links or loopholes in the protection and utilization of Zayton Port Heritages. During the Cultural Revolution (1966–1976), many relics of Zayton were destroyed. Nowadays, besides the environmental degradation and change, weathering and corrosion of heritage body, etc., the most significant pressures are industrialization, modernization, urban development and mass tourism. A typical case is Shiposi Site, the only "Ancient Customs" site preserved in China today. Shiposi Site was formally established in 1087 AD., specializing in handling cargo and controversial trade matters. After Fujian Shiposi was moved to Fuzhou in 1472 AD., part of the site of the Zayton Shibosi was rebuilt into the Narcissus Palace. Shibosi sites were gradually abandoned and occupied by more and more dwellings and units, losing its original style and features. Approved by the Quanzhou Municipal Government in 2003, the Zayton Shibosi Site was handed over to the Watermen Community Protection Team, which were composed of six elderly people and without any salary. Therefore, it is not difficult to understand that every time We found in the recently survey, visitors came to the Shibosi Site with interest but returned with disappointment [6]. This case just reflects the problems and defects in the concept and consciousness of Zayton heritage protection, protection mechanism and system, protection organization and financial support.

3 Discussion

Based on the analysis above, key factors affecting the protection and utilization of Zayton heritage are summarized as belows.

3.1 Coupling Factors of Spatial Distribution

Different factors such as historical culture, population quantity, topography, rivers, and other factors might have close relationship with the heritage's spatial distribution[7].Thus, Mapwise software tools were used to input the spatial characteristics and other features of the above 24 heritage sites and analyze theme systematically.

(a) From the perspective of administrative jurisdiction, 22 heritages are distributed in coastal regions including Licheng District, Fengze District, Luojiang District, Quangang District and Hui'an County, Jinjiang City, Shishi City, while only 2 representative sites are located in Anxi County, Yongchun County, Dehua County, and Nan'an City where are relatively far away from the coastal zone. Based on the logical judgment, Fujian coastal areas enjoy the transportation and market benefits advantages from the trade ports. As an ancient port, Zayton is a natural harbor, which is narrow inside and wide outside (43 km wide, 30 m deep, an average water depth of 4.37 m and a tidal range of 6.4–7.7 m), forming the port cluster of Fashi Port, Houzhu Port, Luoyang Port, and Hanjiang Port. In The Travels of Marco Polo, Zayton port was as famous as Alexandria Port in Egypt. It was known as the largest port in the East and the world economic and cultural center in the song and Yuan Dynasties.

(b) In terms of the convenience of land and water transportation resources, it was found that the heritage site of the Zayton Port are basically distributed in "one bay and two rivers" zoon: Quanzhou Bay, Jinjiang River and Luoyang River. Convenient water transportation is another decisive factor in the selection of commodity production bases along the Maritime Silk Road. Take porcelain as an example, it is heavy and fragile and can be easily damaged by land transportation. Therefore, almost all ceramic production bases of Song-Yuan Dynasties in Fujian Province were close to rivers. Located near the Jiujiu River, a tributary of Jingjian River, the porcelain products of Jinjiaoyi Mountain Kiln site can be shipped directly to the mouth Jinjiang River. For Dehua porcelains, they were first transported by land to Xugang Port in Yongchun County and shipped to the destination along the Dongxi River, the upper tributary of Jinjiang River, down to the Jinjiang River estuary (Figs. 1 and 2).

(c) From the perspective of spatial span, the distribution of classified heritage sites in transportation and production bases are very scattered. For example, the driving distance between lighthouses-Houzhu Port and Liusheng Tower is 26 km, and the driving distance between Qudougong Kiln Site and Jinjiaoyi Hill of Cizao Kiln Site is 110 km. Moreover, the surrounding areas of these heritage sites are lack the support of convenient commercial service systems. As a result, the point divergence distribution of these sites imposes some constraints and difficulties on the protection and utilization of Zayton Port sites especially for centralized management and mass tourism development. On the contrary, small-scale in-depth cultural experience and study tour must be a good path for heritage protection and utilization.

Fig. 1 Porcelain waterways in Zayton

3.2 Vital Factors

3.2.1 Relics Legislation

Laws and regulations are the principles that control human behavior. Without legal constraints, ancient Maritime Silk Road heritages can be easily damaged due to industrialization, urbanization, building construction, etc. One of the important reasons why Zayton Port sites are relatively well protected is the priority of legislation. Three of them are additionally designated as National Scenic and Historic Areas, which are protected by National and Province Regulations, and twelve sites are located in the historical downtown conservation areas, which are protected by the Regulations on the Conservation of Historic and Cultural Cities, Towns and Villages (2008).

In addition to cultural heritage protection regulations such as the "Cultural Relics Protection Law of the People's Republic of China" and the "Regulations on the Management of Cultural Relics Protection of Fujian Province", special regulations on the cultural heritage of Quanzhou Maritime Silk Road have also been promulgated. In November 2003, "Measures for the Protection and Administration of the Cultural Heritage of Fujian Province along the Maritime Silk Road: Historical Records of

Fig. 2 River boat in Dongxi river (English translation: Boad on Yongchun River. In history, many Yongchun people took such boats and sailed down the stream, then sailed across the sea through Quanzhou port or Xiamen port to Southeast Asia to make a living, and finally won the reputation of "No Yongchun people, No market open".)

Quanzhou" was promulgated, which is two years ahead of the "Guangzhou Maritime Silk Road Historical Records Protection Regulations" and other similar legislations in other areas. Later in June 2007, the first national cultural ecological protection zone in China-the Minnan Cultural Ecological Protection Experimental Zone was designated in Quanzhou. Then, "The Conservation and Management Plan for the Historic Monuments and Sites of Ancient Quanzhou (Zayton) 2016–2030" was officially approved in January 2016, which is a legal document that gives effect to the management framework: overarching goals, principles, identifies measures for sites. There are also principles and measures for conservation, research, coordination of stakeholders, interpretation and tourism, and monitoring. In December 2019, the Decision of the People's Government of Fujian Province on Amending the Measures for the Protection and Management of the Cultural Heritage of the "Ancient Quanzhou (Zayton) Historical Relics" in Fujian Province was passed, which clearly stipulated the planning management, protection measures, funding guarantee, and legal responsibility etc.

In particular, the plan that 44th World Heritage Committee will be held in Fuzhou, which has had a great impact on the protection and utilization of Zayton heritage. For Quanzhou, this committee is the last and only chance to apply for the United Nation World Heritage List. That's why the local government has promulgated various policies and regulations to carry out large-scale historical heritage survey, investigation and environmental renovation, effectively promoting the protection and inheritance of Maritime Silk Road cultural heritage.

However, it was also found that these legal also tend to lead to another tendency in practice like neglecting protection or even destroying other cultural heritage that are not included in the protection list. The effectiveness of the regulation is related to the implementation of the universal heritage protection concept and protection measures.

3.2.2 Protection Concept

The development and characteristics of cultural heritage is a long-term process. Only by maintaining a dialectical relationship between the protection of cultural heritage and the promotion of cultural heritage can the authenticity, integrity and sustainability of cultural heritage be fully guaranteed development of. We should avoid taking utilitarianism as the leading factor, blindly seeking quickness, innovation, and change, and one-sided emphasis on formal, decorative, and superficial things, and ignore the essence of rational, scientific, humanized and ecological protection of cultural heritage [8]. From the selection of the heritage list, to the organizational structure and protection methods of heritage protection, it has been revealed that there are many shortcomings in Zayton's inscription that need to be improved.

The most disturbing thing is that the 2018 Zayton inscription did not include the Dehua Kiln Heritage Site which is the most important production base for export products. And there are two production bases included in the heritage sites added in the 2020 inscription list. All these reflect the vacillation in understanding and control of the overall integrity of the heritage. Based on our field survey, the pre-conservation of some newly added heritage observation points this year is disappointing: the original appearance of the heritage is incomplete, and the heritage space is occupied by modern buildings.

For protection methods, the World Heritage Committee has denounced that the Jiangkou Dock and estuary docks are a combination of older dock foundations and newer upper parts that have been restored in recent times, which has been affected by modern developments and it violates the principle of authenticity and integrity of world heritage. Another site, Shihu Dock, was also impacted by the nearby construction of a modern harbour, and the landscape context of the Kiln Sites of Jinjiaoyi Hill of Cizao is somewhat overwhelmed by the shelter covering the site and other new constructions, and so on.

Taking the opportunity of successfully applying for World Heritage, it is urgent to fully popularize the concept of heritage protection and utilization applied by the United Nations World Heritage Committee and comprehensively improve the quality of Zayton heritage protection and utilization.

3.2.3 Consumption Demand

Meeting consumer demand is the basis of heritage tourism operation. The differences in consumption patterns in different periods will also impose certain restrictions on the protection and utilization of cultural heritage.

Compared with the sightseeing tourism era, nowadays, the cultural tourism and in-depth immersion consumption are becoming more popular. In particular, since the government vigorously promoted study travel since 2016, the ancient kiln sites, which used to be visited only by a few people looking for in-depth cultural experience, are now receiving large-scale of student groups for study tour. On one hand, study travel greatly promotes tourism development and utilization of Zayton sites these years. On the other hand, it may threaten the protection of the cultural heritage ontology itself and maintenance of the heritage site environment. For example, after some Maritime Silk Road sites became tourist attractions, the number of tourist service facilities has been increased and the surrounding commercial atmosphere has been getting stronger, which greatly reduced the toursits' cultural experience.

3.2.4 Technology

Modern science and technology is crucial for heritage conservation and utilization. Firstly, technology directly affects or even determines the course of heritage survey and archaeological excavation. Meanwhile, the application of modern technology, especially new information technology such as AR(augmented reality)/VR(virtual reality), is key for heritage tourism development, especially for those ancient port sites such as Jiangkou Wharf, where the wharf is seriously silted up or buried with sediment due to the change of hydrologic environment. When tourists visit or intend to visit these sites, they can use VR/AR to transcend the limitation of time and space, experience the magnificent scenes of these historic sites, increase the experience of tourism and improve the satisfaction of tourism. The use of 3D modeling and innovative immersive virtual reality tools can further promote consumers' accessibility to cultural heritage through a more attractive and innovative way [9]. VR and AR environments, which can augment the reality at the destination or immerse the consumers in a new and completely challenging tourism experience, may be used to promote a destination or site in the future [10].

In fact, Quanzhou Maritime Transportation Museum has used a large number of modern technologies to display and protect cultural relics, which have achieved very good dissemination and education effects. In October 2018, under the guidance of archaeological experts and the cooperation of professional technical teams, Zayton had restored the Deji Gate in Song- Yuan Dynasties with modern 3D holographic projection technology. However, only a few heritage sites have implemented those modern technologies currently. The virtual roaming system of all the Zayton Port is under development according to the local government the latest plan.

3.2.5 Social Participation

Social participation has also been proved to be an effective mode for cultural heritage protection. Cultural heritage is a kind of public resource shared by all mankind beyond borders and races. The complexity of public affairs and the rise of non-governmental forces with self-organization and management capabilities force the government to reposition its functions objectively. Non-governmental organizations, enterprises and the general public have gradually become active participants in the field of cultural heritage conservation and utilization. Among them, youth groups play an important role [11]. At present, whether in the United States, the United Kingdom or other developed countries, social forces have participated effectively in the protection of cultural heritage. It has become a consensus to establish a cultural heritage conservation and utilization system integrating national protection and social participation.

According to the survey, Quanzhou residents have played an important role in tracing clues, protecting cultural relics, donating cultural relics, public supervision, or opening private museums and managing porcelain kilns. The protection of the Shiposi Site mentioned above is a typical case. Private investors are also important in heritage protection. For example, Wu Jintian, a ceramic studio known as "guardian of the Dehua memory of the Millennium", gave up Shanghai's urban life in 2009 and run ancient Yueji kiln in Dehua county which is the only firewood porcelain kiln for more than 400 years. Now, the Yueji kiln and International Contemporary Ceramics Center have attracted nearly 100 international ceramicists. Dozens of studios have settled in the New Yueji kiln Creative Industrial Park as well. However, some community residents do not care about heritage protection, and are not very enthusiastic or even indifferent to tourists.

3.2.6 Financial Support

Financial resources are another important factor which can perplex the ancient port sites. Exploration, excavation, monitoring, experimentation, collection, exhibition, research and development and even the construction of road traffic infrastructure require funds.

According to the relevant laws and regulations, the county-level's Government where the cultural heritage is located shall incorporate the funds required for heritage protection into the overall financial budget of the same level, and shall be used exclusively for the planning, protection, management, repair, display and utilization of the heritage. Unfortunately, it was found that some heritage buildings are in disrepair for a long time, and the surrounding environment is lack of renovation as well. In particular, some heritage sites surrounded by old neighborhoods lack enough space for heritage display, public leisure activities, and supporting facilities like parking lot etc. Additionally, due to financial constraints and institutional staffing restrictions, some cultural protection units have to streamline their staff and employ peasants with low education level in rural areas as cultural security personnel. They are paid as low as RMB 2500 per month, and some are even unpaid volunteers.

4 Conclusions

(a) Zayton port is one of the most important samples for the protection and utilization of the Maritime Silk Road heritage in China. It has made a lot of successful attempts and efforts in local heritage legislation, social mobilization and participation, heritage exhibition and tourism utilization, providing important historical and cultural support for the construction of the core area of the 21st Century Maritime Silk Road.

(b) Heritage protection and the development of heritage tourism are deeply influenced by national strategy in China. However, there is still a lot of work to be done, from heritage concept to technical support, to form a long-term mechanism for the heritage protection and tourism development of the Maritime Silk Road heritage (especially relevant to those heritage sites that are not listed in the government's key protection).

(c) Comprehensive consideration on reasonable protection and utilization of heritage and market satisfaction, in the face of different cultural demand markets, we should precisely subdivide the deep cultural experience oriented cultural tourists and "casual cultural tourists" to provide the corresponding heritage tourism products and services with environmental impact differentiation. Considering the spatial distribution and supporting service facilities of the Zayton Port heritages, study tour is one of the current rational choices and key development directions.

(d) Extensive and lasting community participation is one of the important signs of building the most popular destinations for study tour and heritage tourism. How to further build and improve the long-term mechanism of the social participation in the protection and utilization of Maritime Silk Road heritage is an important issue of social governance innovation: such as the bottom-up approach of heritage conservation and utilization planning, balancing the conflicting interests and power disparity of various stakeholders.

Acknowledgements We gratefully acknowledge the financial assistance of:
1. The Fujian Provincial Department of Education Projects, Study Tour Development of Ancient Port Site Along the Maritime Silk Road in Fujian (JAS180404).
2. The University Philosophy and Social Sciences Fundamental Project of Fujian Provincial, Conservation and Utilization of Maritime Silk Road Heritage: a case of porcelain kiln sites in Fujian (JSZM2020064) .

References

1. Xin, J.: Quanzhou's role in the Maritime Silk Route and its development. Econ. Res. Guid. **28**, 147 (2019)
2. Graham, B., Ashworth, G.J., Tunbridge, J.E.: A geography of heritage: power, culture, and economy. London Arnold (2000)
3. The Plan for the Construction of the 21st Century Maritime Silk Road Core Area of Fujian Province. http://www.fujian.gov.cn/zwgk/ztzl/sczl/, 1 January, 2016 (2015)
4. UNESCO: World Heritage List(Quanzhou: Emporium of the World in Song-Yuan China). http://whc.unesco.org/en/list/1561 (2021)
5. UNESCO: Extended 44th session of the World Heritage Committee.16–31 July (2021)
6. Yumei Xie: Quanzhou Shibosi Site decline, and six retired old people are obliged to guard it. http://qz.fjsen.com/2013-03/01/content_10751878_2.htm,1Mar (2013)
7. Qifu Wu: The temporal and spatial distribution of world cutural heritages in China: and Study on the world cultural heritage application in China. Tour. Sci. **24**(5), 25–31 (2010)
8. Jamieson, W.: Cultural heritage tourism. The George Washington University Career Education Program, Washington (2002)
9. Bekele, M.K., Pierdicca, R., Frontoni, E., et al.: A survey of augmented, virtual, and mixed reality for cultural heritage. Acm J. Comp. Cult. Herit. **11**(2), 7:1–7:36 (2018)
10. Guttentag, D.A.: Virtual reality: applications and implications for tourism. Tour. Manag. **31**(5), 637–651 (2010)
11. Zeynep Yazıcıoğlu Halu et al.: Public participation of young people for architectural heritage conservation. Soc. Behav. Sci. **225**, 166–179 (2016)

Effects of Destination-Language Proficiency on Tourists' Motivation

Yinan Li, Raúl Hernández-Martín, and Pablo Rodríguez-González

Abstract The language barrier has been typically studied as a constraint in international tourism. Little research has focused on how learning the destination language could affect the potential tourists' motivations, perceptions, and intentions. This paper investigates this topic through a survey aimed at Chinese university students as potential visitors to Spain. The primary objective is to explore how these differences influence their travel motivation, perceived cultural distance, perceived destination image of Spain, and behavioural intentions to visit Spain. Statistical analyses, including exploratory factor analysis and one-way ANOVA tests, were conducted to examine these factors. Our findings reveal the statistically significant differences among the students with different Spanish language proficiency. Practical implications are provided for Spanish destination management on attracting more Chinese tourists after the pandemic of COVID-19.

Keywords Travel motivations · Perceived cultural distance · Destination image · Behavioural intentions · Spain · COVID-19

1 Introduction

Spanish is generally considered a valuable and significant language in international communication. According to data published by Instituto Cervantes [1], it is the second most spoken language with more than 585 million speakers worldwide, which means that 7.6% of the world population can communicate in Spanish. It is also the second-most-studied foreign language with over 22 million students in the world [1]. In China, due to the rapid development of political-economic relations with the

Y. Li (✉) · R. Hernández-Martín · P. Rodríguez-González
University of La Laguna, San Cristóbal de la Laguna, Santa Cruz de Tenerife, Spain
e-mail: alu0100735147@ull.edu.es

R. Hernández-Martín
e-mail: rahernan@ull.edu.es

P. Rodríguez-González
e-mail: prodrigg@ull.edu.es

Hispanic countries, an increasing number of young Chinese people are learning and speaking Spanish as a foreign language. Spanish language proficiency is becoming one of the most requested professional skills due to its relevance in the labour market. As a result, Spain has become an ideal tourist destination for Chinese students to improve their Spanish skills and cultural knowledge.

Given the increasing number of Chinese tourists in Spain, academic attention has been drawn to understanding this large tourist source market [2–6]. Much of this research identifies the language barrier as one of the most significant constraints for Chinese tourists visiting Spain. Similar findings were also reported in previous studies about Chinese tourists in other Western destinations (e.g., see [7] and [8]). However, these studies have only focused on how the language gap causes troubles and misunderstandings in tourist-host intercultural communications [9, 10] and how the lack of destination-language fluency negatively affect tourists' experiences [8, 11], satisfaction [13], and travel patterns [12]. Nevertheless, little effort has been made to explore how knowing the destination language affects potential tourists, particularly their motivations, perceptions towards the destination, and intentions to visit it. Hence, our study attempts to fill this gap by investigating the effects of Spanish language proficiency on potential Chinese tourists to Spain.

The COVID-19 pandemic has caused a tremendously negative impact on the Spanish tourism industry. Spain was the world's second most visited country in 2019 and has experienced a dramatic decrease in international tourist arrivals amid global travel restrictions [14]. Unlike other sectors, tourism is a crucial field for Spain's economy. Hence, the recovery of the tourism industry for Spain will be particularly important. In contrast, China had the world's largest outbound tourism market in pre-pandemic times. Following the country's effective control of COVID-19 transmission, the Chinese tourist sector is gradually recovering and the confidence of Chinese tourists about travelling abroad is also increasing. Many professionals have estimated that a strong rebound of Chinese outbound tourism will likely take place when mobility between countries returns to normal. However, until now, research regarding the recovery of Spanish tourism has only focused on providing strategies for recovering domestic tourism demand [14, 15]. Therefore, through an analysis of potential Chinese tourists, our paper aims to give recommendations for improving the attractiveness of Spain as a destination for a future wave of Chinese tourists after the COVID-19 pandemic ends.

To achieve these objectives, the remaining part of this paper is structured as follows. The second section reviews travel motivations, perceived destination image, perceived cultural distance, and tourist behavioural intentions. The third section presents the research design and the methodology. The firth section shows the study's findings, followed by a discussion of its implications related to the COVID-19 pandemic. The last section concludes the research and identifies its contributions and limitations.

2 Literature Review

2.1 Tourist Motivation

Motivation is the key driving force behind people's behaviours. Travel motivation can be defined as *"the global integrating network of biological and cultural forces which gives value and direction on travel choices, behaviours, and experience"* [16]. Scholars usually classify travel motivations as *push* and *pull* factors [17–19]. According to Dann [19], *pull* factors are the external resources that attract tourists to one destination over another, and *push* factors refer to internal forces that predispose a tourist to travel. Baloglu and Uysal [20] argue that *push* factors are related to individuals' desires, including personal escape, psychological or physical health benefits, thrill and adventure, and social interactions. In contrast, *pull* factors are related to the attributes of the chosen destination, such as natural and historical attractions [20]. Crompton [17] identifies and classifies nine motivations for pleasure vacations, including two *pull* (cultural) and seven *push* (social-psychological) motives. The two cultural motives were *novelty* and *education*. The seven social-psychological motives comprised *escape from routine, self-discovery, relaxation, improving family relationships, facilitating social interaction, prestige*, and *regression*. To date, the concept of the *push* and *pull* model has been well accepted by most studies on tourist motivations, and no other tourist motivational model has survived the full rigour of empirical verification [21, 22].

In the case of Chinese travellers, some studies have attempted to explore their travel motivations in the context of Western destinations. For example, according to push and pull factors, Prayag et al. [23] identified three types (e.g., *Essentials, Exigent* and *Low personalisation*) of young Chinese travellers to Western Europe. Pung and Del Chiappa [24] found that the primary motivation to travel to Europe was exploring different cultures. Lojo [25] analysed the differences between young Chinese and more mature Chinese tourists in Spain. The results showed that the younger Chinese tourists give more importance to increasing knowledge and getting to know the Western culture.

2.2 Perceived Destination Image

Tourist destination image is generally defined in the literature as an individual's knowledge, feelings, and overall perception of a particular destination [17]. Kotler and Gertner [26] also describe the destination image as the sum of people's beliefs and impressions about a place. Existing research reveals two main destination image components: cognitive and affective. The cognitive image refers to functional or tangible elements, while the affective image involves physical or intangible components, such as positive or negative impressions of the place [27, 28]. It is widely accepted that tourists' perceptions of a destination influence the destination selection process [29, 30] and their behavioural intentions [31, 32].

Considering the importance of the perceived destination image, a large and growing body of tourism literature has investigated factors that influence people's perception of particular destinations. For example, Beerli and Martín identified that the motivations influence the affective components of the image, and the level of experience positively affects the cognitive dimensions of the destination image [33]. Hudson and Wang [34] indicate that films can change viewers' perceptions of a place—in the case of their study, South America. After watching a film, a large percentage of the study participants expressed a desire to visit the country. San Martín & Del Bosque [35] argue that the destination image which the individual has before the trip is partially affected by the cultural distance between their origin country and the destination. In other words, tourists with similar values to the destination's culture will positively perceive the destination. Similarly, Kastenholz [36] also confirmed the impact of cultural proximity on destination image. As a result, the question *"Does learning the destination language, in our case Spanish, affect potential Chinese tourists' perception of Spain as a tourist destination?"* arises very naturally. The findings will help us understand how the destination image of Spain is perceived by potential Chinese travellers, a topic that has not yet been thoroughly investigated.

2.3 Perceived Cultural Distance

Cultural distance has been acknowledged as the extent to which a tourist's home country's culture is different from or similar to that of a destination [37]. According to Crompton [17], international tourists have two common reasons for travelling: escape from their everyday environment and the search for novelty. Namely, people decide to travel abroad because they want to experience something new and different. In this way, cultural distance is commonly considered as a motivational factor that can push individuals towards destinations with different cultures. Therefore, the greater the cultural distance, the more attractive the destination will be to the tourist. However, other researchers have identified the adverse effects of cultural distance on tourists' behaviours [38, 39]. For example, Lepp and Gibson [38] found that people perceived greater travel risk when visiting destinations with more cultural differences due to ignorance of the local language and customs. This negative relationship between cultural distance and tourists' intention to visit a destination was also confirmed by Ng et al. [39] in the context of the Australian tourists' intentions to visit international destinations.

A more recent study argues that the effect of cultural distance on international travel is not absolutely positive or negative. Bi and Lehto [40] developed an inverted U-curve model to account for this relationship and calculated the safe cultural distance for Chinese outbound tourists' destination choice as 2.8757. In the same study, they also calculated the cultural distance between China and Spain (2.7747), which was quite close to the optimal point. That means, other conditions being equal, Spain could attract more Chinese tourists because of its close to optimal cultural distance. Other researchers like Liu et al. [37] reported that perceived cultural distance does not significantly impact international destination choice except when cultural motivation moderates. Specifically, people with higher levels of cultural motivation to travel were more likely to visit culturally distant destinations.

Many factors affect individuals' perceptions of cultural distance. Generally, familiarity with the destination decreases the perceived cultural distance; on the contrary, geographic and psychological distance are negative antecedents. Based on extant literature, the present study proposes the following research question: *What is the impact of learning Spanish on Chinese tourists' perception of the cultural distance between China and Spain?*

2.4 Tourist Behavioural Intention

Behavioural intention is an essential concept for understanding tourists' selection of destinations and future behaviours. It is defined as *"an indication of how hard people are willing to try, of how much an effort they are planning to exert, in order to perform the behaviour"* [41]. According to Prayag et al. [42], tourist behavioural intentions can be divided into two dimensions: intention to visit a particular destination and willingness to recommend that destination. The current study is interested in understanding the possible effect of learning Spanish on Chinese people's intention to visit Spain and recommend Spain as a tourist destination.

3 Methodology

3.1 Research Design

Our study investigates how Spanish language proficiency affects Chinese tourists' motivations to travel, the perceived destination image of Spain, the perceived cultural distance between China and Spain, and the intention to visit and recommend Spain as a tourist destination. A quantitative method involving a self-administered survey was adopted to achieve these objectives. The targeted population was divided into three comparison groups with different levels of Spanish proficiency: Spanish-major students (Group 1), non-major Spanish learners (Group 2), and students who had never learned Spanish (Group 3). To ensure the sample's representativeness, we set a quota of 200 responses for each group.

3.2 Data Collection

The final questionnaire was distributed between September 2019 and February 2020 via the Wenjuan online platform, which allows the participants to access the survey within WeChat (*Weixin* in Chinese) by scanning a quick response (QR) code. To increase the completion rates, we employed monetary incentives at the end of the survey. Each participant completing the survey received a digital red packet that contained virtual cash transferrable to the participant's WeChat wallet. A total of 642 surveys were well finished and used in the study.

The main sample was made up of university students. Previous studies in tourism have considered university students as a homogenous population in terms of age and education [17, 52]. As such, lecturers and professors from three large public universities in China helped distribute the questionnaire. Group 1 consisted of students who majored in Spanish and mainly came from the Department of Spanish Philology of Tianjin Foreign Studies University. The second group (G2) included people who had studied Spanish but not majored in it. The main population of Group 2 were students who learned Spanish as an optional course at Beijing Information Science and Technology University. The last group (G3) was mainly composed of students from the Dalian Neusoft University of Information, and they had never studied any Spanish before the survey.

3.3 Measurement

A five-part structured questionnaire was designed based on a review of relevant literature. All continuous variables in the survey were measured using a five-point Likert Scale, which has been noted to increase response rate and response quality while reducing respondents' frustration levels [43, 44]. The first section of the questionnaire examined the respondents' motivations for taking an overseas trip. The measures were assessed via 29 five-point Likert Scale questions, ranging from 1 *(not at all important)* to 5 *(extremely important)*. These items roughly covered the *pull* and *push* motives, including *novelty, education, escape from routine and relaxation, self-discovery, prestige,* and *improving family relationships/social interaction*. All these items were rephrased into statements consistent with the context of Chinese tourists' motivations.

The second section dealt with measuring Spain's destination image perceived by Chinese tourists. First, cognitive images of Spain were measured with 25 items covering four aspects: *natural/cultural resources, infrastructure and socioeconomic environment, social conditions,* and *atmosphere* [27, 28, 30, 31, 45]. Respondents were asked to indicate their agreement level for each item on a five-point Likert scale, ranging from 1 *(strongly disagree)* to 5 *(strongly agree)*. Moreover, respondents were also given a choice to reply to *N/A (No answer)* to avoid false neutral evaluations [46]. Second, the affective components were assessed with four 5-point semantic differential scales: *sleepy-arousing, distressing-relaxing, gloomy-exciting,* and *unpleasant-pleasant*. Last, the overall destination image was measured by asking respondents to indicate their general feelings toward the destination. A five-point measurement scale ranging from 1 *(strongly negative)* to 5 *(strongly positive)* was adopted from Baloglu and McCleary [27].

The third section captured respondents' behavioural intentions, which consisted of the intention to visit Spain and recommend it. The first variable was estimated with three items: (1) *I intend to visit Spain in the future*; (2) *I want to visit Spain*, and (3) *It is likely that I will visit Spain in the future* [47, 48]. The recommendation variable was measured by asking the respondents to answer: (1) *I will recommend Spain to my friends or family as an ideal travel destination;* (2) *I would say positive things about Spain to other people*; (3) *I will encourage my friends or family to visit Spain* [37, 49]. All items were scored on a five-point Likert Scale, measuring whether the respondents' agreed or disagreed with each statement.

The fourth section of the questionnaire comprised three questions on tourists' perceived cultural distance. The first question was adapted from Liu et al. [37]: *How do you perceive the cultural distance between China and Spain?* Participants were asked to rate cultural distance on a scale of 1 to 5 (1 = *very small*, 5 = *very large*). The other two items were adopted from various recent studies [39, 50, 51]. Respondents were asked how difficult it would be to adapt to the Spanish language environment and the Spanish lifestyle. Both items were measured with 5-point Likert Scale from 1 (*very easy*) to 5 (*very difficult*). The questionnaire's final section assessed sociodemographic information (i.e., *gender, age, language proficiency, monthly income,* and *previous visits to Spain*).

The questionnaire was initially developed in Spanish and then translated into Chinese and revised by two bilingual experts. To ensure the accuracy of meaning, items selected from studies in English were translated directly into Chinese. The translated version was further verified by a Chinese professor who is proficient in English.

4 Findings

4.1 Profile of Respondents

Within the sample of 642 respondents, female students accounted for 63.9%, while male students made up 36.1%. The gender imbalance was more severe in the Spanish major students compared with the other groups. All the respondents were considerably young in terms of age, and more than half of the participants (60.4%) were between 19–21 years old. Regarding monthly household income, most respondents had a gross monthly household income between RMB ¥5,000–15,000 which is roughly China's middle-class income. The sociodemographic characteristics of the sample are presented in Table 1.

Table 1 Sociodemographic profile of the three sample groups

Sociodemographic characteristics		Total (n = 642)		G1 (n = 208)		G2 (n = 175)		G3 (n = 259)	
		n	%	n	%	n	%	n	%
Gender	Male	232	36.1	43	20.7	56	32.0	133	51.4
	Female	410	63.9	165	79.3	119	68.0	126	48.6
Age	16–18	94	14.6	35	16.8	37	21.1	22	8.5
	19–21	388	60.4	122	58.7	99	56.6	167	64.5
	22–24	93	14.5	24	16.3	15	8.6	44	17.0
	25 and above	67	10.4	17	8.2	24	13.7	26	10.0
Monthly household gross income	Less than 5,000	87	13.6	28	13.5	14	8.0	45	17.4
	¥5001–10,000	161	25.1	63	30.3	31	17.7	67	25.8
	¥10,001–15,000	107	16.7	33	15.8	35	20.0	39	15.1
	¥15,001–20,000	63	9.8	19	9.1	19	10.9	25	9.7
	¥20,001–30,000	45	7.0	16	7.7	19	10.9	10	3.9
	¥30,001 and above	26	4.1	6	2.9	9	5.1	11	4.2
	N/A	152	23.7	43	20.7	48	27.4	62	23.9

4.2 Factor Analysis of Variables

An Exploratory Factor Analysis (EFA) was conducted to identify the underlying dimensions of travel motivations and the Spanish destination image. The Principal Component method and varimax rotation were applied. The total variance explained was 56.619% for motivations and 62.910% for destination image. The Kaiser–Meyer–Olkin (KMO) measure of sampling was 0.901 and 0.928, respectively. Bartlett's test of sphericity values was both significant ($p = 0.000$), which means the data was very suitable for EFA. Items with lower factor loadings than 0.5 were deleted. Reliability analysis was also performed, and Cronbach's alpha values demonstrated an acceptable level of internal consistency (Cronbach's alpha of perceived cultural distance = 0.602, which is also acceptable according to Griethuijsen et al. [53]). Mean ratings of all items obtained from EFA are also provided in Table 2.

4.3 Estimating the Effects of Spanish Language Learning

As there were statistically significant differences between the three groups with different Spanish language abilities, a series of one-way analyses of variance (ANOVA) were performed alongside Tukey's post hoc test to identify which groups have means that differ significantly. As illustrated in Table 3, there was a statistical difference between the three groups regarding travel motivations' composite

Table 2 Factor analysis results (n = 642)

Variables/Items	M	SD	Factor loading	Cronbach's alpha
Travel motivation				
[TM1] Culture and Novelty seeking	4.13	0.67		0.765
To discover new culture and lifestyle	4.31	0.83	0.607	
To visit places related to my personal interests	4.26	0.84	0.768	
To have unpredictable experiences	4.18	0.91	0.689	
To feel the different atmosphere of the destination	4.08	0.93	0.568	
To visit cultural and historical attractions	3.85	1.07	0.604	
[TM2] Escape and Relax	3.94	0.85		0.793
To feel inner harmony/peace	4.12	0.97	0.73	
To seek release from work/study pressure	3.99	1.01	0.552	
Being free to act as I feel	3.86	1.16	0.816	
Feeling accomplished	3.79	1.15	0.73	
[TM3] Ego-enhancement and Self-development	3.68	0.81		0.781
To meet new and different people	3.94	1.05	0.599	
To enrich myself intellectually	3.7	1.07	0.709	
To interact with local people	3.64	1.09	0.643	
To develop skills and abilities	3.63	1.08	0.681	
To learn something from the trip	3.39	1.2	0.664	
[TM4] Enhancement of social relationships and Prestige	2.8	0.93		0.823
To go to a famous or prestigious place	3.02	1.28	0.746	
Travelling abroad makes me feel prestigious	3	1.28	0.684	
To go to places that friends have not visited	2.94	1.31	0.68	
To be able to tell friends about holiday experiences	2.82	1.23	0.719	
To visit friends or relatives	2.65	1.26	0.586	
To go to fashionable places	2.37	1.26	0.777	
Cognitive image				
[COG1] Natural and cultural resources	4.12	0.54		0.837
Architecture	4.24	0.75	0.678	
Culture attractions	4.17	0.75	0.729	
Costumes	4.17	0.7	0.73	
History	4.13	0.69	0.746	
Gastronomy	4.07	0.8	0.75	
Cultural activities	4.06	0.74	0.522	

(continued)

Table 2 (continued)

Variables/Items	M	SD	Factor loading	Cronbach's alpha
Adventure	3.78	0.88	0.74	
[COG 2] Atmosphere and social environment	3.96	0.53		0.733
Exotic	4.2	0.7	0.57	
Reputation	3.9	0.67	0.725	
Climate	3.87	0.7	0.712	
Peace	3.82	0.7	0.541	
[COG 3] Infrastructures and socioeconomic environment	3.6	0.6		0.837
Connection	3.9	0.77	0.701	
Accessibility	3.66	0.83	0.693	
Price-quality	3.61	0.75	0.584	
Shopping	3.59	0.82	0.738	
General infrastructures	3.5	0.79	0.744	
Price	3.21	0.9	0.659	
Affective image	**3.94**	**0.76**		**0.882**
Sleepy—arousing	3.92	0.91	0.854	
Distressing—relaxing	3.91	0.98	0.853	
Gloomy—exciting	3.9	0.95	0.858	
Unpleasant—pleasant	3.96	0.98	0.857	
Negative—positive	4.03	0.74	0.714	
***Perceived cultural distance**	**2.57**	**0.71**		**0.602**
[PCD1] Perceived cultural distance between China and Spain	2.28	0.86	0.585	
[PCD2] How difficult it is to adapt to the Spanish language environment	2.61	1.04	0.824	
[PCD3] How difficult it is to adapt to the Spanish lifestyle	2.81	0.95	0.81	
Behavioural intentions				
[INT] Intention to visit Spain	3.96	0.96		0.912
I intend to visit Spain in future	3.88	1.09	0.869	
I want to visit Spain	4.05	1.02	0.85	
It is likely that I will visit Spain in future	3.98	1.03	0.87	
[REC] Intention to recommend Spain as destination	3.71	0.91		0.907
Recommend Spain to my friends or family	3.79	0.97	0.794	
Say positive things about Spain	3.71	0.95	0.886	
Encourage friends or family to visit Spain	3.62	1.05	0.878	

* All items of perceived cultural distance were reversed scored

Table 3 ANOVA multiple comparisons and post hoc test

Variables	Mean			F value	Sig	Post hoc test results		
	G1	G2	G3			G1 vs G2	G1 vs G3	G2 vs G3
TM	3.492[b]	3.6	3.654[a]	3.909	0.021*	−0.108	−0.162*	−0.054
TM1	4.118	4.250[a]	4.109[b]	2.712	0.067	−0.132	0.009	0.141
TM2	3.703[b]	3.82	3.865[a]	2.406	0.091	−0.117	−0.162	−0.045
TM3	3.617[b]	3.702	3.717[a]	0.962	0.383	−0.844	−0.099	−0.015
TM4	2.597[b]	2.734	2.997[a]	11.615	0.000***	−0.137	−0.401***	−0.264**
COG	4.101[a]	3.961	3.762[b]	16.764	0.000***	0.141*	0.339*	0.199*
COG1	4.346[a]	4.215	3.894[b]	37.696	0.000***	0.132*	0.452***	0.321***
COG2	3.759[a]	3.607	3.554[b]	4.303	0.014*	0.152	0.206*	0.053
COG3	4.098[a]	4.056	3.829[b]	13.239	0.000***	0.042	0.269***	0.227***
AI	4.168	4.200[a]	3.687[b]	36.771	0.000***	−0.032	0.482***	0.513***
PCD	2.726[a]	2.535	2.462[b]	8.398	0.000***	0.191*	0.264*	0.073
PCD1	2.25	2.220[b]	2.340[a]	1.048	0.351	0.032	−0.082	−0.114
PCD2	3.000[a]	2.54	2.360[b]	23.942	0.000***	0.458***	0.639***	0.181
PCD3	2.930[a]	2.85	2.690[b]	3.741	0.024*	0.082	0.234*	0.152
BI	4.207[a]	4.004	3.402[b]	60.526	0.000***	0.203*	0.806***	0.603***
INT	4.448[a]	4.222	3.482[b]	72.938	0.000***	0.227*	0.966***	0.740***
REC	4.045[a]	3.834	3.345[b]	40.995	0.000***	0.211*	0.700***	0.489***

TM = Travel motivations; COG = Cognitive image; AI = Affective image; PCD = Perceived cultural distance; BI = Behavioural intentions; INT = Intentions to visit; REC = Intentions to recommend
* $p < 0.05$; ** $p < 0.01$; *** $p < 0.001$
[a] The highest rating among the three groups; [b] The lowest rating among the three groups

mean score. Furthermore, the post hoc test revealed that the travel motivations of students who had never learned Spanish (G3) were statistically significantly higher than Spanish major students (G1). The results also indicated that generally, all participants scored highest on *culture and novelty seeking* (TM1) and lowest on *Enhancement of social relationships and Prestige* (TM4). Moreover, the non-major Spanish learners (G2) were more motivated by *culture and novelty seeking* (TM1) compared to the other two groups. There was no significant difference between the major and non-major Spanish students (G1 vs. G2) for any of the four motivation factors.

In regard to destination image evaluations, the ANOVA analysis revealed statistical differences across the three groups for all cognitive and affective components. Respondents who major in Spanish (G1) rated Spain's cognitive image highest, while those who never studied Spanish (G3) gave the lowest scores. The affective image of Spain was generally perceived more positively by the non-major Spanish learners (G2) than other groups. Overall, the major and non-major Spanish students (G1, G2) had nearly the same scores, except for Spain's natural and cultural image (COG1), which were slightly different.

As Table 3 shows, significant differences exist among the three groups regarding the perceptions of cultural distance between China and Spain. The Spanish major students (G1) gave the highest composite mean score, while students without any Spanish language abilities (G3) gave the lowest one. More concretely, the PCD2 (language adaption) and PCD3 (lifestyle adaption) were significantly higher rated by the Spanish major students (G1) than other participants. Additionally, no significant difference was found between G2 (non-major Spanish students) and G3 (Students without Spanish proficiency) for any dimensions. The results indicate that Spanish language learning has a significantly positive influence on perceived cultural distance, especially regarding the destination's language and lifestyle differences.

For the behavioural intentions, the data shows that Spanish major students (G1) have more positive intentions to visit Spain and recommend it as a tourist destination compared to individuals from the other two groups. A post hoc test revealed that the mean differences between the three groups on all dimensions of behavioural intentions were statistically different.

5 Discussions and Implications

5.1 *Key Findings and Discussions*

These findings are important for several reasons. First, they determine the dimensions of young Chinese travellers' motivations. The EFA extracted four underlying motivational factors: (1) *Culture/Novelty seeking*; (2) *Escape/Relax*; (3) *Ego-enhancement/Self-development*; and (4) *Enhancement of social relationships and Prestige*. Among these dimensions, *cultural/novelty seeking* were most important for young Chinese travellers. *Discovering new cultures and lifestyles* was the *push* motive with the highest mean score. The participants also highly rated *escape and relaxation*, especially in *feeling inner harmony/peace*. These findings are similar to the young Chinese travellers' motivations identified in earlier studies [23–25]. The results of the ANOVA tests indicated the existence of a significant difference ($\alpha = 0.05$) in travel motivations between the Spanish major students and the students without any Spanish knowledge. More specially, students who had never studied Spanish were more motivated to travel abroad than the Spanish-major students. This finding was unexpected considering the large proportion of students from this sample group (55.6%) without any Spanish proficiency and with only a basic level of English. In the previous studies, language barriers were mainly described as one of the top inhibitors for Chinese tourists travelling abroad [7]. Our study does not find evidence of this inhibitory effect on tourists' overseas travel motivations.

Second, *pull* motives associated with cognitive destination attributes were highest rated by the Spanish major students. A possible explanation for this result may be the close relationships between language and culture. Learning Spanish, especially as a university major, inevitably involves learning Spanish culture. The students' strong inclination toward Spanish culture may help them generate a more positive image of Spain as a tourist destination. However, the non-major Spanish students perceived a slightly more favourable affective image of Spain than the Spanish major students. Interestingly, in this study, the non-major Spanish students were also the most motivated by *cultural* and *novelty seeking*. As mentioned in the literature review, the affective image refers to the individual's feelings or emotions toward the tourist destination [28]. It is affected by some psychological motivations (i.e., *leisure, knowledge, social interaction*) [54]. In this regard, the results support previous observations about the positive impact of culture on tourists' affective destination image [18, 35, 54].

Third, the differences in perceived cultural distance among the three groups were statistically significant. However, these differences were not obvious when we asked the respondents about their general perception of cultural distance between China and Spain. Indeed, students who had never studied Spanish rated a slightly higher mean score for this item. That is to say, the ignorance of the destination language may not affect perceived cultural distance for potential Chinese young travellers. Significant differences were only found on items related to language distance and lifestyle differences. Students who had learned Spanish rated higher scores on these two items. These results confirm that Spanish learning can positively influence the perceived cultural distance between China and Spain. This effect is more significant on some particular aspects (i.e., *linguistic distance*). Finally, Spanish-major students showed relatively higher behavioural intentions compared to other respondents. Moreover, non-major Spanish learners also demonstrated higher intentions than students who had never studied Spanish, which indicates that even a moderate amount of language ability positively affects tourists' behavioural intentions.

5.2 Theoretical and Practical Implications

Academically, these findings offer several contributions to the extant literature. First, this research represents one of the first attempts to test the effects of foreign language learning on tourist behaviours. Second, young Chinese travellers' overseas travel motivations were empirically identified and compared based on their Spanish language proficiency. This new understanding should improve predictions regarding the impact of language barriers on Chinese outbound tourists' travel motivations. Third, by investigating the Chinese tourists in Spain, this paper extends studies on Chinese tourists into a new Western context. Finally, destination-language learning (i.e., Spanish language learning) positively affected tourists' perceptions of cultural distance, contributing to the lack of research on antecedents of perceived cultural distance. Moreover, this research has optimised the perceptual measure of cultural distance by adding new dimensions.

The research findings have some practical and managerial implications for the post-crisis recovery of Spanish tourism. First, the multidimensional measure of Chinese young people's motivations for travelling abroad allows tourism authorities and stakeholders who have limited knowledge about Chinese tourists to understand how to capture a share of this source market. Generally, two important motivations factors can be highlighted from the results. The most important one is cultural and novelty seeking, especially discovering the culture and lifestyle of the destination country. Thus, marketers and specialist organisations in Spain should focus on promoting culture-related tourism products and activities in the recovery process. However, the results also demonstrated that escaping to relax and achieve inner peace is very important for Chinese travellers, especially after suffering a severe lockdown due to the COVID-19 pandemic. Thus, classic Spanish tour packages designed to visit several city destinations like Madrid or Barcelona in a few days should not be as widely promoted as before. Mass tourism should be planned more cautiously. Youth travellers from China may prefer a niche package, incorporating wellness services and cultural attractions. Spanish destinations which were unpopular with Chinese tourists before the pandemic may benefit from changes to tourism patterns.

Second, language and education-based tourism can help create a better image of Spain as a tourist destination and provide marketing opportunities for destination management organisations (DMOs). Spanish-major students can be identified as relatively stable consumers for the Spanish tourism market. DMOs should enhance cooperation with universities and language institutions in Spain and educational establishments in China. Virtual exchange programmes could be designed and offered to Chinese students during the pandemic. Both Spanish language courses and diverse cultural activities should be included in these programmes. Marketing strategies should emphasise language and education activities during the recovery of Spanish inbound tourism. Being a type of tourism that involves a more extended stay, it naturally generates more revenue for the destination. Moreover, language tourism could also fulfil the emerging needs of Chinese tourists after the pandemic, that is, travelling less frequently but spending more time at the destination [55]. Spanish language students in China also could play a key influential role in cultural transmission, primarily through digital channels. DMOs should work on cooperating with them through Chinese social media platforms to target more potential travellers.

6 Conclusion and Limitations

The present study was designed to explore the effects of Spanish language learning on travel motivations, perceived cultural distance, perceived destination image, and the behavioural intentions of young Chinese travellers. A quantitative method using questionnaire survey data was applied. Measurement scales of proposed variables were developed following the previous literature and validated based on Chinese travellers to Spain. Data analysis methods, including descriptive analysis, factor analysis, and ANOVA tests, were performed to examine the data. The findings confirmed the positive effects of Spanish language proficiency on young Chinese people's travel motivations, perceptions, and intentions to visit Spain as a tourist destination. This research contributes to studies of Chinese outbound travellers in the context of Western countries and provides valuable insights into the potential role of language tourism in Spain's tourism recovery plan after the pandemic.

Several limitations should be considered for future research. These findings are limited to university students, who do not sufficiently represent Chinese young people as a whole. Moreover, samples were mainly collected from three universities, which may not accurately represent the whole student population. Due to the size of samples and sampling methods, future research should use a larger sample from more diverse backgrounds. Furthermore, the perceived cultural distance was measured by three items extracted from different studies. The use of this construct has not previously been empirically tested in the field. Hence, future research may focus on improving the measurement of perceived cultural distance and validating the scale presented within.

References

1. Instituto Cervantes: *El español: una lengua viva. Informe 2020*, https://cvc.cervantes.es/lengua/espanol_lengua_viva/pdf/espanol_lengua_viva_2020.pdf. (2020)
2. Andreu, R., Claver, E., Quer, D.: Destination attributes and Chinese outbound tourism to Europe 目的地特性和中国对欧洲的对外旅游. J. China Tour. Res. **10**(3), 275–291 (2014)
3. Lojo, A.: Chinese tourism in Spain: an analysis of the tourism product, attractions and itineraries offered by Chinese travel agencies. Cuadernos de Turismo, 243–268 (2016)
4. Lojo, A., Li, M.: Segmentation by experiential familiarity and travel mode of the Chinese outbound market to Spain. J. China Tour. Res. **14**(1), 100–121 (2018)
5. Lin, J., Guia Julve, J., Xu, H., Cui, Q.: Food habits and tourist food consumption: an exploratory study on dining behaviours of Chinese outbound tourists in Spain. J. Policy Res. Tour. Leisure Events **12**(1), 82–99 (2020)

6. Tan, Y., Huang, S.: Open Chinese tourism market for coastal destinations in Spain—taking Majorca Island as an example. In: Tourism Product Development in China. Asian and European Countries, pp. 109–119. Springer, Singapore (2020)
7. Sparks, B., Pan, G.W.: Chinese outbound tourists: Understanding their attitudes, constraints and use of information sources. Tour. Manage. **30**(4), 483–494 (2009)
8. Ying, T., Wen, J., Wang, L.: Language facilitation for outbound Chinese tourists: importance-performance and gap analyses of New Zealand hotels. J. Travel Tour. Mark. **35**(9), 1222–1233 (2018)
9. Reisinger, Y.: Tourist—host contact as a part of cultural tourism[J]. World Leisure Recr. **36**(2), 24–28 (1994)
10. Mancini-Cross, C., Backman, K.F., Baldwin, E.D.: The effect of the language barrier on intercultural communication: a case study of educational travel in Italy[J]. J. Teach. Travel Tour. **9**(1–2), 104–123 (2009)
11. Gu, Q., Huang, S.: Profiling Chinese wine tourists by wine tourism constraints: A comparison of Chinese Australians and long-haul Chinese tourists in Australia[J]. Int. J. Tour. Res. **21**(2), 206–220 (2019)
12. Ma, E.J., Duan, B., Shu, L.M., Arcodia, C.: Chinese visitors at Australia wineries: preferences, motivations, and barriers[J]. J. Tour. Herit. Serv. Market. **3**(1), 3–8 (2017)
13. Li, G., Song, H., Chen, J.L., Wu, D.C.: Comparing Mainland Chinese tourists' satisfaction with Hong Kong and the UK using tourist satisfaction index: 基于旅客满意指数比较中国大陆旅客对香港和英国的满意度. J. China Tour. Res. **8**(4), 373–394 (2012)
14. Moreno-Luna, L., Robina-Ramírez, R., Sánchez, M.S.O., Castro-Serrano, J.: Tourism and sustainability in times of COVID-19: the case of Spain. Int. J. Environ. Res. Public Health **18**(4), 1859 (2021)
15. Rodríguez-Antón, J.M., Alonso-Almeida, M.D.M.: COVID-19 impacts and recovery strategies: the case of the hospitality industry in Spain. Sustainability **12**(20), 8599 (2020)
16. Pearce, P.L., Morrison, A.M., Rutledge, J.L.: Motivation influence in tourism demand. Tourism: Bridges across continents. Roseville NSW, Australia: McGraw-Hill Book Company (1998)
17. Crompton, J.: Why people go on a pleasure vacation. Ann. Tour. Res. **6**(4), 408–424 (1979)
18. Dann, G.M.S.: Anomie, ego-enhancement and tourism. Ann. Tour. Res. **4**, 184–194 (1977)
19. Dann, G.M.S.: Tourist motivation: an appraisal. Ann. Tour. Res. **8**, 187–219 (1981)
20. Baloglu, S., Uysal, M.: Market segments of push and pull motivations: a canonical correlation approach[J]. Int. J. Contemp. Hosp. Manag. (1996)
21. Uysal, M., Li, X., Sirakaya-Turk, E.: Push-pull dynamics in travel decisions. Handbook Hospit. Market. Manag. **2009**, 412–439 (2008)
22. Dann, G.M.: Tourist motivation and quality-of-life: In search of the missing link. In Handbook of tourism and quality-of-life research (pp. 233–250). Springer, Dordrecht (2012)
23. Prayag, G., Disegna, M., Cohen, S.A., Yan, H.: Segmenting markets by bagged clustering: Young Chinese travelers to Western Europe. J. Travel. Res. **54**(2), 234–250 (2015)
24. Pung, J.M., Del Chiappa, G.: Understanding Chinese travellers' motivations to visit Europe. In Tourist Behavior (pp. 187–201). Springer, Cham (2018)
25. Lojo, A.: Young Chinese in Europe: Travel behavior and new trends based on evidence from Spain. Tour. Int. Interdis. J. **68**(1), 7–20 (2020)
26. Kotler, P., Gertner, D.: Country as brand, product, and beyond: a place marketing and brand management perspective. J. Brand Manag. **9**(4), 249–261 (2002)
27. Baloglu, S., McCleary, K.W.: U.S. International pleasure Traveller's images of four mediterranean destinations: a comparison of visitors and non-visitors. J. Travel Res. **38**(2), 144e152 (1999)
28. Pike, S., Ryan, C.: Destination positioning analysis through a comparison of cognitive, affective, and conative perceptions. J. Travel. Res. **42**, 333–342 (2004)
29. Mayo, E.J., Jarvis, L.P.: The psychology of leisure travel. CBI Publishing Company, Inc., Effective marketing and selling of travel services (1981)
30. Fakeye, P.C., Crompton, J.L.: Image differences between prospective, first-time, and repeat visitors to the Lower Rio Grande Valley. J. Travel. Res. **30**(2), 10–16 (1991)

31. Chen, C.F., Tsai, D.C.: How destination image and evaluative factors affect behavioural intentions? Tour. Manage. **28**(4), 1115–1122 (2007)
32. Wang, C.Y., Hsu, M.K.: The relationships of destination image, satisfaction, and behavioral intentions: an integrated model. J. Travel. Tour. Mark. **27**(8), 829–843 (2010)
33. Beerli, A., Martin, J.D.: Factors influencing destination image. Ann. Tour. Res. **31**(3), 657–681 (2004)
34. Hudson, S., Wang, Y., Gil, S.M.: The influence of a film on destination image and the desire to travel: a cross-cultural comparison. Int. J. Tour. Res. **13**(2), 177–190 (2011)
35. San Martín, H., Del Bosque, I.A.R.: Exploring the cognitive–affective nature of destination image and the role of psychological factors in its formation. Tour. Manage. **29**(2), 263–277 (2008)
36. Kastenholz, E.: 'Cultural proximity' as a determinant of destination image. J. Vacat. Mark. **16**(4), 313–322 (2010)
37. Liu, H., Li, X.R., Cárdenas, D.A., Yang, Y.: Perceived cultural distance and international destination choice: the role of destination familiarity, geographic distance, and cultural motivation. J. Destin. Mark. Manag. **9**, 300–309 (2018)
38. Lepp, A., Gibson, H.: Tourist roles, perceived risk and international tourism. Ann. Tour. Res. **30**(3), 606–624 (2003)
39. Ng, S.I., Lee, J.A., Soutar, G.N.: Tourists' intention to visit a country: the impact of cultural distance. Tour. Manage. **28**(6), 1497–1506 (2007)
40. Bi, J., Lehto, X.Y.: Impact of cultural distance on international destination choices: the case of Chinese outbound travelers. Int. J. Tour. Res. **20**(1), 50–59 (2018)
41. Ajzen, I.: The theory of planned behavior. Organ. Behav. Hum. Decis. Process. **50**(2), 179–211 (1991)
42. Prayag, G., Hosany, S., Odeh, K.: The role of tourists' emotional experiences and satisfaction in understanding behavioral intentions. J. Destin. Mark. Manag. **2**(2), 118–127 (2013)
43. Babakus, E., Mangold, W.G.: Adapting the SERVQUAL scale to hospital services: an empirical investigation[J]. Health Serv. Res. **26**(6), 767 (1992)
44. Sachdev, S.B, Verma, H.V.: Relative importance of service quality dimensions: a multisectoral study[J]. J. Serv. Res. 4(1) (2004)
45. Lin, C.H., Morais, D.B., Kerstetter, D.L., Hou, J.S.: Examining the role of cognitive and affective image in predicting choice across natural, developed, and theme-park destinations. J. Travel Res. **46**(2), 183–194 (2007)
46. Shoemaker, P.J., Eichholtz, M., Skewes, E.A.: Item nonresponse: distinguishing between don't know and refuse. Int. J. Public Opin. Res. **14**(2), 193–201 (2002)
47. Lam, T., Hsu, C.H.: Predicting behavioral intention of choosing a travel destination. Tour. Manage. **27**(4), 589–599 (2006)
48. Zhang, H., Gursoy, D., Xu, H.: The effects of associative slogans on tourists' attitudes and travel intention: The moderating effects of need for cognition and familiarity. J. Travel Res. **56**(2), 206–220 (2017)
49. Yoon, Y., Uysal, M.: An examination of the effects of motivation and satisfaction on destination loyalty: a structural model. Tour. Manage. **26**(1), 45–56 (2005)
50. Fan, D.X., Zhang, H.Q., Jenkins, C.L., Lin, P.M.: Does tourist–host social contact reduce perceived cultural distance? J. Travel Res. **56**(8), 998–1010 (2017)
51. Ang, T., Liou, R.S., Wei, S.: Perceived cultural distance in intercultural service encounters: does customer participation matter? J. Serv. Mark. **32**(5), 547–558 (2018)
52. Hung, K., Petrick, J.F.: Testing the effects of congruity, travel constraints, and self-efficacy on travel intentions: an alternative decision-making model. Tour. Manage. **33**(4), 855–867 (2012)
53. van Griethuijsen, R.A.L.F., van Eijck, M.W., Haste, H., et al.: Global patterns in students' views of science and interest in science[J]. Res. Sci. Educ. **45**(4), 581–603 (2015)
54. Dann, G.M.: Tourists' images of a destination-an alternative analysis. J. Travel Tour. Mark. **5**(1–2), 41–55 (1996)
55. Wen, J., Kozak, M., Yang, S., et al.: COVID-19: potential effects on Chinese citizens' lifestyle and travel[J]. Tour. Rev. (2020)

Destination Image of Spain Perceived by the Chinese Tourists During the Pandemic

Dongmei Ren and Dolores Sánchez-Aguilera

Abstract This research aims to examine the image of Spain as a tourist destination for the Chinese market before and after the pandemic outbreak using an unstructured method with an open questionnaire. The study considers that the analysis of the image of a destination can contribute to the design of strategies to overcome the negative effects of the perception of risk on the attitudes and intentions of tourist visits during the expansion of the pandemic. Finally, the study suggests possible implementation measures that could contribute to improving the security and attractiveness of the image and, eventually, to maintaining the functionality and attractiveness of a destination.

Keywords Destination image · COVID-19 outbreak · Unconstructed method · Spain Image · Marketing strategy

1 Introduction

The spread of the COVID-19 pandemic has posed an unprecedented threat to the global tourism industry. Mobility restrictions have slowed tourist flows around the planet. But after the COVID-19 outbreak, elements such as the perception of risk are of interest as a key factor that influences travelers to make their travel decisions.

Spain is one of the European countries that has been most affected by the COVID-19 pandemic since March 2020. The expansion of the pandemic has devastated the Spanish tourism industry, which is a strategic sector and may affect the expansion of the booming Chinese outbound tourism in Spain, a very attractive component due to its potential and high purchasing power.

Unlike other goods and services, tourism is an intangible product which cannot be experienced until well after purchase. For this reason, the projection of an attractive

---

D. Ren (✉)
University of Barcelona, Barcelona, Spain
e-mail: 18801950203@163.com

D. Sánchez-Aguilera
Department of Geography, University of Barcelona, Barcelona, Spain

image of a destination and the destination brand promotion are particularly important in tourism [1]. Meanwhile, tourism has become more reliant on image [2, 3]. It can be said that previous researchers reached an agreement about the importance of image for a destination's success in tourism [3–5].

Reilly (1990) also recommended "an accurate assessment of the appropriate image of whatever is to be promoted is a prerequisite to designing an effective marketing strategy". Above, it has been stated that the destination image is an important factor due to its effect on supply-side factors, such as marketing. Despite this, the destination image is generally viewed as an important factor in impacting the behavior of tourists in particular decisions on the demand-side [1, 4, 6–11]. As supported by previous research, in addition to the image of the destination, risk perception is one of the critical selection factors that determines preferred destinations [12]. As natural threats become more prevalent (E.g…, pandemic diseases, natural disasters), security issues have become a pressing issue for tourists, increasing the perceived level of travel risk and preventing tourists from traveling [13].

Spain has been selected by this study since it is a Mediterranean destination with an influential, positive image [6] and has replaced the US as the world's second most popular tourist destination, according to the UN World Tourism Organization (UNWTO). However, Spain is only the fourth favorite destination of Chinese tourists in Europe and Chinese tourists represented only 0.8% (699.108) of the number of Spanish international tourists (83,701.011). Consequently, their total expenditure represented only 1.4% of Spain's total tourism revenue. In this way, Chinese customers do not appear to be strategic customers of Spain. Actually, this is not the case. International Chinese travelers have been ranked number one worldwide since 2013. In accordance with the INE (2019), spending by Chinese tourists in Spain comes in first with an average of 2563 euros spent per person. Meanwhile, the arrival of Chinese outbound tourists in Spain has multiplied by 40 times in the last 20 years with an annual average of 21.62% growth. So, by looking at the increasing number, we can see the potential. Spain is starting to recognize the Chinese market´s potential and redouble its efforts to capture a more significant market share. Nevertheless, from March of 2020, Spain has been one of the worst-hit countries of the pandemic, which has caused a variety of perceived risk factors. In line with the study by Reisinger and Mavondo (2005), perceptions of risk are not only correlated with travelers' anxiety but can also influence destination choice among tourists [14]. At a time of a global health crisis, the perception of risk is very important in public awareness, which can have a negative impact on the selection of Chinese tourist destinations.

Despite an incredible increase in the number of Chinese tourists to Spain, there is, however, an intriguing gap in terms of tourism images of Spain evaluated by Chinese tourists. Apart from that, relatively little attention has been given in the academic literature on the destination image of Spain from the perspective of Chinese tourists. As a result, our analysis focuses on the evolving image Chinese tourists have of Spain as a tourism destination before and after the COVID-19 outbreak. More specifically, our analysis studies the image of Spain by employing unstructured methods. It is possible that Spain's tourism marketing specialists will have to influence international decision-making in an increasingly complex and competitive global market. Consequently, this paper is expected to offer useful strategies for sector authorities to understand the risks associated with the tourism destination image.

2 Literature Review

A review of earlier studies of the destination image shows that the concept of the destination image has been widely regarded as a concept of attitude consisting of the mental representation of a person's mental representation of knowledge (beliefs), feelings, and global impression about an object or destination [1, 4, 15–18]. This image is created gradually through the processing of information from different sources [1, 17, 19]. As mentioned above, individuals can have an image of a destination even if they have never visited. Moreover, the image may not be what the product really is, but rather the perception that the tourist's beliefs, attitudes, level of awareness and expectations tend to build [20]. This means that the destination image changes before and after the visit. What is more, the formation of the destination image is a dynamic process affected by various sources of information, which include non-tourism information sources, i.e., organic image and trade information sources, i.e., and induced image [21]. Later on, the destination image formation was conceptualized by Fakeye and Crompton [1] as evolving from an organic image, through an induced image, to a complex image. The organic and induced images are shaped before visiting a specific destination, while the complex image is constructed once the tourist has visited the destination [22] and encompasses the destination experience. As the induced image is generated when tourists actively seek information about the destination, on the supply side, building a better induced image may play a positive role in destination marketing. On the other hand, in terms of demand, several studies have shown that destination image has a strong influence on decision-making, behavior [4, 15, 19, 23–27], and satisfaction [8–10]. Based on the above considerations, C. Echtner and Ritchie [19] conceptualized destination image as a whole that consists of attribute-based images, holistic impressions, and functional, psychological, unique, and general traits, meanwhile, they argued that it is essential to design more appropriate and stringent destination images in order to implement an efficient tourism marketing strategy. Therefore, a combination of structured and unstructured methods is presented, which is essential for the complete measurement of the target image [28]. This article has drawn on their non-structural methods to measure holistic, unique, functional and psychological characteristics of Spain's destination image in context of the COVID-19 outbreak.

As advocated by Gartner (1994), the destination image consists of three distinct but hierarchically interrelated elements: cognitive, affective, and conative. From his perspective, the cognitive image is a summary of the beliefs and evaluation of the well-known attributes of a destination. The emotional component of the image is relevant to travel motivation and relates to how a tourist feels about a destination, including perceptions of safety and security [29] in the context of the pandemic disease. With the rise in the incidence of global pandemics and epidemics, such as SARS, 'Bird flu' and Ebola, the perceived destination risk in the emotional component of the image was a major concern [12, 30] to create behavioral intention [7, 9, 31]. We should note that the perceived destination risk was considered to be remarkably affecting the destination image and future travel behavior [12, 32, 33]. Thus, it is necessary to build strong and long-term marketing strategies based on the assessment of the cognitive and the affective components of destination images to increase the competitiveness of tourism destinations [7].

3 Methodology

The COVID-19 crisis could be a watershed for Spain's image as an international tourist destination in China. As we mentioned in the introduction, the overall objective of this paper is to analyze the impact of Spanish destination image in the context of COVID-19, an issue of particular importance from the point of view of the commercialization of tourist destinations. To achieve this, different techniques for the measurement of a tourist's destination image are reviewed as presented in Table 1 and the dominance of the structured approach common in western academic circles over the unstructured approach prevalent in China [34]. Table 1 presents a summary of advantages and disadvantages of techniques used in the past for research on product image measurement. Given the facts shown in Table 1 image measurement. Given the facts shown in Table 1, both types of measurements show strengths and weaknesses. For this reason, Echtner and Ritchie [28] point out that it is preferable to combine the two methods to completely capture the components of the target image attribute. However, an unstructured technique, such as open-ended questions, is most effective for capturing the unique and holistic image [28].

Our research is based on open-ended questions, following Echtner and Ritchie's [28] proposal, and was carried out based on three main questions, whose objective is to measure the holistic, psychological and unique picture of Spanish destinations on the Chinese market as follows:

(1) What images or characteristics come to mind when you think of Spain as a vacation destination before the COVID-19 pandemic? (Functional holistic component)
(2) What images or characteristics come to mind when you think of Spain as a vacation destination after the COVID-19 outbreak?
(3) How would you describe the atmosphere or mood that you would experience while visiting Spain before the COVID-19 pandemic? (Psychological holistic component)
(4) How would you describe the atmosphere or mood that you would expect to experience while visiting Spain after the COVID-19 outbreak?
(5) Please list any distinctive or unique tourist attractions that you can think of in Spain before the COVID-19 pandemic? (Unique component)

Table 1 Techniques used in the past for research on product image

Dimensions	Structured	Unstructured
Measurement	They force the respondent to think about product image in terms of the attributes specified by the scales	The respondent is allowed to more freely describe his/her impressions of a destination. The attributes of image are not specified at the onset of the research
Techniques used	Based on a set of standardized attributes Differential or Likert type scales Close-ended questionnaire A set of semantic	Free form descriptions Focus groups Open-ended survey questions Content analysis Various sorting Categorization techniques Interactive interviews Visual aspect of image
Advantages	Quite effective for measuring the common and attribute-based components of image They are easy to administer, simple to code and the results can be analyzed using statistical Sophisticated techniques	More conducive to measuring the holistic components of product Image and also to capturing unique features and auras
Disadvantages	Attribute lists may be incomplete by failing to incorporate all Of the relevant functional and psychological characteristics of the destination image They are not useful for capturing the unique and holistic components	Qualitative nature of the data, statistical analyses of the results are limited Qualitative research with consumers is expensive and time consuming
Cases of previous studies	The scale items: 5- point Likert-scales 6- point Likert-scales 7- point Likert-scales Check list of attributes Semantic Differential Scale	Free elicitation Content analysis Cognitive mapping Correspondence analysis Analysis of linguistic structure of destination image Analysis on Google keyword search volumes

Source Adapted from Echtner and Ritchie [19, 28]; Jenkins [15], Pan and Li [35], Wu et al. [34]

(6) Please list any distinctive or unique tourist attractions that you can think of in Spain after the COVID-19 outbreak?

The target population in the sample was Chinese tourists from different regions of China, who took at least one pleasure trip in the last 12 months. Given the language barrier, to facilitate the Chinese' response, the English text was translated into Chinese. Each respondent has been authorized to provide up to six responses, but the questionnaires are considered valid and contain at least one response to each question. In terms of sample size, 615 questionnaires were completed between

October 13 and October 17, 2020, using two methods. The first was carried out with the help of a Chinese online polling platform called Wenjuanxing. The second was for selected Chinese tourism groups WeChat. Finally, the actual analysis is made up of 458 valid and complete responses.

There are some limitations associated with this study which are important to mention. From a methodological perspective, this study, like all empirical research work, has certain limitations which affect the evaluation and generalization of its results. First, Echtner and Ritchie [28] illustrated that "a combination of structured and unstructured methodologies is necessary to measure the destination image" [28]. However, as this study only applies the unstructured methodologies, it does not fully capture the components of the destination image. Second, the target group is limited as it is an online survey, so the results have a bias for those who do not use the Internet regularly and cannot access the questionnaire. Moreover, the demographic characteristics of respondents are unknown, and their understanding of the questionnaire may vary. Finally, the generalization of the results is another limitation, since the research can only generalize the results for the sample population.

4 Results

The questions asked of respondents, as mentioned above, focused on a holistic, psychological, and unique image of Spain as a tourist destination prior to and during the COVID-19 pandemic. Respondents were encouraged to describe Spain in simple terms. Content analysis, such as various sorting and categorization techniques is used to determine the image dimensions. The responses were coded into categories and represented in Figs. 1, 2, 3, 4, 5 and 6, which provide the most frequent responses to the six open-ended questions in the questionnaire. The answers were coded as categories and we selected the top 15 answers for each question.

The first and second questions focused on the imagery associated with Spain as a travel destination. Responses were used to examine holistic images before and after COVID-19 outbreak. Analysis of Figs. 1 and 2 gives considerable insight into the holistic image of Spain among the entire sample and highlights differences among the respondents. In general, the image of respondents is very different, and there is hardly any consensus. Furthermore, by comparing the two figures below, it is clear that the overall impression of Chinese tourists towards Spain has changed significantly as a result of the pandemic intervention.

A first conclusion is that the image of Spain prior to the COVID-19 pandemic is mostly positive among Chinese tourists mentioning "Bullfighting", "Hospitable people", "Beaches-Sunlight-Sea", "Football", "Romance", "Cuisine, Spanish Hams, Paella", and "Scenic beauty" as the most frequent terms.

On the contrary, when the pandemic emerged seriously in Spain, the potential Chinese tourists surveyed began to have a negative image of Spain. Terms such as "Dangerous- unsafe-afraid" and "Serious Virus" accounted for more than half of the total responses and became the global image of Spain after the outbreak of the

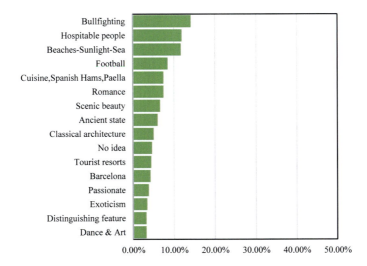

Fig. 1 Description of Spain as a holiday destination prior to the COVID-19 pandemic. *Source* Own elaboration based on survey

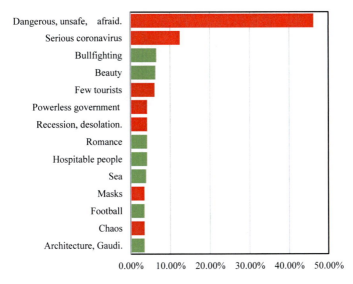

Fig. 2 Description of Spain as a holiday destination after the COVID-19 outbreak. *Source* Own elaboration based on survey

pandemic. These descriptions of the image have completely changed the perception of Spain before the pandemic. And other negative concepts appear, such as "Impotent Government", "Recessions, desolation", "Masks" or even "Chaos". Nevertheless, some terms used to describe pre-pandemic Spain were still present in respondents, but at lower rates as a result of the pandemic response. In particular, we must note

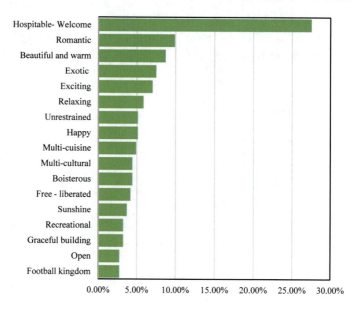

Fig. 3 The atmosphere or mood expected when travelling to Spain prior to the COVID-19 pandemic. *Source* Own elaboration based on survey

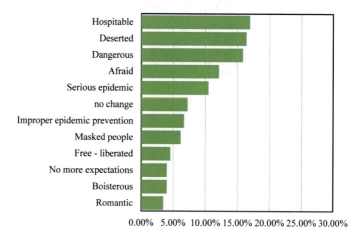

Fig. 4 The atmosphere or mood that you experience after the COVID-19 outbreak. *Source* Own elaboration based on survey

the "bullfighting" image, located as a frequent answer to all sex questions, which is a widely spread but fixed and simplistic image of Spain as a destination. Analysis of the data from this study shows that " bullfighting " is not only anchored in the holistic picture of Spain, providing a very popular identity ground in the tourist destination,

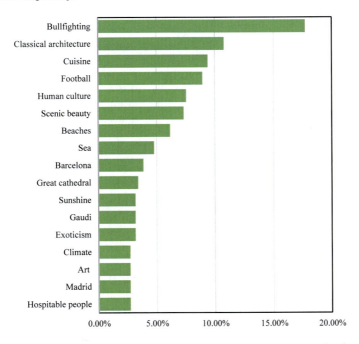

Fig. 5 Distinguishing or unique tourist attractions in Spain prior to the COVID-19 pandemic. *Source* Own elaboration based on survey

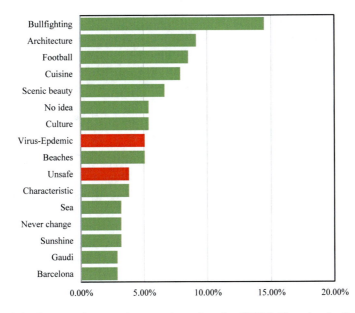

Fig. 6 Distinctive or unique tourist attractions after the COVID-19 outbreak. *Source* Own elaboration based on survey

but also regarded as an idiosyncratic spectacle belonging to the Spanish cultural tradition.

As suggested by previous researchers, the data in the third and fourth questions mainly generated the psychological image [28]. According to the survey findings (Fig. 3), the expected atmosphere of Spain by Chinese tourists surveyed prior to COVID-19 was positive. "Hospitality" is the head image, and the atmosphere is described with terms like "Romantic", "Beautiful and warm", "Exotic", "Exciting" or "Happy".

However, after the worst outbreak in Spain, perceptions changed, and the positive images fell to the second half of the rankings. While the proportion of "hospitality" in the fourth question is still at the top of the list, it is 10% lower than before the COVID-19 pandemic. We may consider that such an expectation has not entirely changed in the context of Spain being confirmed more infections than in any other in the European Union. The data strongly suggest that Spain has established a really long tradition of genuine hospitality, and that Spaniards are considered a friendly group who know how to make tourists feel welcome in their country. Not surprisingly, Spain is the second most visited country in the world, with 81.8 million visitors in 2019. However, respondents feel that tourism may be scarce this year due to lockdowns and other COVID-19 restrictions. They expressed a belief that the formerly bustling and noisy spanish tourist resorts must be deserted in terms of functional and psychological characteristics.

Therefore, in Fig. 4 only 6.45% of the answers consider that Spain's psychological image will not change due to the pandemic. Meanwhile the remaining key features that made an impression on respondents all related to negative perceptions of danger, fear, and scarcity, or a severe pandemic. It refers to the fact that the cognitive picture of Spain is completely disrupted by the pandemic, rendering the picture of Spain as a country with good ambiance that is romantic, beautiful, hot, exotic, relaxing, etc. no longer dominates. Finally, the fifth and sixth questions were asked to determine some of the responses that respondents considered specific to the destination before and after the outbreak. Figures 5 and 6 contain the descriptors of the unique spanish image offered by the global sample. The highest proportions of single image statements (Figs. 5 and 6) are "bull-fighting", which corresponds to the respondent's description of the overall impression of Spain in Fig. 1. The second most mentioned descriptors refer to the architecture, whether it is before or after the outbreak. The following common description of distinctive or unique tourist attractions across the sample can be summarized into two categories: cultural heritage and natural heritage. The first includes "Cuisine", "Football", "Human culture", "Great cathedral", "Gaudi", "Art", or "Sagrada Familia" the latter consists of "Scenic beauty", "Beaches, Sea",

"Sunshine" and "Climate", although some little differences existed before and after the outbreak in Spain.

It should be noted that, following the outbreak of the pandemic in Spain, the respondents' unique impression of Spain was also affected. In fact, only two percent of respondents believe that the pandemic will not change the uniqueness of Spain. Individual attractions will have their own identity, which in many cases will be masked by the overall brand image of the specific political entity of the local attraction (Reilly 1990). As shown in Fig. 6, among the categories "Pandemic Virus" as well as "Unsafe" are part of the respondents' unique impression of Spain.

5 Discussion and Conclusion

As the preceding examples demonstrate, the analysis of descriptive adjectives provides an overview of Spain's image across the sample and highlights the differences between images from different periods of the pandemic. Furthermore, open-ended questions were carried out based on three main questions, which provides a powerful but simple method for examining the image that potential or actual tourists hold of a tourist destination. The findings can then be used in the design of marketing efforts in various ways. The overall image of Spain during COVID-19 as a tourist destination should be considered as the interaction of all the holistic, psychological, and unique components. As a consequence, this research has attempted to illustrate the whole destination image with word clouds to easily produce a summary of surveys and to visualize data (Figs. 7 and 8).

The size of a word indicates the frequency with which it is displayed in a survey. Figure 7 results confirmed that before the COVID-19 pandemic, Spain had an image of a joyful, free and relaxing destination that was particularly popular for a welcoming environment. In addition to the famous beaches, the sun, and the sea, there were bullfights and soccer matches. In the meantime, the result suggested that Spain was the destination with picturesque beauty, Mediterranean cuisine and diverse culture, plus a romantic style and a taste of the exotic.

However, when Spain faced the worst coronavirus infection rate in Western Europe, the overall image of Spain changed, according to the study. Past investigations have found that perceived risks to travel, such as infectious diseases, are the

Fig. 7 Overall image of Spain before the COVID-19 pandemic. *Source* Own elaboration based on survey

Fig. 8 Overall image of Spain after the COVID-19 outbreak. *Source* Own elaboration based on survey

number one consideration for travelers when choosing a destination [33]. Figure 8 shows that after the COVID-19 outbreak, Spain was described as a dangerous and unsafe place where Chinese respondents were afraid to go. Even worse, Spain became the first country in Western Europe to record one million cases of coronavirus. The people interviewed believed that the streets of Spain were deserted with no vibrant street life because of the strict containment of the coronavirus. In this sense, it is clear that Spain's image has to reinvent itself. Except for the above-mentioned image, Fig. 8 also suggests that the COVID-19 crisis has not totally devastated the previous image of Spain. Certain perceptions such as the "bullfighting" history of the country, the "hospitable culture", and the bewitching "architecture", the famous "football team", the Spanish "cuisine" and the "picturesque beauty" remain in the minds of the Chinese surveyed. However, these categories show frequencies significantly reduced compared to those in Fig. 7 Previous research findings demonstrate that "a destination image can act as a mediator between perceived risks and revisit intention"[12]. On the other hand, destinations associated with high risk can be eliminated from the traveler's choice at the beginning of the decision-making process [36]. Based on W. C. Gartner and Hunt [16], unless an attraction is at the upper end of the single ladder, destination success will be largely determined by state image [16]. It is clear that Spain's image has to reinvent itself after the outbreak of the pandemic. Law (2006) advocated that if the travel destinations that are vulnerable to the main types of risks don't want to suffer long-term negative impacts of similar risk factors, they should integrate crisis management in all of their sustainable development and marketing strategies. In other words, without understanding the types of perceived risks specific to tourist destinations and their impact on the destination image, general strategies to enhance the destination image may not be successful in urging tourists to travel to risky destinations [37].

Therefore, the "safe tourism" quality seal applied to destinations that have successfully dealt with the pandemic and that have a low risk of infection could put Chinese holiday makers at ease. Clearly, it is not sufficient to rely exclusively on the above measures. Caber et al. (2020) states that "perceived travel risks had a negative effect on cognitive and affective destination images" rather than real risk circumstances of destination [12, 38]. As a matter of fact, the frequency of media coverage sometimes creates unnecessary fears and exaggerates the scope of perceived risks [30, 39]. Gartner and Hunt [16] affirmed that "Changing the image of a destination is usually a slow and tedious process," but it plays a key role in enhancing the image and capturing the economic benefits of tourism [16]. More than that, recent results also suggest that although certain risks cannot be controlled by destination managers, effective e communication strategies on social networks used by destination marketers can reduce the negative impact on the destination and then achieve the goal of restoring a positive image [40–42]. In this sense, Spain's tourism industry needs to develop a digital marketing strategy using social media services such as WeChat, Weibo, Live stream and other online forums and communities to be able to fully exploit Spain's great potential as a premium tourist destination for Chinese outbound tourism. Chinese tourists in Spain are already very impressed by the hospitable people, bullfighting, natural beauty, relaxing atmosphere, etc. so making sure tourists leave satisfied and with a good impression of Spain is essential in attracting other Chinese tourists, who will be more inclined to visit Spain through hearing the experience of other tourists who have traveled there. Again, special attention to the management of Spain's destination image and tourist communities are necessary to make sure that a very good impression of Spain is all that tourists can get. This would allow not only to improve Spain's image, but also to rebuild its international markets.

Acknowledgements This research was funded by the project: "Tourism and the city: analysis and evaluation of the synergies, conflicts and challenges generated by tourism development in Spanish cities" (PGC2018-097707-B-100) financed by the European Regional Development Fund (ERDF)/Ministerio de Ciencia, Innovación y Universidades—Agencia Estatal de Investigación (AEI) (Ministry of Science, In- novation and Universities—State Research Agency (AEI).

References

1. Fakeye, P.C., Crompton, J.L.: Image differences between prospective, first-time, and repeat visitors to the lower Rio Grande Valley. J. Travel. Res. **30**(2), 10–16 (1991)
2. Lepp, A., Gibson, H., Lane, C.: Image and perceived risk: a study of Uganda and its official tourism website. Tour. Manga. **32**(3), 675–684 (2011)
3. Tasci, D.A., Gartner, W.C.: Destination image and its functional relationships. J. Travel. Res. **45**(4), 413–425 (2007)
4. Hunt, J.D.: Image as a factor in tourism development. J. Travel. Res. **13**(3), 1–7 (1975)
5. Campa, J.L., López-Lambas, M.E., Guirao, B.: High speed rail effects on tourism: Spanish empirical evidence derived from China's modelling experience. J. Transp. Geogr. (2016)
6. Baloglu, S., Brinberg, D.: Affective images of tourism destinations. J. Travel. Res. **35**(4), 11–15 (1997)
7. Agapito, D., Oom do Valle, P., da Costa Mendes, J.: The cognitive-affective-conative model of destination image: a confirmatory analysis. J. Travel. Tour. Mark. **30**(5), 471–481 (2013)

8. Chon, K.: The role of destination image in tourism: a review and discussion. Tour. Rev. (1990)
9. Çakmak, E., Isaac, R.K.: What destination marketers can learn from their visitors' blogs: an image analysis of Bethlehem, Palestine. J. Destin. Mark. Manag. (2012)
10. Molina, A., Esteban, Á.: Tourism Brochures. Usefulness and image. Ann. Tour. Res. **33**(4), 1036–1056 (2006)
11. Prayag, G.: Tourists' evaluations of destination image, satisfaction, and future behavioral intentions-the case of mauritius. J. Travel Tour. Mark. (2009)
12. Chew, E.Y.T., Jahari, S.A.: Destination image as a mediator between perceived risks and revisit intention: a case of post-disaster Japan. Tour. Manag. (2014)
13. Gabor, M.: Tourism eclipsed by crime Gabor. J. Travel. Tour. Mark. **15**(April 2015), 1–18 (2008)
14. Björk, P., Kauppinen-Räisänen, H.: A netnographic examination of travelers' online discussions of risks. Tour. Manag. Perspect. (2012)
15. Jenkins, O.H.: Understanding and measuring tourist destination images. Int. J. Tour. Res. **1**, 1–15 (1999)
16. Gartner, W.C., Hunt, J.D.: An analysis of state image change over a twelve-year period (Utah 1971–1983). J. Travel. Res. **26**(2), 15–19 (1987)
17. Baloglu, S., McCleary, K.W.: A model of destination image formation. Ann. Tour. Res. (1999)
18. Xie, C., Huang, Q., Lin, Z., Chen, Y.: Destination risk perception, image and satisfaction: The moderating effects of public opinion climate of risk. J. Hosp. Tour. Manag. **44**(January), 122–130 (2020)
19. Echtner, C., Ritchie, J.: The meaning and measurement of destination image. J. Tour. Stud. **2**(2), 2–12 (1991)
20. Moutinho, L.: Consumer Behaviour in Tourism, **21**(10) (1987)
21. Howell, R.: Vacationscape: designing tourist regions. Ann. Tour. Res. **16**(3), 445–447 (1989)
22. Almeida-García, F., Domígunez-Azcue, J., Mercadé-Melé, P., Pérez-Tapia, G.: Can a destination really change its image? The roles of information sources, motivations, and visits. Tour. Manag. Perspect. **34**(February), 100662 (2020)
23. Pearce, P.L.: Perceived changes in. Ann. Tour. Res. 145–164 (1982)
24. Kent, W.E.: Underground Atlanta: the untimely passing of a major tourist attraction. J. Travel. Res. **22**(4), 2–7 (1984)
25. MacKay, K.J., Fesenmaier, D.R.: An exploration of cross-cultural destination image assessment. J. Travel. Res. **38**(4), 417–423 (2000)
26. Rodríguez del Bosque, I., San Martín, H.: Tourist satisfaction a cognitive-affective model. Ann. Tour. Res. **35**(2), 551–573 (2008)
27. Kim, H., Richardson, S.L.: Motion picture impacts on destination images. Ann. Tour. Res. **30**(1), 216–237 (2003)
28. Echtner, C.M., Ritchie, J.R.B.: The measurement of destination image: an empirical assessment. J. Travel. Res. (1993)
29. Beerli, A., Martín, J.D.: Tourists' characteristics and the perceived image of tourist destinations: a quantitative analysis—a case study of Lanzarote, Spain. Tour. Manag. (2004)
30. Rittichainuwat, B.N., Chakraborty, G.: Perceived travel risks regarding terrorism and disease: the case of Thailand. Tour. Manag. **30**(3), 410–418 (2009)
31. Boulding, K.E.: The image: knowledge and life in society. Univ, Michigan Press (1956)
32. Michael Hall, C., Timothy, D.J., Duval, D.T.: Safety and security in tourism: relationships, management, and marketing. Saf. Secur. Tour. Relationships, Manag. Mark, 1–340 (2012)
33. Kozak, M., Crotts, J.C., Law, R.: The impact of the perception of risk on international travellers. Int. J. Tour. Res. (2007)
34. Wu, B.Q., Wu, J.F., Zhou, F.R., Yang, CH.H.: 旅游目的地形象清晰度及测评方法. J. Zhejiang Univ. **45** (2018)
35. Pan, B., Li, X.: The long tail of destination image and online marketing. Ann. Tour. Res. **38**(1), 132–152 (2011)
36. Solomon, M.R., Joseph, S., Wolny, J.: Delivered by Ingenta to: guest user. J. Cust. Behav. **14**(2), 127–146 (2016)

37. Baker, D.: The effects of terrorism on the travel and tourism industry. Int. J. Relig. Tour. Pilgr. **2**(1), 58–67 (2014)
38. Khan, M.J., Chelliah, S., Ahmed, S.: Factors influencing destination image and visit intention among young women travellers: role of travel motivation, perceived risks, and travel constraints. Asia Pacific J. Tour. Res. (2017)
39. Baxter, R., Hastings, N., Law, A., Glass, E.J.: [UNWTO report 2017], vol. 39, no. 5 (2008)
40. Clayton, A., Boxill, I.: Worldwide hospitality and tourism themes. Tour. Themes Iss **4**(4), 98–100 (2012)
41. Barbe, D., Pennington-Gray, L., Schroeder, A.: Destinations' response to terrorism on Twitter. Int. J. Tour. Cities (2018)
42. Oliveira, A., Huertas-Roig, A.: How do destinations use twitter to recover their images after a terrorist attack? J. Destin. Mark. Manag. **12**(April 2018), 46–54 (2019)

Exploration and Innovation of Zhoushan Marine Tourism Industry in the Context of Free Trade Zone

Xu Guo and Park Jaepil

Abstract Zhoushan is one of the most important node city on the maritime Silk Road. Zhoushan Islands have distinct geographical advantages and abundant tourism resources. Marine tourism has become one of the pillar industries in Zhoushan. In 2017, the China (Zhejiang) Pilot Free Trade Zone was launched in Zhoushan, which once again provided new development opportunities for the marine tourism industry in Zhoushan. This paper uses the SWOT-AHP analysis method to analyze the profound impact of constructing Free Trade Zone on the development of marine tourism industry in Zhoushan. Analyzes the distinct advantages of Zhoushan marine tourism industry; abundant tourism resources; government supports and guidance; low level of tourism reception services; outstanding shortcomings in inter-island transportation; overseas markets to be developed; major national strategic opportunities; strong demand on consumer markets; improved infrastructure construction; fragile of island ecological environment; intensified competition in the marine tourism market; low coupling between the development of the marine tourism industry and national strategies in the context of the Free Trade Zone. This paper proposes a new path for the development of marine tourism industry in Zhoushan; including smart tourism and tourism service reconstruction; government-enterprise cooperation and regional integration; cultural integration and cultural tourism integration; and the combination of free trade zones to tap the potential of international tourism.

Keywords Marine tourism · Free trade zone · China (Zhejiang) pilot free trade zone · Exploration and innovation

---

X. Guo (✉) · P. Jaepil
School of Economics and Management, Zhejiang Ocean University, Zhoushan 316004, China
e-mail: 104675331@QQ.COM

Department of Economics, Kunsan National University, Kunsan 54150, South Korea

1 Introduction

Zhoushan Islands locate on the East China Sea in Zhejiang Province. With its unique geographical advantages, it has been an important node city along the East China Sea lane since ancient times, and it has been an important part of the ancient Maritime Silk Road. China's Pilot Free Trade Zone (hereinafter referred to as the "Free Trade Zone") is known as the "upgraded version of the Special Economic Zone Experiment of China", and it is a new milestone in China's reform and opening-up measures following the Shenzhen Special Economic Zone in the 1980s [1]. With the official launch of the Zhejiang (Zhoushan) Pilot Free Trade Zone in April 2017, Zhoushan Islands became the core area and regional development highland for the "Maritime Silk Road" construction in the 21st Century. Zhoushan marine tourism industry has ushered in new development opportunities in the context of the "One Belt and One Road" Initiative and the Free Trade Zone.

2 Overview of Free Trade Zone

Free Trade Zone refers to a small specific area within a country or region that implements preferential tax and special regulatory policies. Free Trade Zone is a trade market established in a specific region by the laws and regulations of the country (region). It is an act outside the borders of a country (region). Its function is to facilitate trade exchanges and reduce trade costs [2].

2.1 Overview of the World's Major Free Trade Zone

Free Trade Zone is different from bilateral or multilateral Free Trade Area (FTA). FTA refers to more than two countries or regions, through the signing of Free Trade Agreement [3], mutually eliminate tariffs and non-tariff barriers to goods, remove market access restrictions for related sectors, and open investment to promote goods and services to freely flow with capital, technology, personnel and other production factors to achieve complementary advantages and promote common development [1]. At present, the major Free Trade Zone in the world include Hamburg Freeport in Germany, Hong Kong Freeport, Singapore Freeport, Dubai Free Trade Area, and Busan Jinhae Economic Free Zone in South Korea.

From the middle of the eighteenth century to the middle of the nineteenth century, Britain, which was the first to complete the capitalist revolution, began to implement free trade policies. Thereafter, France, Germany, and the United States successively introduced free trade policies to establish economic free zones. In the early 1950s, the United States proposed that Free Trade Zone could develop manufacturing with export processing as its main goal. In the following ten years, developing countries followed the example of the United States established special industrial zones and developed them into export processing zones. After the 1980s, many countries in the world began to change the development model of the Free Trade Zone from the original labor-intensive industry to the technology-intensive industry (Table 1).

2.2 Overview of China's Free Trade Zone

China's Free Trade Zone started relatively late. In 2013, The State Council of China approved the establishment of the China (Shanghai) Pilot Free Trade Zone, which opened a new chapter in constructing China's Free Trade Zone and then developed rapidly. The establishment of China's Free Trade Zone is no less important than that of the special economic zones, and Pudong New Area established in the last century. So far, the number of China's Free Trade Zone has expanded to 18, forming a "1 + 3 + 7 + 1 + 6" wild goose-style matrix, covering areas from south to north, from coastal to inland, including Shanghai, Guangdong, Tianjin, Fujian, Liaoning, Zhejiang, Henan, Hubei, Chongqing, Sichuan, Shaanxi, Hainan, Shandong, Jiangsu, Hebei, Yunnan, Guangxi, Heilongjiang. All China's coastal provinces are Free Trade Zone; they are Liaoning, Hebei, Tianjin, Shandong, Jiangsu, Shanghai, Zhejiang, Fujian, Guangdong, Guangxi, and Hainan from north China to south China [5].

In June 2015, the National Tourism Administration held a meeting in Tianjin, proposing to use the Free Trade Zone as a new highland for tourism opening up, a test field for deepening reform, and a demonstration area for institutional innovation to accelerate forming new advantages for the development of the tourism industry. It's the first time the national level has clearly defined the development of tourism trade in the Free Trade Zone [3]. In 2017, the Zhejiang Free Trade Zone established in Zhoushan Islands, which means that Zhejiang's economic development has since entered the era of the Free Trade Zone. The Free Trade Zone can make use of the advantages of the tourism resources of the Zhoushan Islands and focus on advancing the development of marine tourism [6]. So that it embarks on the international road with the launch of the Free Trade Zone, and the marine tourism industry in Zhoushan has ushered in new opportunities for development.

3 SWOT Analysis of Zhoushan Marine Tourism Industry Development in the Context of Free Trade Zone

According to relevant statistics, in 2018, Zhoushan received 63.214 million tourists, an increase of 16.87% over the previous year; its total tourism revenue reached 94.22 billion yuan, an increase of 17.77% over the previous year. In recent years, the tourist reception and tourism revenue have both increased by more than 15%, and the tourism industry in Zhoushan is in a rapid development stage. In terms of

Table 1 Major free trade zone in the world

Free trade zone (port)	Country	Time of establishment	Area and scale	Preferential policy
Freeport of Hamburg	Germany	1888	16.2 km^2	Foreign goods are free to enter and leave the Free Trade Zone from the water. Some goods need to be declared, and some goods are not required to be declared. No customs duties impose; foreign exchange transactions don't restrict [4]
Hong Kong free trade port	China		All over Hong Kong	Freedom of trade, freedom of business operation, opening financial markets, and freedom of personnel
Singapore free trade port	Singapore	1969	30,000 m^2	Except for automobiles, petroleum products, and tobacco, no tariffs impose on other commodities
Dubai free trade zone	United Arab Emirates	1985	135 km^2	Foreign investment can be 100% wholly-owned, not subject to the 49% foreign investment and 51% domestic investment provisions in the UAE Company Law; foreign companies enjoy 15 years of exemption from income tax, which can extend for another 15 years after expiration; no personal income tax; free import tax; currency is freely convertible [4]

(continued)

Table 1 (continued)

Free trade zone (port)	Country	Time of establishment	Area and scale	Preferential policy
Jinhae free economic zone in Busan	Korea	2003	104 km²	Taxes on free zones are reduced by 100% within 7 years and by 50% in the following 3 years. The lease period is 50 years, the government subsidizes 30% of the land acquisition fee and 50% of the building rental fee for two tears based on 1% of the land price each year

the domestic market, Zhoushan has a relatively concentrated source of tourists; they mainly come from the Yangtze River Delta and Fujian. Among them, tourists who come from Zhejiang Province accounted for 44%, tourists who come from Jiangsu and Shanghai accounted for 16.4% and 13% respectively, Jiangsu and Shanghai were respectively the second largest tourist source and the third largest tourist source. In terms of international markets, in 2017, Zhoushan received 344,313 international tourists, of which the tourists were mainly Japanese, accounting for nearly 20%, which was followed by Filipino and Singapore tourists, the number of tourists from Filipino and Singapore are over 7,000.

3.1 Analysis of Development Advantages of Zhoushan Marine Tourism Industry (S)

1. **Obvious location advantage (S1)**

Zhoushan locates in the Yangtze River Delta region; it backs by the entire Yangtze River Basin. Yangtze River Basin is also one of the most active areas in China's economy. Zhoushan Islands have many deep-water ports, and its port economy has developed to a certain stage. Zhoushan Islands have a unique geographical advantage. In the northeast, it faces South Korea and Japan across the sea, and in the south, it is adjacent to Treasure Island Taiwan. It has obvious geographical advantages as a commodity transit trade. Zhoushan is far from the mainland, which facilitates innovation in customs supervision. Zhoushan Islands have many tourism resources and is a well-known tourist city in China. The launch of the Free Trade Zone can form a joint development with Zhoushan tourism. The "Maritime Silk Road" is an important opportunity for Zhoushan Islands to develop international tourism. In 2013, after President Xi proposed the concept to create the 21st Century Maritime Silk Road, promoting the launch of the new area in Zhoushan Islands has become an important goal of local government. Zhoushan can learn experience from marine tourism development in the starting areas to realize its international development. The launch of the Free Trade Zone provides policy support and top-level design opportunities for the development of island tourism in Zhoushan. As long as we grasp the dual opportunities brought by the Maritime Silk Road and the Free Trade Zone, Zhoushan Island Tourism will certainly develop to a new stage.

2. **Rich tourism resources (S2)**

Zhoushan has 1,390 islands and more than 800 tourism items, of which more than 200 tourism items are in excellent grade, accounting for about 25% of total tourism items. As of 2019, Zhoushan has a total of 5A-level scenic spots, 4 4A-level scenic spots, 15 3A-level scenic spots, 11 2A-level scenic spots, 7 1A-level scenic spots, and a total of 38 scenic spots. Zhoushan has two national-level scenic spots including Shengsi Islands and Putuo Mountain. Dinghai is the only island cultural city in China, which has huge brand development potential. In addition, Zhoushan also has Shenjiamen fishing port, Nandong, Dongji Island and other tourist attractions with marine characteristics. The distribution of the Free Trade Zone is similar to that of tourism resources in Zhoushan, which has brought opportunities for the further development of Zhoushan tourism.

3. **Government support and guidance (S3)**

In recent years, with the increased support from the central and Zhejiang governments at all levels for the marine economy in Zhoushan, it has injected vitality into the development of marine tourism industry in Zhoushan. In 2011, the Plan for the Zhejiang Marine Economy Development Demonstration Zone was approved by the State Council, which incorporated the Zhejiang Marine Economy Demonstration Zone into the national strategy, which has a landmark significance in the history of the marine economy development in Zhejiang. The establishment of "Zhoushan Archipelago New Area" signifies that the launch of the Zhoushan Archipelago New Area was formally incorporated into the national development master plan [7], allowing Zhoushan a key development object supported by the state. In 2019, the integration development between the Ningbo and Zhoushan written into the work report of the provincial government of Zhejiang province for the first time. Zhejiang province explicitly supports the integration development between the Ningbo and Zhoushan [8]. Zhoushan local government has also introduced various preferential policies to focus on training local leisure tourism brands. The local government of Zhoushan has implemented preferential policies on finance, taxes and fees, guaranteed the development of tourism industry funds, land and other resource elements, deepened the reform of the tourism management system and mechanism, and optimized the tourism development environment to actively support the development of the marine tourism industry.

3.2 Analysis of the Development Disadvantages of Zhoushan Marine Tourism Industry (W)

1. **Low levelled tourist reception service (W1)**

Due to the special nature of the island, the infrastructure conditions in islands are generally poor, resource elements are not easy to concentrate, development costs are high, and tourism investment is weak. As a tourism city, the accommodation costs in Zhoushan are comparable to the provincial capital Hangzhou, but its high costs do not seem to bring corresponding service levels. The uneven reception service has become one of the factors restricting the development of tourism in Zhoushan. Hotels and hostels fail to update their basic equipment in time. Old bedding and aging electronics equipment will undoubtedly bring tourists a bad experience. Marine tourism practitioners are mostly local islanders and fishermen. They do not have high quality and cultural level, they lack corresponding service awareness and management level, and they do not put customer experience first. Therefore, the development of tourism industry in Zhoushan needs to implement tourists as the center, start from the details, improve the service quality, and do a good job in tourism reception services.

2. **Weak inter-island transportation (W2)**

Zhoushan Islands are far from the mainland, and a considerable part of the scenic spots are scattered islands, so the transportation problem has played a crucial role in restricting the development of Zhoushan tourism. Before the Zhoushan Cross-sea Bridge was completed and opened to transportation, in 2008, Zhoushan received only 15.164 million passengers, and the total tourism revenue was 10.196 billion yuan. After the Zhoushan Cross-sea Bridge was completed and opened to transportation, Zhoushan enjoyed a huge transportation bonus. In 2018, Zhoushan received 63.214 million people in boat tourism throughout the year, achieved a total tourism revenue of 94.22 billion yuan.

At present, tourists can generally travel to Zhoushan in the following three ways: (1) By air, they can fly directly to Putuo Airport. The air ticket is relatively high, and the carrying capacity of tourists is limited. (2) By ship: Ningbo and Shanghai both have direct routes to Zhoushan, but shipping takes too long, and its' carrying capacity is limited, restricting the number of tourists. (3) Highway mode. Since the Cross-sea Bridge has been completed and opened to transportation, Zhoushan has got rid of the predicament of relying solely on shipping to facilitate tourists to Zhoushan for sightseeing. The highway mode is currently the most important mode for transportation. Zhoushan has not opened a railway so far, and transportation is still the weakness. The lack of the railway system with strong carrying capacity will undoubtedly put Zhoushan Cross-sea Bridge under tremendous transportation pressure. The transportation on Zhoushan Island is not optimistic. According to statistics, as of 2018, the total mileage of Zhoushan City's highways has reached 1921.8 km. However, due to the densely packed mountains in Zhoushan, the urban area and the hillside are intertwined, which severely backlogs the scalability of urban highways, and the public transportation system still has problems. The weak transportation system has brought unpleasant experiences to tourists, which has become one of the factors hindering tourists' trip for the once more.

3. **Development of overseas market (W3)**

According to the statistics of the Zhoushan Statistics Bureau, in 2017, Zhoushan received 54.732 million domestic tourists throughout the year, generating 79.323 billion in revenue, while receiving less than 350,000 foreign tourists and generating only 1.329 billion in foreign exchange revenue. Comparatively speaking, the overseas market in the tourism industry in Zhoushan is basically at a blank stage. The limited foreign tourists are mainly related to the following reasons: the level of service is low, and it is not in line with international standards. At present, the employees in the tourism industry in Zhoushan can't provide a service that can meet the needs of overseas tourists. Before improving the service level, even if the number of foreign tourists increased, the tourism industry in Zhoushan could not complete the normal reception service. Zhoushan tourism industry has a low international reputation. At present, Zhoushan is an important tourist city in the province, but it can only be regarded as a rising star in the country and is still an unknown generation internationally. It can't tightly combine culture and tourism. It is the biggest attraction for foreign tourists to experience traditional Chinese culture while enjoying the beautiful scenery. Zhoushan still has a long way to go in tightly combining culture and tourism.

3.3 *Analysis of Development Opportunities of Zhoushan Marine Tourism Industry (O)*

1. **Major national strategic opportunities (O1)**

The 21st Century "Maritime Silk Road" and China (Zhejiang) Pilot Free Trade Zone have provided significant development opportunities for the development of marine tourism industry in Zhoushan. Zhejiang is an important position on the 21st Century Maritime Silk Road. As the only Free Trade Zone consisting of land and marine anchorages in China, the Zhejiang Free Trade Zone is China's leading area in the Pacific Rim Economic Circle, and it is an important window for establishing cooperation with countries along the Belt and Road Initiative. The Zhejiang Free Trade Zone divides into three major areas including Zhoushan Islands, North Zhoushan Island and Southern Zhoushan Island. The outlying area of Zhoushan Island has a high similarity with that of Daishan Scenic Area and Shengsi Scenic Area. The northern area of Zhoushan Island is not far from the characteristic villages in the islands such as Nandong and Ma'ao, while the southern area of Zhoushan Island has some similarities with Zhujiajian, Taohua Island, Putuo Mountain and other attractions. Free Trade Zone in Zhoushan will undoubtedly bring significant benefits and huge opportunities to Zhoushan tourism.

2. **Strong consumer market demand (O2)**

On the one hand, China's tourism industry has entered a new era. With the increase of income level and the satisfaction on material needs, spiritual happiness has become a further pursuit of human. Inland attractions have caused many tourists to produce aesthetic fatigue, and marine tourism has become a new target for people because of its uniqueness. Marine tourism ushers in new development opportunities. Facing the upsurge of marine tourism, Zhoushan has become an emerging destination for domestic marine tourism with its many excellent tourism resources.

On the other hand, the development of the Maritime Silk Road and the launch of the Free Trade Zone have brought a large number of people and new consumer groups to Zhoushan. Taking Yushan Island as an example, Yushan Island locates in the gray sea ocean area 4 miles from the Daishan Island in Zhoushan. Before the launch of the Free Trade Zone, it was only a backward island with a population of about 3,000. However, since the launch of the TTZ in 2017, the government plans to build Yushan Island into an international green petrochemical base. In just three years, the 40-million-ton/year refining and chemical integration project in the Yushan Island Green Petrochemical Base is about to be completed. At the same time, it equipped with nearly 60,000 migrant workers, all of whom are potential tourism growth items. The development and construction of major projects has brought huge transportation to Zhoushan and has become a new potential driving force for Zhoushan tourism.

3. **Improvement of infrastructure construction (O3)**

To accelerate the launch of the Zhejiang Pilot Free Trade Zone, the Zhejiang and Zhoushan municipal governments have significantly accelerated the launch of the transportation, medical, and water supply projects in Zhoushan. The launch of the Zhouzhou high-speed railway will end its non-railroad era. By then, the strong carrying capacity of the railway will greatly enhance its transportation capacity and alleviate the transportation pressure of the Zhoushan cross-sea bridge during the peak tourist period. The main passageway of Ningbo-Zhoushan Port mainly includes the three major projects of the Fuchimen Bridge, the main passage section and the Yushan Bridge. After the completion, tourists from Ningbo to Zhujiajian can directly take the Zhoushan Expressway next to the Fuchimen Bridge; they can reach the destination in an hour and a half, further reducing the travel time cost of tourists. After the completion of Yushan Island, it connected Yushan Island and Daishan Island, making it only 6 min to drive from one island to the other.

After the third phase of the Zhoushan Water Diversion Project is put into operation, the average annual water diversion capacity of Zhoushan will reach 127 million cubic meters. In this way, the water shortage in Zhoushan Island or Zhoushan Native Island caused by the influx of tourists during the peak tourist season will be relieved, which will further enhance the tourism carrying capacity in Zhoushan Island.

The three items above are only part of measures improving its infrastructure during the launch of the Free Trade Zone. These measures will directly or indirectly promote the development and prosperity of Zhoushan tourism.

3.4 Threats to the Development of Zhoushan Marine Tourism Industry (T)

1. **Island ecological environment is fragile (T1)**

The island ecosystem is a unique type of ecosystem. On the one hand, the island is far from the mainland, which shapes its special species composition, that is, there is a specific relationship between the number of species that it lives and the area it occupies. The total number of species in the island has remained stable; on the other hand, due to the lack of species diversity, island ecosystems are relatively fragile, and once artificially damaged, it is difficult to recover by itself. During the development of the marine tourism industry and the resources, if there are problems including improper disposal of garbage, pollution of offshore waters, and discharge of pollutants, the ecological structure of the island will be unbalanced. To prevent pollution of the marine environment and degradation of island resources, human beings cannot blindly pursue economic benefits during the development of marine tourism. We should also consider rationally controlling the intensity of island development and the number of tourists to maintain the ecological balance on the island.

2. **Increased competition in the marine tourism market (T2)**

The mature island tourism destinations abroad have no small market challenges for China's marine tourism. At the same time, the development of marine tourism industry in Zhoushan has challenged by similar coastal cities such as Sanya, Xiamen, and Qingdao. China's marine tourism industry is still in the development stage. Development planning and operation management are not standardized and perfect. The development of ideas, models, and management in the marine tourism industry in coastal areas are homogeneous and highly replaceable. The Zhoushan Cross-sea Bridge across the whole line, which has changed the state of exchange of funds, technology and information between Zhoushan and external cities, which is of great strategic significance effect for the rapid, healthy and coordinated development of Zhoushan. Zhoushan marine tourism is bound to retain tourists to obtain greater benefits, and then improve its service level and quality of tourism products. With the opening of the Zhoushan Cross-sea Bridge, convenient transportation can attract more tourists. Due to the shortened time cost, a large number of tourists in surrounding areas choose to travel and return on the same day, which is not conducive to retaining tourists. At the same time, the high cost for crossing the sea bridge has hindered the development of Zhoushan tourism economy to a certain extent.

3. **Low coupling between marine tourism industry development and national strategy (T3)**

The twenty-first century "Maritime Silk Road" and the launch of the Zhejiang Free Trade Zone are extremely important development opportunities for the marine tourism industry in Zhoushan. However, Tourism in Zhoushan has not made full use of this opportunity. Compared with Hainan Island, it has many similarities with

Hainan. Hainan is also an FTA. It is also an important position in the Maritime Silk Road. However, Hainan is taking advantage of the Free Trade Zone and the opportunity to build the Maritime Silk Road to further accelerate its internationalization. It strives to open 100 international routes within three years between 2018 and 2020. In the first quarter of 2018 alone, Hainan opened 6 international routes including the Haikou-Sydney direct route and the Haikou-Manila route, which extended the layout of Hainan's international routes to Oceania for the first time. Throughout 2018, Hainan has opened more than 16 target routes to London and other overseas destinations. However, Zhoushan Airport is still in its infancy. At present, there are 14 domestic airlines in China, and only 13 cities are open to navigation.

4 Application of AHP Method in SWOT Analysis for Zhoushan Marine Tourism Industry

The SWOT analysis method mostly conducts qualitative analysis of the research objects. To make up for the shortcomings of the quantitative analysis in the SWOT analysis method, this study combines the qualitative and quantitative analysis for the research objects with the Analytic Hierarchy Process (AHP) to improve the reliable results. Analytic Hierarchy Process is an organic combination of quantitative and qualitative analysis. It is necessary to find out the main factors in the decision-making process, and then divide them into corresponding hierarchical models according to the internal organizational structure. Through calculation, we compare the various factors to obtain the relative importance of the factors, and finally performs a comprehensive analysis to obtain the results [9].

This paper uses the Delphi method to issue a Zhoushan marine tourism industry development SWOT-AHP questionnaire to 30 experts in the marine, tourism, and economic fields in October 2019. They separately analyzed the advantages and disadvantages of the marine tourism industry in Zhoushan. Opportunity factors and challenge factors assigned to the four system-level elements for evaluation. Finally, 22 valid questionnaires obtained. After the original data transposed by SPSS 23.0 software, YAAHP 7.5 software is used to carry out a qualitative and quantitative comprehensive analysis on the development status and various index factors of Zhoushan marine tourism industry and put forward the corresponding development suggestions for Zhoushan marine tourism industry.

Table 2 SWOT strategic hierarchy structure of marine tourism industry development in Zhoushan

	System layer	Variable level	Label
SWOT strategic hierarchy structure of marine tourism industry development in Zhoushan	Strengths (S)	Obvious location advantage	S1
		Rich tourism resources	S2
		Government support guidance	S3
	Weaknesses (W)	Low levelled tourist reception services	W1
		Inter-island transportation weakness	W2
		Overseas markets to develop	W3
	Opportunities (O)	Major national strategic opportunities	O1
		Strong consumer market demand	O2
		Improvement of infrastructure construction	O3
	Threats (T)	Fragile island ecological environment	T1
		Increased competition in the marine tourism market	T2
		Low coupling between marine tourism industry development and national strategy	T3

4.1 The Hierarchical Structure of Marine Tourism Industry in Zhoushan Development Strategy

The advantages, disadvantages, opportunities, and threats selected in the SWOT analysis on Zhoushan marine tourism industry constitute a hierarchical structure (Table 2) and a structural model (Fig. 1).

4.2 Using AHP to Determine the Development Status of Zhoushan Marine Tourism Industry

1. **Construct a judgment matrix and perform consistency check**

First, a comparison matrix including strengths group, weaknesses group, opportunities group, and threats group forms according to the SWOT hierarchy structure (Table 2). The four sets of comparison matrices are converted into judgment matrices, as shown in Tables 3, 4, 5 and 6, then the indicator layer factors are calculated according to this judgment matrix table. The priority factors (W_i) of the target layer factors compared, and consistency checked. The consistency ratio CR is used to check the

Exploration and Innovation of Zhoushan Marine Tourism Industry ...

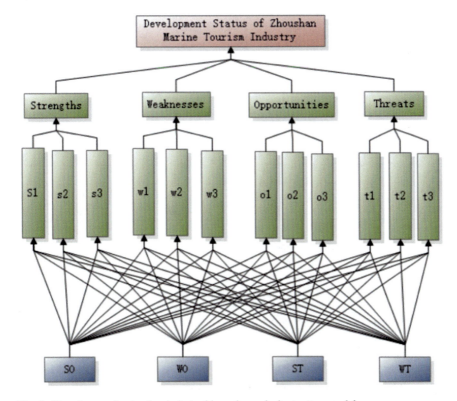

Fig. 1 Zhoushan marine tourism industry hierarchy analysis structure model

Table 3 Judgment matrix for the dominant group

Strengths	S1	S2	S3	Wi
S1	1.0000	3.0000	3.0000	0.5889
S2	0.3333	1.0000	2.0000	0.2519
S3	0.3333	0.5000	1.0000	0.1593

Note Consistency test result CR = 0.518 <0.1, it is acceptable

Table 4 Judgment matrix for disadvantaged group

Weaknesses	W1	W2	W3	Wi
W1	1.0000	3.0000	2.0000	0.5485
W2	0.3333	1.0000	1.0000	0.2106
W3	0.5000	1.0000	1.0000	0.2409

Note Consistency test result CR = 0.0176 <0.1, it is acceptable

Table 5 Judgment matrix for opportunity group

Opportunities	O1	O2	O3	Wi
O1	1.0000	2.0000	2.0000	0.4905
O2	0.5000	1.0000	0.5000	0.1976
O3	0.5000	2.0000	1.0000	0.3119

Note Consistency test result CR = 0.517 <0.1, it is acceptable

Table 6 Judgment matrix for the challenge group

Threats	T1	T2	T3	Wi
T1	1.0000	2.0000	2.0000	0.5000
T2	0.5000	1.0000	1.0000	0.2500
T3	0.5000	1.0000	1.0000	0.2500

Note Consistency test result CR = 0.000 <0.1, it is acceptable

consistency of the matrix, and to judge whether the satisfaction between different levels in the matrix is consistent: When the CR is less than 10%, the consistency of the matrix is satisfactory, indicating that the evaluators' thinking is similar and the results are acceptable. Otherwise, adjust the judgment matrix and re-compare until the consistency check passes.

After sorting each group of SWOT factors, the largest priority index factor of each group selects to form a new SWOT judgment matrix (Table 7). All the judgment matrices have passed the consistency test, which shows that the consistency results are satisfactory, and the AHP analysis results are feasible.

2. Zhoushan marine tourism industry development strategy hierarchy

From the overall ranking shown in Table 8, we can see that the impact of each factor of SWOT on the development of Zhoushan marine tourism industry is as follows: rich tourism resources, fragile island ecological environment, low leveled tourism reception services, obvious location advantages, low coupling between marine tourism industry development and national strategy, increased competition in the marine

Table 7 Inter-group judgment matrix

Inter-group	S	W	O	T	Wi
S	1.0000	2.0000	5.0000	1.0000	0.3923
W	0.5000	1.0000	2.0000	1.0000	0.2223
O	0.2000	0.5000	1.0000	0.3333	0.0940
T	1.0000	1.0000	3.0000	1.0000	0.2913

Note Consistency test result CR = 0.0225 <0.1, acceptable

Table 8 Zhoushan marine tourism industry development strategy hierarchy

SWOT factors	S	W	O	T	Hierarchical weight
	0.3923	0.2223	0.0940	0.2913	
S1	0.5889				0.0988
S2	0.2519				0.2310
S3	0.1592				0.0625
W1		0.5485			0.1219
W2		0.2106			0.0468
W3		0.2409			0.0536
O1			0.4905		0.0186
O2			0.1976		0.0461
O3			0.3119		0.0293
T1				0.5000	0.1460
T2				0.2500	0.0726
T3				0.2500	0.0728

tourism market, government support and guidance, overseas markets to be developed, outstanding transportation weakness, strong consumer market demand, improved infrastructure construction, and major national strategic opportunities.

5   Recommendations for Zhoushan Marine Tourism Industry

5.1   Reconstruction of Smart Tourism and Tourism Services

Smart tourism can integrate Zhoushan marine tourism resources through the Internet cloud computing method, thereby intelligently customizing suitable travel plans and tourism products for tourists and improving the tourist experience. The government and relevant agencies should fully integrate the Internet and actively promote the launch of a public information disclosure platform for the tourism industry. The government and relevant agencies should dynamically update information on tourism resources, tourism economy, tourism activities, and tourists through the Internet platform to create new smart tourism. Reconstruction of smart tourism and tourism services not only enables tourists to enjoy the convenience of travel in the modern technology era but also enables tourists to supervise scenic spots through tourism product information that the platform dynamically updates.

5.2 Government-Enterprise Cooperation and Regional Integration

Marine tourism should actively play the role of enterprises in the market, promote government-enterprise cooperation, deepen the PPP model, and actively cultivate new engines for development. Tourism PPP is a semi-social public service; it pursues both economic benefits and social services. It can mobilize more social resources to participate in the development of tourism and improve the effectiveness of tourism investment. Zhoushan marine tourism development is inseparable from the active expansion of tourism PPP projects. First, the government should issue corresponding policies and regulations to support the development of tourism PPP. At the same time, the government should improve its credibility, thereby enhancing the confidence of enterprises in developing tourism PPP projects. Finally, scientific price formation and sound financial subsidy mechanisms are needed to encourage Zhoushan marine tourism development.

In addition to government-enterprise cooperation, Zhoushan should actively respond to regional integration, especially in integrating boat-boat integration and the Yangtze River Delta. At present, although Zhoushan has joined the "Five City Tourism Association in Southeast of Zhejiang", the tourism resources of Ningbo and Zhoushan still cannot be effectively shared. It is necessary to accelerate the integration of infrastructure, accelerate the reform and opening up integration, accelerate the integration of industrial development, accelerate the integration of market development, accelerate the integration of public services, and accelerate the integration of environmental protection. In the integration of the Yangtze River Delta, Zhoushan should base its development on characteristics and accelerate its integration into the Yangtze River Delta. Vigorously developing the marine economy is the top priority of Zhoushan economic development, is also the dislocated Zhoushan economic development in the integration process of the Yangtze River Delta.

5.3 Cultural Integration and Cultural and Tourism Integration

With the continuous extension of the global tourism concept, public cultural consumption constantly transformed into characteristic tourism products, and cultural tourism has become a hot trend. Zhoushan has a distinctive marine culture, and it is extremely promising to combine marine civilization and tourism. The integration of cultural and tourism is more than just admiring the scenery on the surface. It is more to reflect the fact that young people are no longer satisfied with simple-way travelling, but more willing to feel and pursue the cultural charm behind tourism products. Therefore, Zhoushan marine tourism can realize the integration of culture and tourism by creating characteristic island villages and developing boutique island tours.

5.4 Exploiting International Tourism Potential with Free Trade Zone

Zhoushan is an important position on the 21st Century Maritime Silk Road. Looking at the tourist hot spots along the Maritime Silk Road, Taiwan, Hong Kong, Phuket, Singapore and other places have developed unique international island tourism. Zhoushan can learn from it, with the experience of these regions, Zhoushan can take advantage of Free Trade Zone to develop their international tourism projects. Zhoushan can strengthen international cooperation in island tourism. There is not only competition in island tourism, but also a rich basis for cooperation. The 2019 International Island Tourism Conference provided the direction for the development of international island tourism in Zhoushan. The purpose of the conference is to promote the exchange and trade in the entire industrial chain of marine island tourism development, create a diplomatic platform that China and the world island tourism countries and regions share, and cast the IP symbol for the international island tourism industry.

Increasing airport flights is overwhelming. At present, Zhoushan has only one airport, Putuo Airport, it only has domestic flights, which prevents foreign tourists from reaching Zhoushan directly, which increases the cost of travel for international tourists. Therefore, opening international flights at the right time is also a top priority. In recent years, the cruise business has been an important breakthrough in the development of international island tourism, but there are few Zhoushan cruise tourism products. At present, the launch of the Free Trade Zone has brought about a turnaround in the development of the cruise industry. With the improvement of the marine transportation network, Zhoushan is also expected to build an international cruise port and develop cruise tourism products.

6 Conclusions

Since the outbreak of COVID-19, global economic activity has been severely impacted by the epidemic. The COVID-19 pandemic has made a huge impact on the tourism economy. Marine becomes a natural barrier to the spread of the virus. Due to the special geographical environment of islands, the relationship between epidemic prevention and control with economic performance is quite different compared with other parts of the mainland. Zhoushan has taken timely and scientific epidemic prevention measures to ensure that the prevention and control of COVID-19 epidemic is under control.

There is still a lot of room for development in Zhoushan marine tourism industry. Seizing the opportunity of the Free Trade Zone, Zhoushan should review the existing deficiencies, actively explore new tourism products, increase its popularity, and strive to become a golden business card for China's marine tourism, and finally make Zhoushan marine tourism international.

References

1. Junlu, R., Ying, W., Yafang, P., Zhuying, D., Fengzhi, S., Yinghua, S.: Research on the evaluation system of Zhoushan marine tourism industry cluster competitiveness. Mod. Econ. Inform. (09), 494–495 + 498 (2016)
2. Jinbo, J.: New development of China's tourism industry in the context of the free trade pilot zone. J. South China Univ. Technol. (Soc. Sci. Edn.) **18**(02), 1–8 (2016)
3. Jingci, W., Sheng, Z.: Research on the development strategy of island leisure industry based on SWOT-AHP method-taking Zhoushan as an example. Mar. Dev. Manag. **35**(03), 109–115 (2018)
4. Ying, L., Zhibo, T., Jiajia, D., Hanglu, Z., Yichun, D.: Suggestions for the development of Zhoushan shipping service industry based on SWOT analysis. Water Transp. Manag. **40**(02), 9–11 + 20 (2018)
5. Zhuyu, W.: Discussion on the development model of "medical + global tourism" from the perspective of Hainan free trade zone. Natl. Circ. Econ. **34**, 84–85 (2018)
6. Liushen, D., Liqing, M.: Exploration of Zhoushan marine tourism development strategy under the new normal. Jiangsu Commer. Theory (01), 86–87 + 95 (2019)
7. Wenyan, D., Guo, X.: Research on the development of Zhoushan fishery and farmhouse tourism. Manag. Obs. **15**, 184–187 (2017)
8. Guangyu, Z., Weiwei, H.: SWOT analysis of sports tourism development in island areas—taking Zhoushan as an example. Spec. Econ. Zone (07), 117–119 (2016)
9. Ting, W., Liuwu, C., Xiaojun, W.: Fujian Free Trade Zone and the "21st Century Maritime Silk Road" Deep Connection Research. Fujian Forum (Humanities and Social Sciences) **10**, 189–196 (2018)

Minority Women's Willingness to Participate in Tourism Poverty Alleviation—A Case Study

Yujing Chu, Songmao Wang, Yang Yang, and Tong Ding

Abstract Tourism poverty alleviation is the potential and driving force for tourism employment. It is one of the forecast targets of employment behavior. This paper investigates the willingness of 660 Kazak women in 33 rural areas of Xinyuan County to participate in tourism poverty alleviation. The Probit model is used to study the influencing factors of Kazakh women's willingness to participate the poverty alleviation activities. The results show that 51.9% of the respondents are willing to participate in tourism poverty alleviation work. Among the Kazakh women to participate in tourism poverty alleviation affecting factors, the positive factors of their employment intention are Chinese level, ethnic food making skills, tourist souvenir making skills, government's attention to tourism poverty alleviation, etc. Age, tourism poverty alleviation accuracy, tourism poverty alleviation employment environment, the distance between residence and scenic spot, the number of family children, per capita grassland area showed negative effects. Education years, Halal diet care degree, singing and dancing skills, per capita cultivated land area, etc. did not pass the significant test.

Keywords Kazakh women · Willingness · Tourism poverty alleviation · Influencing factors

Y. Chu
College of Tourism, Shanghai Normal University, Shanghai, People's Republic of China
e-mail: chuyujing@163.com

S. Wang
College of Economics and Management, Shandong Agricultural University, Taian, Shandong, People's Republic of China

Y. Yang (✉) · T. Ding
College of Tourism, Shanghai Normal University, Shanghai, People's Republic of China
e-mail: gogotaurus@outlook.com

© The Author(s), under exclusive license to Springer Nature Singapore Pte Ltd. 2022
Y. Luo et al. (eds.), *Tourism, Aviation and Hospitality Development During the COVID-19 Pandemic*, https://doi.org/10.1007/978-981-19-1661-8_8

1 Introduction

After the epidemic, international tourism suffered huge impact, the emergence of the epidemic led to the damage of China's tourism image, and the World Health Organization was listed as an emergency of the public health incident in the international concern, thus, the inbound and outbound tour was suffered serious restrictions, meanwhile, the implementation of China's tourism poverty alleviation has brought heavy blows.

Tourism poverty alleviation refers to the industrial poverty alleviation mode [1] in areas with certain tourism resources to drive the local poor people out of poverty and become rich through the development of tourism. Since the 1980s, the government and scholars have paid attention to the poverty alleviation through tourism. In recent years, the national government has placed great hopes on the poverty alleviation through tourism. Policy documents have been issued to emphasize that the role of tourism development should be brought into full play in poverty alleviation. Xinyuan County, Yili, has the characteristics of rich tourism resources, high quality of ecological environment, weak economic foundation, wide range of poverty and Kazakh ethnic agglomeration. Tourism poverty alleviation is a new, ecological and efficient way of poverty alleviation, which can effectively drive Xinyuan county to develop ecological economy and achieve the best choice of poverty alleviation and prosperity. In 2017, Xinyuan County formulated the tourism development strategy of "one core, two lines, one triangle and six groups", focusing on the construction of the industrial layout of "integration of the whole region and world quality products". In 2016, Xinyuan county established a "tourism poverty alleviation experimental area" relying on Nalati scenic spot, and vigorously supported a group of poor households to set up agricultural (animal husbandry, fishery) family entertainment, family hotels, etc., and the tourism poverty alleviation effect was remarkable. The development of tourism in Xinyuan county has a great impact on the local economy and society, especially on the local women's social and economic status and employment mode. However, influenced by the national customs and habits, the traditional idea of "men are in charge of the outside world, and women are in charge of the interior", there are a series of special difficulties in Kazakh women's employment. The tourism industry includes "food, housing, transportation, tourism, shopping, entertainment" and other aspects. Compared with other industries, it has the characteristics of low threshold and strong accessibility. Kazakh women play an important role in the production and inheritance of ethnic characteristic diet and national handicraft industry. Under the background of the comprehensive implementation of targeted tourism poverty alleviation, local women's willingness to participate in poverty alleviation through tourism should be improved, it will help to solve the problem of women's employment and improve the benefit of tourism poverty alleviation.

2 Literature Review

DFID put forward the concept of Pro-poor Tourism [2] at the conference of sustainable development in 1999. With the popularization of PPT concept in foreign countries, domestic scholars gradually transfer the object and target of tourism poverty alleviation from regional level to poverty level. Xinhong Zhou and others believe that 'poverty alleviation' is the essence of poverty alleviation tourism. In the process of helping the poor, the development of tourism is the means to achieve the goal of poverty alleviation [3]. Subsequently, more and more domestic scholars have studied poverty alleviation through tourism from the perspective of the development and benefits of the poor population. Jia Li et al. Studied the perception of poverty alleviation and participation behavior of tourism poverty alleviation among residents in Sanjiangyuan area of Qinghai Province [4]. Taking Liupanshan tourism poverty alleviation experimental area in Ningxia as an example, Jianhong Xiao and others studied the tourism poverty alleviation approach for the poor population [5]. At present, the research on the effect of tourism poverty alleviation is mainly based on the macro and micro perspectives. Taking Alexandra town and Madikwe reserve as examples, Rogerson makes a comparative study on the role of tourism poverty alleviation in promoting the economic development of different urban and rural areas [6]. Shu Guo this paper studies the poverty alleviation effect of tourism from the perspective of industrial chain [7]. Based on the residents' perception theory, Li Jiang and others conducted a questionnaire survey on Jiulongjiang community residents. The results showed that local residents had obvious perception of the social and economic effects of tourism poverty alleviation, were not sensitive to environmental effects, and had strong willingness to participate in tourism. However, restricted by economic and cultural factors, their actual participation ability was insufficient [8]. Xiaohai Deng studied the economic and social effects of tourism on local residents by using grey correlation method [9]. Based on the theory of planned behavior, Lu Chong and others studied the willingness and influencing factors of poverty-stricken farmers and herdsmen in Sichuan Tibetan areas by using the double threshold model [10].

Since the 1970s, some scholars began to pay attention to the relationship between women and tourism. The foreign research mainly includes the attitude and cognition of rural women tourism workers in poverty alleviation [11, 12], the wage status and work experience of female employees in tourism enterprise [13, 14]. At present, the domestic research on women and tourism poverty alleviation can be divided into two categories: first, the impact of tourism poverty alleviation and development on local women. Using grounded theory and taking rural tourism as an example, Daowei Mao studied the changes caused by women's participation in tourism poverty alleviation [15] from three aspects of economy, psychology and social culture [16]. Secondly, from the perspective of women as participants in tourism poverty alleviation, this paper analyzes the advantages and disadvantages of women in tourism poverty alleviation, and puts forward suggestions on promoting the advantages and avoiding the disadvantages of women tourism employment [17, 18].

At present, most of the literature about poverty alleviation through tourism is in underdeveloped areas, especially in minority areas. As a powerful force of modernization, tourism is changing the social structure and the social role of people, which has a great impact on local women. It is of great significance to explore the willingness and influencing factors of ethnic minority women in poverty-stricken areas for improving the employment rate and accuracy of tourism poverty alleviation. So far, under the background of traditional culture and ethnic customs, there is still a lack of research on minority women's participation willingness and influencing factors in tourism poverty alleviation.

Taking Kazakh as an example, this paper analyzes women's willingness to participate in tourism poverty alleviation and its influencing factors from four aspects of personal characteristics, tourism employment skills, tourism poverty alleviation perception and family environment, which will enrich the research field of tourism poverty alleviation and provide theoretical support for the local government to issue tourism poverty alleviation policies.

3 Research Hypothesis, Theoretical Model and Research Method

3.1 Overview of the Study Area

Xinyuan County, located in the east of Yili Prefecture, has always been known as "the Pearl of grassland, Xinjiang wine town". With a total area of 7581 km^2, the county governs 11 towns and 77 administrative villages, with a total population of 321,700. Among them, the Kazakh population is 150,100, which is about one tenth of the total Kazakh population in China. It is the county with the largest number of Kazakh people living in the country. The agricultural population of Xinyuan County accounts for 74% of the total population of the whole county, and it is a non-key county for poverty alleviation and development in the autonomous region. There are 12 key villages for poverty alleviation and development. Xinyuan county is rich in tourism resources, famous scenic spots are Nalati scenic spot, Künes National Forest Park, West Region wine culture museum, etc. In recent years, the tourism industry in Xinyuan county has developed rapidly. In 2016, the number of tourists received was 3.3728 million, and the tourism income was 1.159 billion yuan, increasing by 31.2% and 37.2% respectively (Fig. 1).

3.2 Influencing Variables and Research Hypotheses

Based on the previous research results and previous research on Kazakh women's willingness to participate in tourism poverty alleviation, this paper constructs a

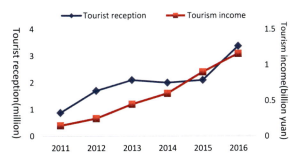

Fig. 1 Tourism development of Xinyuan county from 2011 to 2016

theoretical framework that influences Kazakh women's willingness to participate in tourism poverty alleviation from four aspects: personal characteristics, tourism employment skills, tourism poverty alleviation perception and family environment.

3.2.1 Personal Characteristics

(1) Age

In the tourism industry, there are many jobs with high labor intensity, such as tour guide, hotel service personnel, scenic spot staff, etc. Secondly, young people have stronger adaptability and are easier to master new tourism skills. Moreover, unmarried young people have less family burden to take care of the elderly and children, and have more opportunities to go out to work. Therefore, the following assumptions are put forward.

H1-1: age has a significant negative impact on Kazakh women's willingness to participate in tourism poverty alleviation.

(2) Years of education

Education can enable people to acquire knowledge, master skills and increase know ledge. The more years of education, the stronger the willingness of Kazakh women to go out for employment, at the same time, the more opportunities for tourism employment. Therefore, the following assumptions are put forward.

H1-2: the number of years of education has a significant positive impact on Kazakh women's willingness to participate in tourism poverty alleviation.

(3) Halal diet care

The more the Kazakh people care about their food and drink, the more they care about the Muslim food and drink, the more likely it is for Kazakh women to pay attention to the Muslim food and drink. Therefore, the following assumptions are put forward.

H1-3: there is a significant negative relationship between the degree of halal diet care and the willingness of Kazakh women to participate in tourism poverty alleviation.

(4) Chinese level

Tour guide service, scenic spot service, hotel service and other tourism jobs require the employment to have good Chinese communication skills. Kazakh women with good Chinese proficiency have more opportunities for tourism employment. Therefore, the following assumptions are put forward.

H1-4: there is a significant positive relationship between Chinese level and Kazakh women's willingness to participate in tourism poverty alleviation, that is, the better the level of Chinese, the stronger the willingness to participate in tourism poverty alleviation.

3.2.2 Tourism Employment Skills

(1) Production skills of ethnic food

There are many Kazakh ethnic foods, and tasting Kazakh food is an important content for tourists to choose. Kazakh women with the skills of making ethnic food are more likely to sell special food, run restaurants, farmhouse and other tourism related work in the scenic area, Therefore, the following assumptions are put forward.

H2-1: ethnic food production skills and Kazakh women's willingness to participate in tourism poverty alleviation have a significant positive relationship.

(2) Tourist souvenir making skills

Kazakh embroidery, woolen products and other tourist souvenirs are well-known at home and abroad. With the development of tourism, Kazakh women with tourism souvenir making skills should be more willing to participate in tourism poverty alleviation. Therefore, the following assumptions are put forward.

H2-2: tourism souvenir making skills and Kazakh women's willingness to participate in tourism poverty alleviation have a significant positive relationship.

(3) Performance skills of folk song and dance

The unique ethnic song and dance has a certain role in promoting the development of tourism. Kazakh people are passionate, ebullient, and love dancing and singing. Therefore, the following assumptions are put forward.

H2-3: ethnic song and dance performance skills have a significant positive impact on Kazakh women's willingness to participate in tour ism poverty alleviation.

3.2.3 Perception of Poverty Alleviation Through Tourism

(1) The government attaches great importance to tourism poverty alleviation

The government plays two main roles in the process of poverty alleviation through tourism: one is to formulate policies and regulations to provide software support for tourism poverty alleviation; the other is to improve infrastructure and provide hardware support for tourism poverty alleviation. Therefore, the following assumptions are put forward.

H3-1: the government's emphasis on tourism poverty alleviation has a significant positive impact on Kazakh women's willingness to participate in tourism poverty alleviation.

(2) Accuracy of tourism poverty alleviation

At present, the accuracy of poverty alleviation by tourism in many parts of China is poor, and the phenomenon of "helping the rich but not helping the poor" has emerged, which further widens the gap between the rich and the poor, and inhibits the enthusiasm of local community residents to participate in tourism poverty alleviation. Therefore, the following assumptions are put forward.

H3-2: Tourism poverty alleviation accuracy has a significant positive impact on Kazakh women's willingness to participate in tourism poverty alleviation, that is, the better the accuracy of tourism poverty alleviation, the stronger the willingness to participate in tourism poverty alleviation.

(3) Employment environment for poverty alleviation through tourism

The employment environment for poverty alleviation through tourism is an important factor to attract the employment to choose to engage in tourism. It includes employment safety environment, employment humanistic environment and employment stability. Female employees are more sensitive to job security environment and humanistic environment. Therefore, the following assumptions are put forward.

H3-3: Tourism poverty alleviation employment environment has a significant positive impact on Kazakh women's willingness to participate in tourism poverty alleviation.

(4) Participation of tourism income in poverty alleviation

The economy of Xinyuan county is relatively backward, and the employees are more sensitive to salary. Therefore, the following assumptions are put forward.

H3-4: the economic income of tourism poverty alleviation has a significant positive impact on Kazakh women's willingness to participate in tourism poverty alleviation.

3.2.4 Family Environment

(1) The degree to which family hinders going out to work

Kazakh people believe in Islam, and the traditional idea of "men are in charge of the outside world, and women are in charge of the interior" is relatively serious, which hinders Kazakh women from going out to participate in employment to a certain extent. Therefore, the following assumptions are put forward.

H4-4 has a negative impact on Kazakh women's willingness to go out to work.

(2) Distance between residence and scenic spot

The farther the distance between the residential area and the scenic spot, the less perception of tourism development [19], the less possibility of local community residents to participate in tourism employment. At the same time, the farther the residence is from the scenic spot, the higher the cost of tourism employment. Therefore, the following assumptions are put forward.

H4-2: the distance between residence and scenic spot has a significant negative impact on Kazakh women's willingness to participate in tourism poverty alleviation.

(3) Health status of parents

The health status of parents is closely related to Kazakh women's migrant work. Kazakh believe in Islam, especially respect the elderly. If their parents are not in good health, Kazakh women will choose to stay at home to take care of their parents. Therefore, the following assumptions are put forward.

H4-3: there is a significant positive relationship between parents' health status and Kazakh women's willingness to participate in tour ism poverty alleviation, that is, if their parents are healthy, Kazakh women have strong willingness to participate in tourism poverty alleviation.

(4) Number of children in the family

The national family planning policy stipulates that more than one million people, less than ten million people, can have one more child than the Han nationality. Many Kazakh families will raise 2–3 children, which will also hinder Kazakh women from going out to work. Therefore, the following assumptions are put forward.

H4-4: the number of family children has a significant negative impact on Kazakh women's tourism poverty alleviation willingness, that is, the more the number of family children, the weaker the willingness of Kazakh women to help the poor through tourism.

(5) Per capita cultivated land area

The cultivated land area of Xinyuan county is about 800,000 mu, and the per capita cultivated land area of farmers and herdsmen is about 2.5 mu. Generally speaking, the more cultivated land, the better the family's economic income, and the less likely they are to engage in poverty alleviation through tourism. Therefore, the following assumptions are put forward.

H4-5: there is a significant negative relationship between per capita cultivated land area and Kazakh women's willingness to participate in tourism poverty alleviation.

(6) Grassland area per capita

Kazakh is a traditional nomadic people. Xinyuan county has 7,616,600 mu of the best natural grassland in Xinjiang and even in the whole country. The per capita grassland area of each farmer and herdsman is about 15 mu. Generally speaking, the larger the grassland area and the more livestock raised by families, the better the family's economic income, and the less likely they are to engage in poverty alleviation through tourism. Therefore, the following assumptions are put forward.

H4-6: grassland area per capita has a significant negative relationship with Kazakh women's willingness to participate in tourism poverty alleviation.

Based on the above hypothesis, the theoretical model is established (Fig. 2).

4 Research Methods and Data

4.1 Research Model

According to the above analysis and hypothesis, considering that some explanatory variables are assigned to zero, it is not suitable to apply logistic model, and the sample data basically conforms to normal distribution, which is more suitable for Probit model analysis. Probit model is one of the important models in econometric nonlinear analysis, and is often applied to the study of labor transfer [20]. This paper classifies and processes the data of Kazakh women's employment intention, and classifies the (very willing) and (relatively satisfied) survey results into the (willing) one with the value of 1, while the results of (general), (unwilling) and (very unwilling) are classified into the (unwilling) category as the reference frame, and the value is 0. This transformation can not only reduce the demand for large sample size of 5-point categorical variable regress ion model, it can also meet the requirements of the model for binary dependent variables and improve the accuracy of data analysis between variables in this model. According to the results of the survey data, the factors influencing the willingness to participate in tourism poverty alleviation are complex and diverse. This paper uses a set of variables X to explain the influencing factors of Kazakh women's willingness to participate in tourism poverty alleviation. The relationship function is as follows:

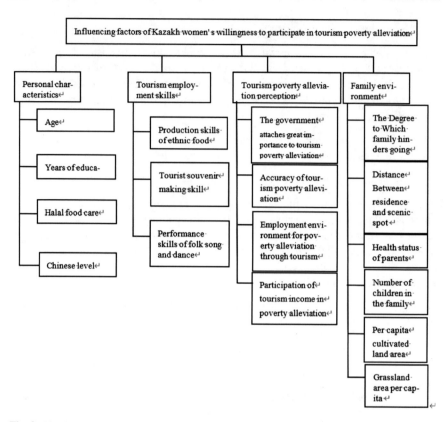

Fig. 2 The theoretical model

Y (willingness to participate in tourism poverty alleviation) = f (personal characteristics, tourism employment skills, tourism poverty alleviation perception, family environment) + random disturbance.

The Probit model of Kazakh women's willingness to help the poor through tourism can be established as follows:

$$\begin{aligned}\text{Prob}(Y=1|X_i) &= \Phi(\alpha_0 + B_1X_1 + B_2X_2 + B_3X_3 + B_4X_4 + \varepsilon_n) \\ &= \Phi(\alpha_0 + \beta_{11}x_{11} + \cdots + \beta_{1n}x_{1n} + \beta_{21}x_{21} + \cdots + \beta_{2n}x_{2n} \\ &\quad + \beta_{31}x_{31} + \cdots + \beta_{3n}x_{3n} + \beta_{41}x_{41} + \cdots + \beta_{4n}x_{4n} + \varepsilon_n)\end{aligned}$$

In the formula, $\text{Prob}(Y = 1X_i)$ represents the probability of Kazakh women's tourism employment, and X_i is the independent variable vector, which mainly refers to personal characteristic variable, tourism employment skill variable, tourism poverty alleviation perception variable and family environment variable. X_{1n} is the nth independent variable under the first independent variable vector, α_0 is the constant term, β_{1n} is the Probit regression coefficient of the nth independent variable under the first independent variable vector, and ξ_n is the disturbance term, that is, the influence of other independent variables not included.

4.2 Research Data

The research team visited Xinyuan county from August 5 to 22 and October 11 to 27, 2016. Three villages were randomly selected from each township, and 20 respondents were randomly selected from each village. The questionnaire was divided into four parts: (1) demographic characteristics; (2) tourism employment skills; (3) tourism poverty alleviation perception; (4) family environment. The liker scale was used to express the degree of problem perception. The questionnaire was compiled in Kazakh language. The questionnaire was divided into two groups, composed of teachers and students of Xinjiang University Tourism College. Each group was equipped with two Kazakh teachers and students to ensure the convenience of data acquisition. Each group was equipped with a supervisor. If the questionnaire was found to be inconsistent or incomplete, the respondents were required to fill in again. Considering the authenticity and privacy of the data obtained, all interviews and surveys were conducted in the interviewees' homes. The Cronbach's α of the questionnaire was 0.763, indicating that the reliability of the questionnaire was good, and the KMO value was 0.712, indicating that the validity of the questionnaire was good. A total of 660 questionnaires were distributed and 632 were recovered. 610 questionnaires were valid, with an effective rate of 92.42%. The influencing variables and their descriptions are shown in Table 1.

5 Results and Analysis

5.1 Sample Descriptive Statistics

According to the analysis of the demographic characteristics of the respondents, the Kazakh women under 25 accounted for 11.7%, 36.1% were 25–35 years old, 35.6% were over 35–45 years old, and 16.5% were over 45–60 years old. The educational background of the respondents was generally low, with junior high school and primary school education accounting for 72.2%, 14.6% and 13.2% respectively, 56.6% of the respondents were in good health. In terms of willingness to participate in tourism poverty alleviation, 49.5% of the respondents chose to participate in tourism poverty alleviation related work, 38.5% of the respondents chose to be ordinary, 8.6% of the respondents were not willing, and the proportion of respondents who were very unwilling and very willing were 0.9% and 2.4% respectively. Among those willing to participate in tourism poverty alleviation, most of the respondents chose to set up stalls in scenic spots, accounting for 25.9%, followed by 23.9% of

Table 1 Statistical characteristics of variables

	Variable	Mean	Standard deviation	Estimated impact	Variable interpretation
	Tourism poverty alleviation willingness (Y)	0.46	0.393		1 = willing to travel for employment 0 = unwilling to travel for employment
Characteristics	Age (X_{11})	27.56	7.323	(−)	Minimum age = 18 Maximum age = 60
	Years of education (X_{12})	6.8	2.872	(+)	Minimum number of years of study = 0 Maximum number of years of study = 18
	Halal food care level (X_{13})	3.87	0.782	(−)	Don't care about 1–2–3–4–5 Very much
	Chinese level (X_{14})	2.13	0.673	(+)	Very poor 1–2–3–4–5 Very good
Tourism employment skills	National characteristic food production skills (X_{21})	3.64	0.583	(+)	Very poor 1–2–3–4–5 Very good
	Tourist souvenir making skills (X_{22})	3.76	0.676	(+)	Very poor 1–2–3–4–5 Very good
	National song and dance performance skills (X_{23})	3.87	0.525	(+)	Very poor 1–2–3–4–5 Very good
Tourism poverty alleviation perception	The government attaches great importance to tourism poverty alleviation (X_{31})	2.82	0.724	(+)	Very poor 1–2–3–4–5 Very good
	Accuracy of poverty alleviation by tourism (X_{32})	2.79	0.678	(+)	Very poor 1–2–3–4–5 Very good
	Tourism poverty alleviation employment environment (X_{33})	3.62	0957	(+)	Very poor 1–2–3–4–5 Very good

(continued)

Table 1 (continued)

	Variable	Mean	Standard deviation	Estimated impact	Variable interpretation
	Economic income from participating in tourism poverty alleviation (X_{34})	3.62	1.231	(+)	Very poor 1–2–3–4–5 Very good
Family environment	Degree of family hindrance from going out to work (X_{41})	2.11	0.663	(−)	Very support 1–2–3–4–5 Very Unsupported
	Distance between residence and scenic spot (X_{42})	15	39	(−)	1: 0–5 km, 2: 5–10 km, 3: 10–15 km, 4: 15–20 km, 5: over 20 km
	Parental health (X_{43})	0.86	0.865	(+)	Healthy or dead = 1 Unhealthy = 0
	Number of children in the family (X_{44})	1.9	0.562	(−)	Minimum number of children = 0 Maximum number of children = 5
	Per capita arable land area	2.5	0.427	(−)	1: 0–1 mu, 2: 1–2 mu 3: 2–3 mu, 4: 3–4 mu 5: 4 mu or more
	Grassland area per capita	15	22	(−)	1: 0–5 mu, 2: 5–10 mu, 3: 10–15 mu 4: 15–20 mu 5: 20 mu or more

scenic spots, 17.1% of the restaurants were operated by themselves. The number of people who choose to work in scenic spots is relatively small, accounting for 3.9%. The number of people who choose tourism transportation and sell local products is the least, only 2%.

5.2 Model Estimation Results

In this paper, Stata software is used for model operation. In order to comprehensively analyze the influencing factors of Kazakh women's willingness to participate in tourism poverty alleviation, stepwise regression method is used to control the scope of independent variables, and the robustness of regression results is verified. The model

Table 2 Regression results of influencing factors of tourism employment

Variable	Model 1	Model 2	Model 3	Model 4
Age (X_{11})	−0.0021*	−0.0032*	−0.0025*	−0.0026*
Years of education (X_{12})	0.0354	0.0278	0.0302	0.0352
Halal food care level (X_{13})	−0.1262	−0.2012	−0.1983	−0.2111
Chinese level (X_{14})	0.2362**	0.2362**	0.2561**	0.2581**
National characteristic food production skills (X_{21})		0.0221*	0.0268*	0.0251*
Tourist souvenir making skills (X_{22})		0.0456*	0.0458*	0.0458*
National song and dance performance skills (X_{23})		0.0521	0.0625	0.0632
The government attaches importance to tourism poverty alleviation (X_{31})			0.0033*	0.0033*
Accuracy of poverty alleviation by tourism (X_{32})			0.0588*	0.0623*
Tourism poverty alleviation employment environment (X_{33})			0.0423*	0.0425*
Participating in tourism poverty alleviation economic income (X_{34})			0.3681***	0.3761***
Degree of family hindrance from going out to work (X_{41})				−0.2211**
Distance between residence and scenic spot (X_{42})				−0.0587*
Health of parents (X_{43})				0.0258*
Number of children in the family (X_{44})				−0.2241*
Per capita arable land area (X_{45})				0.3520
Grassland area per capita (X_{46})				−0.2452*
_cons	−12.3452*	−11.4551*	−11.3456*	−11.5677*
Log likelihood	−3456.22	−3428.15	−3352.16	−3524.13
McFadden R-squared	0.3452	0.3678	0.4123	0.4225
N	615	615	615	615

Note ***, **, * are significant at 1%, 5% and 10% levels respectively

is estimated by maximum likelihood estimation method, and heteroscedasticity is corrected by White test equation. The estimated results are shown in Table 2.

5.2.1 Personal Characteristics

"Age (X_{11})" has a negative impact at the 10% significance level, which indicates that the older the age, the weaker the willingness of Kazakh women to participate in tourism poverty alleviation, which is consistent with Cheng Mingming's view that the older the age, the weaker the willingness of the labor force to go out to work [21]. With the growth of age, Kazakh women's physical health status declined, and their willingness to go out for employment decreased. At the same time, the pressure of supporting the elderly and raising children has increased, and there are more restrictions on going out to participate in tourism.

"Education years (X_{12})" has not passed the significance test, which shows that Kazakh women's willingness to participate in tourism poverty alleviation has no relationship with education years. The reasons are as follows: first, the tourism industry is still a labor-intensive industry, and the education level of migrant workers is not high; second, the labor competitiveness of Uyghur women with higher education level is enhanced, the scope of employment options is increased, and the probability of engaging in tourism industry is reduced.

This is not consistent with the conclusion of Guangming Li and others that the "Halal diet care degree (X_{13})" has a significant negative impact on the Uygur rural labor force's migrant work [22]. The main reason may be that Kazakh women in Xinyuan county go out to participate in tourism. Their working places are basically near their homes, and rarely go out of Xinjiang, so "Halal diet care degree (X_{13})" has not become an obstacle to the willingness of poverty alleviation through tourism.

The better the "level of Chinese (X_{14})", the stronger the willingness to participate in tourism poverty alleviation. Xinyuan County, as a tourist destination with strong Kazakh customs, at tracts many tourists at home and abroad. The ability of Chinese communication has become an important condition for tourism employment. Many Kazakh women have low willingness to go out for poverty alleviation.

5.2.2 Personal Employment Skills

"National food production skills (X_{21})" showed a positive impact at the 10% significance level. Kazakh women who have the skills of making ethnic food are the first choice to sell special food, run restaurants and farmhouse entertainment in scenic spots. The survey shows that the proportion of Kazakh women choosing self-employed restaurants for tourism employment is about 17.1%.

"Tourism souvenir making skills (X_{22})" has a positive impact at the 10% significance level. The survey shows that stall management is the first choice for Kazakh women in tourism employment, accounting for 25.9%. In recent years, Xinyuan county has actively developed ethnic tourism souvenirs, driving Kazakh women to engage in tourism souvenir making enthusiasm, greatly easing the pressure of female employment.

The factor of "performance skills of ethnic song and dance (X_{23})" has not passed the significance test. The main reasons may be: firstly, Kazakh has always been a singing and dancing nation. No matter what industry Kazakh women are engaged in, it will not affect their enthusiasm for singing and dancing. Secondly, some tourism industries need practitioners with ethnic singing and dancing skills, but the demand is still small.

5.2.3 Tourism Employment Perception

"The government at aches great importance to poverty alleviation through tourism (X_{31})" has a positive impact at the 10% significance level, which indicates that the government's attention positively promotes the local Kazakh women's willingness to participate in tourism poverty alleviation. In recent years, the government of Xinyuan County attaches great importance to the development of tourism industry. The local tourism industry has been developed continuously and stably. The characteristics of high efficiency and strong correlation of tourism deeply affect the economic and social life of local residents.

"Tourism poverty alleviation accuracy (X_{32})" has a positive impact at the 10% significance level, which indicates that the more accurate Kazakh women perceive tourism poverty alleviation, the stronger their willingness to participate in tourism poverty alleviation. The survey shows that the perceived value of tourism poverty alleviation accuracy in Xinyuan county is only 2.12. In the future, the government should continue to improve the accuracy of tourism poverty alleviation and increase the willingness to participate in tourism poverty alleviation.

"Tourism poverty alleviation employment environment (X_{33})" shows a positive impact at the 5% significance level, which indicates that the better the tourism employment environment, the stronger the willingness to participate in tourism poverty alleviation. The survey shows that about 62.4% of Kazakh women think that tourism is unstable and obvious in low and peak seasons. When they have jobs in peak season and are dismissed in off-season, and their social status is not high, they are not willing to engage in tourism employment, which is consistent with there search conclusion of Korea Sheng et al. [23].

"Income from participating in tourism Poverty Alleviation (X_{34})" has a positive impact at the significance level of 1%. In the survey, 59.2% of Kazakh women think that tourism employment income is higher than other industries. At present, the employment of Kazakh women in Xinyuan county is still in the primary stage, and economic income is still an important factor affecting Kazakh women's employment.

5.2.4 Family Environment

At the significant level of 5%, the degree of "family hindering going out to work (X_{41})" showed a negative impact. The traditional thought of "men are in charge of the outside world, and women are in charge of the interior" is relatively serious. At the same time, as the Kazakh believe in Islam, drinking is prohibited according to the Koran's canon. Many Kazakhs unilaterally believe that tourism employment is mostly done in hotels, Therefore, Kazakh women are not allowed to go out to participate in tourism employment.

The "distance between residence and scenic spot (X_{42})" showed a negative impact at the 10% significance level, indicating that the closer the distance between the residence and the scenic spot, the stronger the willingness of Kazakh women to help the poor by tourism. There is a long distance between the residence and the scenic spot. Firstly, it costs a lot for Kazakh women to participate in tourism employment; secondly, it is less affected by tourism industry, so they have a vague perception of tourism employment, so they will not choose tourism industry for employment.

The significant level of "parents' health (X_{43})" showed a positive impact at the 10% significant level, indicating that if the elderly in the family are in poor health and need to be taken care of, Kazakh women are less willing to travel to help the poor.

The significant level of "family children (X_{44})" showed a negative impact at the 10% significant level, indicating that the number of family children is large, Kazakh women need to take care of their children, and the willingness to participate in tourism poverty alleviation is small.

The main reason for the "per capita cultivated land area (X_{45})" has not passed the significance test. The main reason may be: in recent years, the agricultural economic income benefit is low, at the same time, the tourism industry in Xinyuan county has developed rapidly, and the tourism industry has shown considerable economic benefits. Even if the Kazakh family with more cultivated land area, women's willingness to participate in tourism poverty alleviation work will exist.

The "per capita grassland area (X_{46})" showed a negative effect at the significant level of 10%. This is not consistent with Yang ali's view that owning grassland or cultivated land resources can gradually accumulate funds for poor farmers and herdsmen, and promote poor farmers and herdsmen to participate in tourism poverty alleviation [24]. The main reasons are as follows: firstly, Kazakh families with large grassland area breed more cattle and sheep; secondly, the family with large grassland area has higher economic income.

6 Conclusions and Policy Recommendations

This paper investigates 660 Kazakh women's willingness to participate in tourism poverty alleviation activities and its influencing factors in 33 villages of Xinyuan county. The results showed that 49.5% of the respondents chose to participate in the tourism poverty alleviation related work, 38.5% of the respondents chose to be ordinary, 8.6% of the respondents said they were not willing, and the proportion of the respondents who were very unwilling and very willing were 0.9% and 2.4% respectively. The influencing factors of Kazakh women's employment intention are Chinese level, ethnic food making skills, tourist souvenir making skills, government's attention to tourism poverty alleviation, economic income from participating in tourism poverty alleviation, family support for working out, and parents' health level; age, tourism poverty alleviation accuracy, tourism poverty alleviation employment environment, the distance between residence and scenic spot, the number of family children, per capita grassland area showed negative effects; education years, Halal diet care degree, singing and dancing skills, per capita cultivated land area, etc. did not pass the significant test. This paper makes a quantitative study on the influencing factors of Kazakh women's willingness to participate in tourism poverty alleviation, but there are still many deficiencies. In the future, we can choose different cases to compare the factors of Kazakh women's willingness to participate in tourism poverty alleviation, or compare the influencing factors of Kazakh women's and Han's women's willingness to participate in tourism poverty alleviation, so as to find out the common points and special points. The conclusion of this paper is helpful for the government to re-examine the willingness and influencing factors of Kazakh women's poverty alleviation through tourism. In order to improve the willingness of Kazakh women to participate in tourism poverty alleviation, we should first popularize Chinese learning and eliminate the language communication barriers of Kazakh female employees. Tourism industry is an industry that needs to communicate with tourists from different places and nationalities. Many Kazakh women have low level of Chinese and weak expression ability, so they can't communicate in Chinese normally. Therefore, the government should popularize Chinese learning of ethnic minorities through various channels, improve language communication ability and enhance tourism employment competitiveness. Secondly, we should strengthen publicity and education, change traditional ideas and correct the cognitive bias of employment. We should break away from the traditional mode of thinking that men are superior to women and put an end to gender discrimination in employment. It is believed that the tourism image of Kazakh people should be less and the concept of employment should be changed. Thirdly, increase learning and training to improve the skills of Kazakh women in poverty alleviation through tourism. The results show that ethnic food making skills and souvenir making skills have a significant positive impact on Kazakh women's willingness to participate in tourism poverty alleviation. The government can actively advocate and organize Kazakh women to learn tourism poverty alleviation related skills, expand the business model of Kazakh tourism products, and increase the economic benefits of Kazakh tourism products. Finally, improve the accuracy of tourism poverty alleviation and increase the benefits of tourism poverty alleviation. In the survey, many Kazakh women in Xinyuan county think that there is unfair distribution of tourism income, and tourism poverty alleviation is not helpful to the real poor community residents. The government should accurately identify the object of tourism poverty alleviation, accurately implement the way of tourism poverty alleviation, accurately establish tourism poverty alleviation security mechanism, and improve the accuracy of tourism poverty alleviation.

This paper is supported by the National Natural Science Foundation of China: (1) Research on the spatial and temporal differentiation and driving mechanism of tourism poverty alleviation efficiency in the four prefectures of Southern Xinjiang (41,661,110); (2) Research on the measurement of tourism specialization level and its relationship with regional economic growth (41,461,114).

References

1. Schilcher, D.: Growth versus equity: the continuum of pro-poor tourism and neoliberal governance. Curr. Issue Tour. **10**(2), 166–193 (2007)
2. Onez Cetin, Z., Ozgor, H.: A critical theoretical evaluation on pro-poor tourism and poverty alleviation. Mustafa Kemal University J. Soc. Sci. Inst. **9**(17),115–133 (2012)
3. Zhou, X.: Pay attention to the core issues of tourism poverty alleviation. Tour. J. **17**(1), 17–21 (2002)
4. Li, J., Zhong, L., Cheng, S.: Research on residents' perception and participation behavior of tourism in poverty alleviation effects in ethnic poverty areas—taking the Sanjiangyuan region of Qinghai province as an example. Tour. Trib. **24**(8), 71–76 (2009)
5. Xiao, J., Xiao, J.: Research on the tourism poverty alleviation (PPT) model for the poor people based on micro economic effects—taking the Liupanshan tourism poverty alleviation experimental area in Ningxia as an example. Soc. Sci. **1**, 76–80 (2014)
6. Rogerson, C.M.: Pro-poor local economic development in South Africa: the role of pro-poor tourism. Local Environ. **11**(1), 37–60 (2006)
7. Guo, S.: Research method of tourism poverty alleviation effect based on the perspective of industry chain. Tour. Trib. **30**(11), 31–39 (2015)
8. Jiang, L.: A study on residents' perceptions and attitudes of the poverty alleviation effect of tourism in Luoxiao mountain area—a case study of Jiulongjiang area in Rucheng national forest park, Hunan. Reg. Res. Dev. **4**, 99–104 (2015)
9. Deng, X.: Analysis of the effects of tourism on poverty alleviation in the counties belonging to Wumeng mountain in Yunnan. Ecol. Econ. **31**(2), 56–60 (2015)
10. Lu, C., Geng, B., Zhuang, T., Yang, H.: Study on the willingness and behavior of poor farmers and herdsmen in Tibetan areas to participate in tourism poverty alleviation: based on a survey of 1,320 households in 23 counties (cities) in Tibetan areas in Sichuan. Tour. J. **32**(1), 64–76 (2017)
11. Mc Gehee, N.G., Kim, K., Jennings, G.R.: Gender and motivation for agri-tourism entrepreneurship. Tour. Manag. **28**(1), 153–171 (2007)
12. Nilsson, P.A.: Staying on farms: an ideological background. Ann. Tour. Res. **29**(1), 67–79 (2002)
13. Skalpe, O.: The CEO gender pay gap in the tourism industry: evidence from Norway. Tour. Manag. **28**(3), 101–122 (2007)
14. Bird, S.R., Sapp, S.G.: Understanding the gender gap in small business success: urban and rural comparisons. Gend. Soc. **18**(1), 87–98 (2004)
15. Mao, D., Zhong, H.: Research on the survival perceptions of women in rural tourism based on grounded theory. Guizhou Soc. Sci. **1**, 158–162 (2016)
16. Wu, Z., Jia, Q.: Ethnic tourism development and Zhuang women's development: taking Guilin Longji terraced fields as an example. J. Guangxi Univ. Natl. **6**, 99–104 (2008)
17. Niu, C., Wang, G.: Analysis of the employment status and advantages and disadvantages of female tourism practitioners in my country. J. Northwest Sci-Tech Univ. Agric. For. **10**(5), 71–76 (2010)
18. Long, L.: Research on the motivation of rural women participating in rural tourism in economically developed areas. Tour. Trib. **2**, 37–42 (2012)
19. Li, D., Zhang, J., Zhang, S.: Spatial differentiation of residents' perceptions and attitudes of tourism impacts: taking Huangshan Scenic area as an example. Geogr. Res. **27**(4), 602–608 (2008)
20. Han, S., Xiang, W.: Analysis of influencing factors of family flow based on order probit model. Econ. Issues **1**, 92–95 (2017)
21. Cheng, M.: An empirical study on the influence of personal characteristics and family characteristics on rural non-agricultural employment. China's Popul. Resour. Environ. **2**, 94–99 (2012)
22. Li, G., Pan, M.: Employment ability, employment expectation and uyghur rural labor's willingness to work outside. Popul. Econ. **2**, 30–38 (2014)

23. Han, G., Li, H., Zhu, F.: Multiple correspondence analysis of residents' willingness to help the poor through tourism in Tiantangzhai community. East China Econ. Manag. **27**(2), 18–23 (2013)
24. Yang, A., Ba, D.: The construction of a community-participatory tourism poverty alleviation mechanism in ethnic areas—taking Gannan Tibetan autonomous prefecture in Gansu province as an example. Inner Mongolia Soc. Sci. (Chin. Edn.) **5**, 131–136 (2012)

Residents' Perception and Its Impact on Community Participation of Tourism Development

Lihua Cui, Xinze Song, and Minhui Song

Abstract The rapid development of local tourism has attracted a lot of attention of the community. The residents of the community can significantly affect the development of local tourism. In fact, community-based tourism marks the trend of tourism development. Taking Xiaolangdi Multipurpose Dam Project (XMDP) scenic area as an example, this paper applies the structural equation modeling (SEM) to study the relationship between community resident's perception of tourism impact and their participation to the tourism development. The results show that the positive perception of the economic, social, and environmental impacts of tourism can improve the residents' attitude towards the tourism development. Our research finding sheds some light on how to increase the attention of community residents during the tourism development.

Keywords Community residents · Perception of tourism impacts · Participation · Structural equation modeling (SEM)

1 Introduction

Since the 1990s, China has witnessed a boom of tourism. The enormous economic benefits and profound social impacts of tourism development arouse the interests of many local governments. Many researchers have been attracted to discuss the development of tourism resources, the innovation of tourism mode, and the improvement of tourism facilities. However, the development of tourism resources inevitably reshapes every aspect of tourist destinations, exerting an immense effect on the life of community residents. As the coronavirus (COVID-19) plagues the world, the tourism impacts are increasingly perceived by the tourism community.

L. Cui (✉) · M. Song
Xiaolangdi Multipurpose Dam Project Management Center, Ministry of Water Resources, Zhengzhou, Henan, People's Republic of China
e-mail: 1165799506@qq.com

X. Song
International College Dalian University, Dalian, Liaoning, People's Republic of China

© The Author(s), under exclusive license to Springer Nature Singapore Pte Ltd. 2022
Y. Luo et al. (eds.), *Tourism, Aviation and Hospitality Development During the COVID-19 Pandemic*, https://doi.org/10.1007/978-981-19-1661-8_9

Most tourism activities cannot proceed without the support from the community. The residents, as a special type of tourism resources, affect the experience of tourists. Besides, the residents bear the various impact of tourism development, positive or negative, and influence the sustainability of local tourism. Therefore, it is necessary for tourism developers to solicit the support from community residents, and encourage them to participate in tourism development. Nevertheless, community participation in tourism development is often insufficient and unattractive, and the participants are paid unequally due to their varied qualities. These phenomena threat the sustainable development of destinations [1].

Located at the junction of Luoyang and Jiyuan, Central China's Henan Province, Xiaolangdi Multipurpose Dam Project (XMDP) is one of the most important water conservancy projects on the Yellow River. The project is responsible for multiple tasks: flood and frost prevention, silt reduction, water supply, irrigation, and power generation. The project area has developed into a boutique eco-tourism scenic area, with both scientific value and esthetic value. Tourists marvel at the technical sophistication of water conservancy engineering, and the long history of Yellow River culture. The XMDP scenic area is rated as a national AAAA-level tourist attraction, and a national water conservancy scenic spot. In the scenic area, the development of tourism undoubtedly affects the life of residents. In return, the attitude of residents bears on the tourism development and management of the scenic area.

Taking the XMDP scenic area as an example, this paper pursues the sustainable development of tourism from the perspective of community residents, quantitatively investigates residents' perception of tourism impacts and their participation in tourism development, and evaluates the relationship between impact perception and participation. The research results shed important new lights on the tourism development of the XMDP scenic area.

2 Literature Review

Much work has been done on tourism activities and community residents. Lichty (1982) pioneered the research into the tourism impacts on communities. Murphy's book *Tourism: A Community Approach*, published in 1985, marked the beginning of systematic studies on tourism from the perspective of the community.

The term "community" was coined by German sociologist F. Tounies to illustrate a social group with a close, supportive, and humane social relationship. It refers to a homogeneous population sharing similar values. There is not yet a unified academic definition of community. Some definitions are based on social groups, some are based on geographic regions, and some are based on identity and belonging [2]. Tourism is an activity carried out among communities [3]. The community participation is critical to the sustainable development of tourism [4].

Concerning the tourism impacts on the community, Andereck et al. [5] divided the tourism impacts on community residents into three categories, namely, economic impact, socio-cultural impact, and environmental impact, drawing on the social exchange theory. The impacts could be positive or negative, depending on the benefits and dedication of community residents. The depth of community participation in tourism is determined by the residents' ability, perception, and willingness of participation [6, 7].

Community residents have a significant impact on the image of destinations. Murphy [8] incorporated community involvement into tourism research for the first time in his book *Tourism: A Community Approach*. To boost community participation in tourism, it is necessary to recognize the knowledge, skills, and abilities of the local people fully and fairly, and show full respect to them. Empowerment and equal opportunities are the merits of community participation. The process of participation is more important than the participation results. The purpose of community participation is to create a sense of ownership among community residents, to forge a fair and just management and partnership mechanism, to pursue common benefits and interests based on mutual respect, equal negotiation, and experience sharing, and to reach a community consensus through necessary compromises [9].

Community residents have a deep understanding and a true experience of the image of the local destination. If tourism development brings negative impacts to local economy, culture, and environment, and if community participation is ignored, the community residents will be excluded from tourism activities, especially during the COVID epidemic. It is beneficial to design a proper incentive mechanism to boost the community participation in tourism development [10].

Currently, the community participation in tourism is far from satisfactory in China. Relatively few community residents are willingness involved in tourism development [11]. In the tourism community, most residents perceive a sense of social exclusion, which four dimensions: economic exclusion, political exclusion, cultural exclusion, and relational exclusion [12].

The failure of community participation in tourism can be attributed to several reasons: power failure, lack of opportunities, and lack of capability. Zuo and Bao [13] combined Marx's land rent theory with modern theory on property rights to analyze the status quo of rural land properties in China, identified the gap between theories and the practice through the case analysis, evaluated the distribution of value-added income from tourism development, and recommended attracting property rights. Their research paves the way of land power transformation, and encourages Chinese rural communities to participate in tourism development. The community is divided on key issues like whether tourism brings more benefits than what it costs, and whether the positive social and economic impacts of tourism outweigh the possible negative impacts [14].

The community residents' perception of tourism impacts is related to many factors, namely, relevance to tourism, mental capacity, government decisions on tourism, and the social media. Horn and Simmons [15] demonstrated that communities with little contact with tourists have a weak perception of tourism impacts, while those in frequent contact with tourists recognize the rapid changes that ensue tourism development. Economic dependence makes community residents positive to tourism development, but the ecological concern propels them to take a negative attitude [16]. Focusing on the scenic area of Zhangjiajie, Cheng et al. [17] found that the perception of tourism impacts varies with demographic features, such as age, residence time, income, gender, and educational background.

Concerning the process of community participation in tourism, Bao and Sun [18] believed that the government and enterprises often neglect community participation in the initial stage of tourism development; with the growing demand for benefits, and rising resident desire and ability of participation, the government and enterprises will expand the space for community participation by providing job opportunities, financial aids, and other benefits; as community participation deepens, however, there will be more and more prominent conflicts between stakeholders.

During tourism development, it is important to coordinate the interests between stakeholders like communities, tourists, tourism developers, and the government. Otherwise, tourism activities will not truly benefit the society. Kibicho [19] held that the advancement of community tourism is affected by five issues: stakeholder involvement, recognition of personal interests and others' interests, legal appointment of managers, goal setting, and decision execution. Campbell [20] suggested that the absence of government planning and intervention is likely to limit the community benefits from tourism development. Therefore, the community participation in tourism should be promoted through moderate communication, extensive involvement, as well as tolerance and information sharing between residents and other stakeholders [21].

3 Hypotheses and Modeling

3.1 Hypotheses

This paper mainly explores the perception and attitude of community residents in tourism development, and how the perception and attitude influence the participation. Several hypotheses were proposed as follows:

(1) **Influence of perception over attitude**

Inspired by the social exchange theory, Priscilla divided the tourism impacts on community residents into positive and negative classes [22]. Whether an impact is positive or negative can be mainly measured by the resident income. The better the perception of tourism impacts, the stronger the residents' support to tourism development. Hence, the following hypotheses were put forward:

H1. The residents' positive perception of the economic impact of tourism promotes their attitude towards tourism development.
H2. The residents' positive perception of the social impact of tourism promotes their attitude towards tourism development.
H3. The residents' positive perception of the environmental impact of tourism promotes their attitude towards tourism development.

(2) Relationship between perception and willingness

Nazneen et al. [23] discovered that the perceived impacts of development, as antecedents, have a direct or indirect impact on residents' willingness to participate in tourism, and revealed the positive correlation between perceived tourism costs and that willingness. The Tourists are more likely to support tourism, even if tourism costs outweigh the benefits. Hence, the following hypotheses were put forward:

H4. The residents' positive perception of the economic impact of tourism promotes their willingness to participate in tourism development.

H5. The residents' positive perception of the social impact of tourism promotes their willingness to participate in tourism development.

H6. The residents' positive perception of the environmental impact of tourism promotes their willingness to participate in tourism development.

(3) Relationship between willingness and supportive attitude

The previous studies rarely talk about the relationship between community residents' supportive attitude towards tourism and their willingness to participate in tourism development. To make up for the gap, the following hypothesis was put forward:

H7. The residents' supportive attitude towards tourism promotes their willingness to participate in tourism development.

(4) Influence of participation capability on participation

The participation capability of the community is a major bottleneck of community participation in tourism development. The improvement of participation capability would result in more comprehensive and effective participation. Hence, the following hypothesis was put forward:

H8. The participation capability promotes the community participation in tourism development.

(5) Influence of supportive attitude over participation

The community residents' enthusiasm for tourism participation depends heavily on their cognition and supportive attitude of the participation. According to the rational behavior theory, positive attitudes lead to supportive behaviors of tourism development. Hence, the following hypothesis was put forward:

H9. The residents' supportive attitude towards tourism promotes their participation in tourism development.

(6) Influence of willingness over participation

If the community residents are reluctant, they would not actively participate in tourism development. If they are willing, they would take part in tourism more actively. Hence, the following hypothesis was put forward:

H10. The community residents' willingness promotes the community participation in tourism development.

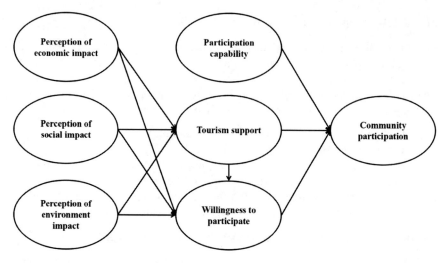

Fig. 1 Conceptual model

3.2 Modeling

Based on the above hypotheses, a conceptual model was designed for the community residents' perception and participation of tourism (Fig. 1).

4 Empirical Analysis

On May 17, 2020, a preliminary questionnaire survey was carried out in the XMDP scenic area. Then, the questionnaire was modified to correct the problems found during the survey. Following nonprobability sampling, a formal survey was performed from May 25 to 28, 2020 in the study area. Out of the 525 questionnaires distributed, 502 (95.6%) valid responses were received.

Among the respondents, 47.8% are males and 52.2% are females. Around 75% of the respondents are middle-aged. In terms of education level, junior college graduates (58.4%) form the largest group of the respondents, followed by graduates from technical secondary school (20.5%). In terms of occupational identity, the largest group is students (32.5%), and the second largest group is enterprise employees (23.9%). Those with a mean monthly income below 2,000 yuan account for 31.3% of all respondents, and those with a mean monthly income between 2,000 and 6,000 yuan take up 20%. 80.7% of the respondents have visited other tourist attractions.

An exploratory factor analysis was conducted on SPSS 23.0 to reveal how tourists are affected by 25 variables of tourist experience. The scores obtained from the formal survey were imported into SPSS, and the factor analysis program was selected. Then, the software automatically calculated the results. After that, varimax rotation was performed through principal component analysis (PCA). Seven common factors were extracted, and the items with a load greater than 0.5 were retained. The items with a load smaller than 0.5 were eliminated, namely, B2, B5, C4, D2, E3, and F3.

Since the overall Cronbach's alpha of the 25 variables (0.931) was greater than the generally accepted level of 0.7, the survey data are internally consistent. According to the Kaiser–Meyer–Olkin (KMO) value (0.718), the common factors are extracted excellently from the survey data. Hence, the factor analysis achieves a high efficiency. The *p*-value of Bartlett's test of sphericity was smaller than 0.001, indicating that the survey data are suitable for factor analysis. The Cronbach's alpha of the 7 common factors was always above 0.7, which is acceptable. Drawing on the relevant research of community participation in tourism, the variables were named in turn as perception of environmental impact, perception of economic impact, perception of social impact, participation capability, tourism support, willingness to participate, and participation.

In addition, the partial least squares algorithm was called for structural equation modeling (SEM) on SmartPLS. This algorithm, which eliminates the need of data normality, is especially suitable for prediction based on small samples [24, 25]. Both theoretical development and verification are integrated in the research.

Referring to Anderson and Gerbing [26], the proposed models were evaluated in two stages: the measurement model was evaluated before the structural model. Both models were obtained through SEM. The measurement model captures the relationship between observed variables and latent variables, while the structural model tackles the relationship between latent variables. Observed variables refer to the contents that can be directly evaluated by the respondents, and latent variables refer to the contents expressed by the observed variables. Each hypothesis was tested by computing the path coefficient and the significance of the external load through bootstrapping, and the predictive validity of the structural model was verified through blindfolding.

As shown in Table 1, the minimum average variance extracted (AVE) was 0.623 in the measurement model, which is greater than 0.5 [27]. The square root of the AVE surpassed the correlation coefficient between the corresponding latent variables (Table 2), indicating a good discriminative validity [28]. The external load of B4 was below 0.4, such that the index was directly deleted. The external load of F1 was smaller than 0.7. In the absence of F1, the AVE and commonality of the Willingness to participate dimension were improved. Hence, F1 was also deleted. The external load for the other items surpassed 0.5. The parameter evaluation of the measurement model confirms that the latent variables are sufficiently reliable and valid.

After the measurement model was validated, the hypotheses in the the structural model were evaluated one by one. Among the 10 hypotheses, only the path relationship between perception of environmental impact and willingness to participate, that between supportive attitude and willingness to participate, failed the test. All the other hypotheses are valid (Table 3 and Fig. 2).

With the aid of SmartPLS, the fitting effect and explanatory power of our model were evaluated by the coefficient of determination (R^2), commonality, and goodness of fit (GoF). Specifically, R^2 represents the explanatory power of exogenous variables to endogenous variables. As shown in Table 4, R^2 was greater than 0.1, reaching the

Table 1 Evaluation results of convergence reliability and validity

Constructs	Indices	External loads	Cronbach's alpha	AVEs
Perception of environmental impact	A1 Environmental beautification	0.611	0.770	0.623
	A2 Infrastructure improvement	0.686		
	A3 Pollution growth	0.827		
	A4 Resource destruction	0.750		
Perception of economic impact	B1 Income growth	0.765	0.773	0.814
	B3 Job growth	0.845		
Perception of social impact	C1 Social security improvement	0.692	0.710	0.771
	C2 Lifestyle change	0.769		
	C3 Custom change	0.775		
Participation capability	D1 Perception capability	0.667	0.735	0.639
	D3 Government encouragement	0.582		
Tourism support	E1 Support of tourism development	0.823	0.856	0.874
	E2 Acceptance of tourism development	0.841		
Willingness to participate	F2 Participation in tourism development	0.757	1.000	1.000
Participation	G1 Participation in tourism decision	0.629	0.824	0.739
	G2 Suggestions on tourism development	0.831		
	G3 Feedbacks on tourism development	0.807		

benchmark level (>10%) recommended by Falk and Miller (1992). The commonality of each latent variable was greater than 0.5, evidence to the high-quality of the latent variables in the model. The GoF (0.393) surpassed the strong critical value 0.360 defined by Wetzels et al. [29], a sign of the good overall fitting effect of our model.

5 Conclusions

This paper processes and analyzes the first-hand data from field survey through partial least squares SEM, which tests the possible paths between the perception of tourism

Table 2 Relevance of the constructs and the square root of AVE

	Supportive attitude	Perception of environmental impact	Perception of social impact	Perception of economic impact	Participation capability	Willingness to participate	Participation
Supportive attitude	0.874						
Perception of environmental impact	0.358	0.623					
Perception of social impact	0.213	0.221	0.771				
Perception of economic impact	0.344	0.414	0.234	0.814			
Participation capability	0.222	0.209	0.130	0.388	0.639		
Willingness to participate	0.310	0.160	0.160	0.216	0.353	1.000	
Participation	0.143	0.178	0.178	0.281	0.534	0.313	0.739

Note The bold font on the diagonal indicates the square of the corresponding AVE

Table 3 Test results on path hypotheses

Original hypothesis	Standard path coefficient	T value	Result
H1. The residents' positive perception of the economic impact of tourism promotes their attitude towards tourism development	0.322	3.781***	Valid
H2. The residents' positive perception of the social impact of tourism promotes their attitude towards tourism development	0.121	2.891***	Valid
H3. The residents' positive perception of the environmental impact of tourism promotes their attitude towards tourism development	0.150	3.628***	Valid
H4. The residents' positive perception of the economic impact of tourism promotes their willingness to participate in tourism development	0.118	2.466**	Valid
H5. The residents' positive perception of the social impact of tourism promotes their willingness to participate in tourism development	0.139	3.195***	Valid
H6. The residents' positive perception of the environmental impact of tourism promotes their willingness to participate in tourism development	0.144	0.019	Invalid
H7. The residents' supportive attitude towards tourism promotes their willingness to participate in tourism development	0.165	0.075	Invalid
H8. The participation capability promotes the community participation in tourism development	0.287	5.559***	Valid
H9. The residents' supportive attitude towards tourism promotes their participation in tourism development	0.125	3.473***	Valid
H10. The community residents' willingness promotes the community participation in tourism development	0.294	3.534***	Valid

Note * means $p < 0.1$ (T = 2.5); ** means $p < 0.05$ (T = 1.96); *** means $p < 0.01$ (T = 1.2); $p = 0.01$, $p = 0.05$, and $p = 0.1$ mean the degree of confidence is 99%, 95%, and 90%, respectively

impacts and community residents' participation in tourism development. The main conclusions are as follows:

(1) The direct positive relationship between the perceptions of economic, social, and environmental impacts on community residents' supportive attitude towards tourism development was proved effectively at the significance level of 0.01. The XMDP scenic area should extend the consumption industry chain, provide more job opportunities to community residents, and diversify their income sources other than tourism. Besides, the scenic area must build a harmonious and beautiful environment for the community, and cultivate an ecological corridor.

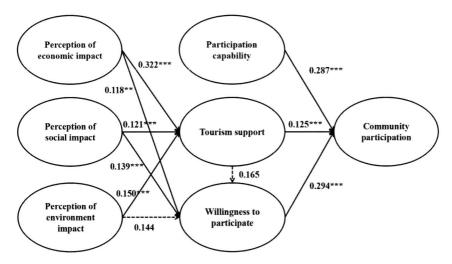

Fig. 2 Path coefficients of the structural model

Table 4 R² of endogenous constructs

Latent variables	Commonality	R²	GoF
Perception of economic impact	0.814		
Perception of social impact	0.571		
Perception of environmental impact	0.623		
Participation capability	0.640		
Supportive attitude	0.874	0.185	
Willingness to participate	1.000	0.135	
Participation	0.739	0.303	
Mean	0.741	0.208	0.393

(2) The direct positive influence of the perceptions of economic and social impacts over the willingness to participate in tourism development was proved effectively at the significance level of 0.05 and 0.01, respectively. As long as the residents of XMDP scenic area perceive the benefits of tourism, they will be willing to participate in tourism development. Hence, it is important to deeply integrate tourism development into community development.

(3) The direct positive influence of the participation capability, supportive attitude, and willingness to participate over the participation in tourism development were proved effectively at the significance level of 0.01. To bolster the tourism participation of XMDP residents, it is necessary to enhance their participation capability through industry training, and upgrade the relevant infrastructure. In this way, the residents will accept and adapt to the trend of tourism development, and benefit significantly from the participation. Facing

the COVID epidemic, the scenic area must also provide the community with alternative income sources, to cope with the impacts of the epidemic on the tourism industry.

References

1. Guo, L., Wang, Z.Z.: On the cultivation of tourism community participant in ethnic region. J. Guangxi Normal Univ. (Philos. Soc. Sci. Edn.) **45**(3), 110–115 (2009)
2. Zhu, Q.M.: Study on the community participation and impact perception of harmonious development in rural tourism-a case study of districts near Lhasa. Zhejiang University (2011)
3. Tang, S.T.: Communitification of tourist destination and community tourism. Geogr. Res. **17**(2), 145–149 (1998)
4. Liu, W.H.: Some theoretical thoughts about community involved tourism development. Tour. Trib. **15**(1), 47–52 (2000)
5. Andereck, K.L., Valentine, K.M., Knopf, R.C., Vogt, C.A.: Residents' perceptions of community tourism impacts. Ann. Tour. Res. **32**(4), 1056–1076 (2005)
6. Dai, W.J.: Research on Behavior of Participation in Tourism of Poor Community Resident-A Case of Shiyang Town. Yunnan Normal University, Dayao County (2018)
7. Zhang, W.K., Wang, Q., Lv, H.Y.: Research on the participatory behavior of rural residents in rural tourism development. Bus. Econ. **3**, 124–125, 193 (2020)
8. Murphy, P.: Tourism: A Community Approach (RLE Tourism). Routledge (2013)
9. Wang, G., Wang, L.P.: Brief discussion on community participation. Urban. Stud. **5**, 53–55 (1998)
10. Scheyvens, R.: Ecotourism and the empowerment of local communities. Tour. Manag. **20**(2), 245–249 (1999)
11. Okazaki, E.: A community-based tourism model: its conception and use. J. Sustain. Tour. **16**(5), 511–529 (2008)
12. Guo, H., Gan, Q.L.: Rural tourism community residents' multi-dimensional perception of social exclusion–a qualitative research on the case of likeng village in Wuyuan, Jiangxi province. Tour. Trib./Lvyou Xuekan **26**(8), 87–94 (2011)
13. Zuo, B., Bao, J.G.: Institutional empowerment: community participation and changes of land property rights in tourism development. Tour. Trib./Lvyou Xuekan **27**(2), 23–31 (2012)
14. Schofield, P.: City resident attitudes to proposed tourism development and its impacts on the community. Int. J Tour. Res. **13**(3), 218–233 (2011)
15. Horn, C., Simmons, D.: Community adaptation to tourism: comparisons between Rotorua and Kaikoura, New Zealand. Tour. Manag. **23**(2), 133–143 (2002)
16. Kaltenborn, B.R.P., Andersen, O., Nellemann, C., Bjerke, T., Thrane, C.: Resident attitudes towards mountain second-home tourism development in Norway: the effects of environmental attitudes. J. Sustain. Tour. **16**(6), 664–680 (2008)
17. Cheng, F.M., Zhong, Y.D., Zhou, M.F., Zhai, G.H.: Study on local residents' attitudes to ecotourism development. J. Cent. South Univ. For. Technol. **29**, 201–205 (2009)
18. Bao, J.G., Sun, J.X.: A contrastive study on the difference in community participation in tourism between China and the west. Acta Geogr. Sin. **4**, 401–413 (2006)
19. Kibicho, W.: Community-based tourism: a factor-cluster segmentation approach. J. Sustain. Tour. **16**(2), 211–231 (2008)
20. Campbell, L.M.: Ecotourism in rural developing communities. Ann. Tour. Res. **26**(3), 534–553 (1999)
21. Matarrita-Cascante, D., Brennan, M.A., Luloff, A.E.: Community agency and sustainable tourism development: the case of La Fortuna. Costa Rica. J. Sustain. Tour. **18**(6), 735–756 (2010)

22. Ananian, P., Perras, A., Borde, M.A.: Living in old montreal: residents' perceptions of the effects of urban development and tourism development on local amenities. Can. Geogr./Géogr. Can. **62**(4), 535–550 (2018)
23. Nazneen, S., Xu, H., Din, N.U.: Cross-border infrastructural development and residents' perceived tourism impacts: a case of China-Pakistan economic corridor. Int. J. Tour. Res. **21**(3), 334–343 (2019)
24. Reinartz, W., Haenlein, M., Henseler, J.: An empirical comparison of the efficacy of covariance-based and variance-based SEM. Int. J. Res. Mark. **26**(4), 332–344 (2009)
25. Hair, J.F., Sarstedt, M., Ringle, C.M., Mena, J.A.: An assessment of the use of partial least squares structural equation modeling in marketing research. J. Acad. Market. Sci. **40**(3), 414–433 (2012)
26. Anderson, J.C., Gerbing, D.W.: Structural equation modeling in practice: a review and recommended two-step approach. Psychol. Bull. **103**(3), 411 (1988)
27. Bagozzi, R.P., Yi, Y.: On the evaluation of structural equation models. J. Acad. Market. Sci. **16**(1), 74–94 (1988)
28. Fornell, C., Larcker, D.F.: Structural equation models with unobservable variables and measurement error: Algebra and statistics. J. Market. Res. **18**(3), 382–388 (1981)
29. Wetzels, M., Odekerken-Schröder, G., Van Oppen, C.: Using PLS path modeling for assessing hierarchical construct models: guidelines and empirical illustration. MIS Quart. 177–195 (2009)

Communication Patterns for Traditional Chinese Culture in Tourism

Liping Ren

Abstract The integration of culture and tourism reflects the worldwide cognitive consensus that cultural resource is among the core resources of tourism development. Chinese tourism classical books, rich in traditional Chinese culture connotations, serve as an inheritor and a communicator. To communicate traditional Chinese culture and promote sustainable development of tourism, especially under the COVID-19 pandemic which hinders the international communication, it is necessary to translate and introduce the classic tourism literature and written material. The simple truth, however, is that the introduction of Chinese classic tourism literature meets with difficulties. The reasons for the difficulties mainly lie in the communication patterns. With a view to be of some reference value to benefit the communication of different cultures, the author makes a research on the current status, causes and solutions of communication problems for traditional Chinese culture in tourism. The author makes a general overview of the current communication of Chinese classic tourism literature, analyses the reasons for the communication difficulties, and creates a 7C-Communication-Model, including 7 communication patterns, based on mass communication model. The model is designed with a hope to benefit the communication in the environment of diversity of world culture.

Keywords Traditional Chinese culture · Tourism classics · Communication patterns

Various national cultures with their own characteristics have stepped onto the global stage. In the integration into world culture diversity, only in closer cooperation and only by sharing the distinguishing features of each culture, can the world culture be multi-win for all. The harmonious coexistence of diverse and various cultures is just as the Chinese proverb says, let a hundred flowers blossom and a hundred schools of thought contend. In this sense, only the cultures with national characteristics are the cultures of the world.

L. Ren (✉)
Shanghai Institute of Tourism/Shanghai Normal University, Shanghai, People's Republic of China
e-mail: renliping001@163.com

Culture communication is not only benefiting the vitality of world culture, but also generating actual economic profit in the field of tourism. There is a natural and close connection between culture and tourism, because tourism activities have cultural attributes. Tourism is an economic undertaking with strong cultural characteristics and also a cultural undertaking with strong economic characteristics. Improving the international communication of traditional Chinese culture is conducive to enhancing the attraction of Chinese tourism.

1 Integration of Culture and Tourism

In the process of maintaining the native ethnic identity, cultures get developed by absorbing new culture elements in the contact and collision with other cultures. In Ji Xianlin's view, the long river of Chinese culture was never in depletion of water although there were times when water was full and times when water was scarce, because new water flowed into this river. Among the numerous water inflows, two torrential ones were remarkable, one from India and the other from the western countries. The driving force of the two water inflows was translation, which was the panacea keeping Chinese culture alive and fresh [1]. The "water inflow from India" refers to translation of the Buddhist classic works, which has deeply influenced the ideology of the Chinese people, while "water inflows from the western countries" refers to the translation of western science and technology books, and the advanced western modern thought in the books at that time opened up a new horizon for the development of Chinese culture. By breaking down the language barrier between different cultures, translators introduced the translated texts of Indian Buddhism and western culture, thus the better understanding of the world culture, and enriching and developing of Chinese culture. Chinese culture, as one of the typical oriental cultures also gives back to other cultures.

For the moment the impact of the COVID-19 pandemic is still strong. It is hindering culture communication. Its direct impact on tourism has been clear in all areas: airline transportation, cruise lines, hotels, nature reserves, and many other tourist attractions. The tourism industry has been greatly impeded, which will further trigger a chain reaction throughout the tourism supply chain from agriculture to fisheries and other services. The tourism industry is highly dependent on natural and cultural resources. How to boost tourism interest and confidence with cultural resources is a topic worthy of in-depth research.

Cultural resource is among the core resources of tourism development. According to Park Jinah and Wu Bihu [2], in the statistical study of data from 31 international tourism journals, the keyword "culture" appears frequently, ranking 13th among the top 20 core keywords in tourism research. Tourism research is interdisciplinary. Currently, it focuses on management, tourism resource development and other branch disciplines, while it remains to be further explored in humanities and social sciences. Tourism development and protection of cultural heritage is a classic topic, which is often discussed and studied in an endless stream. Two reasons for this are "the complexity and diversity of global culture" and "the constant changing concept of cultural inheritance and protection" [3]. Heritage tourism, culture tourism, depth tourism, theme tourism, experience tourism, research tourism and a series of new forms of tourism have sprung up, indicating the integration of culture and tourism is not only a global practical problem, but also a theoretical proposition of universal significance.

China has rich cultural resources, the passing-down of Chinese ancient tourism culture helps to trace the sequence of the development of tourism. The introduction of Chinese tourism culture will help enhance the world's understanding of Chinese culture, and promote exchanges between Chinese fine traditional culture and the cultures of other countries. According to Zhao Defang [4], traditional Chinese culture includes history, philosophy, religion, festivals, architecture, arts, medicine, catering culture and so on. In the long Chinese history, the best records of the traditional Chinese culture are the classic tourism literature and written material, which are referred to hereafter simply as tourism classics in this paper.

In the following parts, Chinese tourism classics resources are briefly introduced in part two. The current situation of the communication of Chinese tourism classics is presented with several examples in part two. The causes of communication dilemma of Chinese Tourism classics are analyzed, and improved communication patterns are suggested in part three. And on the basis of the introduction, presentation and analysis, in part four, the author creates a multi-tier communication model, the 7C-Communication-Model, to help improve the communication of Chinese tourism classics.

2 Communication of Chinese Tourism Classics

2.1 *Tourism Classics Resources*

Tourism classics in the broad sense include ancient poems, travel notes, stone carvings, chronicles, travel logs and so on. The official geography chronicles record the natural landscape and the customs; the ancient travel notes record the scenery and the customs along the way; local chronicles and national geographic chronicles mostly involve territory, astronomy, stars, mountains and rivers, scenic spots, historical sites, customs, products, cities, residence, taxation, schools, election, imperial examination, temples, ancestral temples, personage, art and literature and so on. *"The Si Ku Quan Shu"* 四库全书, or *"Complete Library in the Four Branches of Literature"*[1] completed in 1782, has the world's longest series of books. The work, comprising four traditional divisions of Chinese learning, namely, classics, history, philosophy,

---

[1] It is a large series of books compiled during the Qianlong period of the Qing Dynasty. It was compiled by over 360 senior officials and scholars and transcribed by more than 3,800 people. As the largest cultural project in ancient China, taking thirteen years to complete, it is the most systematic and comprehensive summary of Chinese classical culture.

and belles-letters, contains 3,503 titles bound into more than 36,000 books with a total of 853,456 pages. Tourism classics are mostly in the division of history. The category of geography books in the division of history in "*The Si Ku Quan Shu*" contains 582 kinds of books in total, including 150 kinds of books and the records of 432 kinds of books. Among them the most famous tourism classics are *Tai Ping Huan Yu Ji* 太平寰宇记, *Shui Jing Zhu* 水经注, *Luo Yang Jia Lan Ji* 洛阳伽蓝记, *Da Tang Xi Yu Ji* 大唐西域记, *Fo Guo Ji* 佛国记, *Xu Xia Ke You Ji* 徐霞客游记, and *Dong Jing Meng Hua Lu* 东京梦华录 [5]. The classic *Shan Hai Jing* 山海经, or *The Classic of Mountains and Seas* in the pre-Qin period was classified as geography book in the Tang and Song dynasties because of the rich geographical knowledge. However, in Qing dynasty, it was classified into novel in the division of philosophy, because it contains various contents such as mythology, legends, social customs and so on. And this is also true for some other ancient Chinese classics. Many classics were not classified into the category of geography books, but they also belong to the category of geography books in the broad sense, which shows tourism classics cover a very wide range of bibliography.

2.2 Communication of the Chinese Tourism Classics

Tourism classics serve as an important carrier of traditional tourism culture, and their translation and introduction directly affect the communication of traditional tourism culture. Without translation as a medium, without the translations of the texts and books, the communication of Chinese tourism culture will only be empty talk. According to Ma Zuyi's research, the translation of Chinese classics began between about 508 and 534 AD, during the Northern Wei Period of China's Northern and Southern Dynasties [6]. Since the middle of the last century until now, diverse cultures coexist and live in more harmony, and that was when China systematically translated, published and communicated ancient classics with other countries [7].

During about 20 years from 1981 to 2000, Foreign Languages Publishing House has published more than 200 Panda Books, which is a high-quality English edition of Chinese classics. In 1994, a major national publishing project, the Great China Library has been officially launched, China Foreign Languages Administration took the lead, and 30 publishing institutions participated together. For the first time in Chinese history, Chinese cultural classics in foreign languages have been systematically and comprehensively introduced to the world. Up to now, more than 100 cultural classics have been translated, such as *Luo Yang Jia Lan Ji, Shan Hai Jing, Da Tang Xi Yu Ji, Xu Xia Ke You Ji* and so on. In this paper, information about six representative tourism classics and their translations are gathered and organized into a table. In the table are listed the information about their different English translation versions or editions, publication year, translator, translator's nationality, place of publication, publishing house, overseas library holdings, and the number of sellers on online book buying platform Amazon. It is hoped that the table can help us get a glimpse of the basic situation of the overseas translation and introduction of the tourism classics.

It can be seen from Table 1 that translation and communication of tourism classics started early. For example, *Fo Guo Ji* began to be translated into the English world as early as in the middle of the nineteenth century. The translators of tourism classics were mainly British or American sinologists and Chinese scholars. Most of the English translation publishing houses are internationally renowned and highly qualified. The data of overseas library holdings were borrowed from related scholars' research data from the Global Online Computer Library Center (OCLC) [8]. There is no way to keep track of whether these translated classics have been borrowed or how many times these translated classics have been borrowed. However, it can be assumed that the translated classics in the library should be of interest to readers in the target language. The number of booksellers on Amazon's online book purchase platform is the online data as of August 10, 2020. As Amazon is the world's largest online retailer, sales on Amazon's online book purchase platform basically reflect the popularity of the English translations of the six representative tourism classics. The translations of the tourism classics shown in Table 1 are successful cases of overseas communication, however, compared with the huge volume of Chinese tourism classics, the number of Chinese tourism classics which have been introduced is too small.

3 Dilemma of Communication of Tourism Classics

As exemplified in the previous parts, among the huge volume of Chinese tourism classics, only a few have been introduced and communicated. The reasons are complex and manifold. From the broad sense, we may say that few Chinese tourism classics are translated and introduced into other languages, because, to some extent, the multi-layered and interwoven communication model is hindering Chinese traditional tourism culture communication. In the process of communication of different cultures, translation is an indispensable link, so many people take it for granted that good translation leads to smooth communication of cultures. As a matter of fact, communication cannot be simply understood as an act of good or bad translation of language, high or low quality translation of language. In other words, the quality of translation of classic books alone does not determine whether the translation is accepted, while communication of mindset and culture plays a more important role in the communication of Chinese tourism classics. Xie Tianzhen pointed out that whether the translation would be read by others, the question of acceptability, and the question of influence should all be in consideration [9].

Table 1 English Translation and Communication of 6 Representative Tourism Classics

Tourism classics	English translation						Overseas library holdings	Amazon seller number
	Title of English translation	Publication year	Translator	Translator nationality	Place of publication	Publishing House		
Xu Xia Ke You Ji 徐霞客游记	1. The Travel diaries of Hsu Hsia-ke	1974	Li Chi	America	Hong Kong	The Chinese University of Hong Kong Press	2184	2
	2. The Travels of Xu Xiake	2010	Lu Changhai; Jia Xiuhai	China	Shanghai	Shanghai Foreign Language Education Press		
	3. The Travel diaries of Xu Xiake	2016	Li Wracng	China	Changsha	Hunan People's Publishing House		
Fo Guo Ji 佛国记	1. The Pilgrimage of Fa Hian	1848	J. W. Laidley	UK	Calcutta	J. Thomas, Baptist Mission Press	2161	58
	2. Travels of Fab-Hian and Sung-Yon, Buddhist Pilgrims, from China to India	1869	Samuel Beal	UK	London; New Delhi	Trübner and Co.; Asian Educational Services Trübner & Co.; Kellv & Walsh		
	3. Record of the Buddhistic Kingdoms	1877	Herbert Allen Giles	UK	London; Shanghai	Routledge; Trübner & Co.		

(continued)

Table 1 (continued)

Tourism classics	English translation						Overseas library holdings	Amazon seller number
	Title of English translation	Publication year	Translator	Translator nationality	Place of publication	Publishing House		
	4. A Record of Buddhistic Kingdoms: being an Account by the Chinese Monk Fa-hen of His Travels in India and Ceylon	1886	James Legge	UK	Oxford	The Clarendon Press		
	5. The Travels of Fa-hsien (399-414A. D.) or Record of the Buddhistic Kingdoms	1923	Herbert Allen Giles	UK	Cambridge	Cambridge University Press		
	6. A Record of the Buddhist Countries	1957	Li Rongxi	China	Beijing	The Chinese Buddhist Association		
Shan Hai Jing 山海经	1. The Legendary Creatures of the Shan Hai Ching	1978	John William Scheffler	America	Taiwan	Hwa Kang Press	2097	21

(continued)

Table 1 (continued)

Tourism classics	English translation		Translator	Translator nationality	Place of publication	Publishing House	Overseas library holdings	Amazon seller number
	Title of English translation	Publication year						
	2. The Classic of Maintains and Seas	1999	Anne Maigaret Birrell	America	London	Penguin		
	3. The Classic of Mountains and Seas	2011	Wang Hong	China	Changsha	Hunan People's Publishing House		
Da Tang Xi Yu Ji 大唐西域记	1. Si-Yu-Ki Buddhist Records of the Western World	1906	Samuel Beal	UK	London	Kegan Paul	1756	38
	2. The Great Tang Dynasty-Record of the Western Regions	1996	Li Rongxi	China	Berkeley	Numata Center for Buddhist Translation and Research		
Luo Yang Jia Lan Ji 洛阳伽蓝记	1. Memories of Loyang: Yang Hsien-chih the lost capital (493–534)	1981	William John Francis Jennet	UK	Oxford New York	Oxford: Clarendon Press New York: Oxford University Press	918	9
	2. A Record of Buddhist Monasteries as Lo-Yang	1984	Wang Yitong	America	New York	Princeton University		

(continued)

Table 1 (continued)

Tourism classics	English translation						Overseas library holdings	Amazon seller number
	Title of English translation	Publication year	Translator	Translator nationality	Place of publication	Publishing House		
Chang Chun Zhen Ren Xi You Ji 长春真人西游记	1. The Travels of an Alchemist: The Journey of the Taoist Ch'ang-Ch'un from China to the Hindukush at the Summons of Chingiz Khan	1931	Waley Arthur	UK	London	Routledge & Kegan Paul	583	11

3.1 Translation in the Communication of Tourism Classics

According to Hu Gengshen [10], translation can be summarized as adaptive selection and transformation focusing on three dimensions: language, culture and communication. The exploration of the communication of classic books from these three dimensions gives us a clearer interpretation of the plight and a more objective and pragmatic approach to the enlightenment.

The adaptive selection and transformation of the language dimension is the translator's adaptive selection and transformation of language form in the process of translation. The translation of classic books, represented by Panda Book series and Great China Library, have all the processes strictly checked, including book selecting, translator selecting, translation, revision, typesetting, printing and publishing. In addition to domestic experts, a large number of foreign translators are employed to ensure the quality of translation. Although the translation of classic books is not perfect, it has been improving greatly, thus not a main obstacle in the communication of cultures.

The adaptive selection and transformation of culture dimension is the translator's focus on the transmission and interpretation of bilingual cultural connotation in the process of translation. More attention is given to the differences in nature and content between the culture of the source language and that of the target language. To avoid the distortion of the original text from the cultural perspective of the target language, the whole cultural system that the language belongs to should be in full consideration. According to Edward Hall, cultural context can be divided into High Context and Low Context.[2] In High Context, most of the information exists either in the physical context or is internalized in the individual, while very few are in the clearly transmitted coded message, while Low Context, on the other hand, involves placing large amounts of information in clear coding [11]. Oriental cultures which originated from Buddhism, Taoism and Confucianism mostly belong to High Context culture, while western cultures based on logos and rational debate in ancient Greece mostly belong to Low Context culture. Traditional classical books contain a large number of characteristic cultural elements, and in-depth translation is often used to present to the full the cultural information of source language. One typical example is the translation of *The Analects of Confucius* 论语. This book contains just over 10,000 Chinese characters, however, Simon Leys' translation text runs to 98 pages and the notes run to 105 pages. Huang Jizhong' s translation of *The Analects of Confucius* adopts 991 annotations [12]. In-depth translation promotes western readers' understanding and acceptance of Chinese culture.

The adaptive selection and transformation of communication dimension is the translator's adaptive selection and transformation of communicative intention in the process of translation. In addition to the transformation of linguistic information and the transmission of cultural connotation, translators are required to lay emphasis on the communicative level of selection transformation and pay attention to whether the communicative intention in the original text can be reflected in the translation. Xie

---

[2] According to the accuracy and clarity of information transmission and reception in the process of communication, Edward Hall classified cultures into high-context culture and low-context culture.

Tianzhen pointed out that apart from a few translations that have been well received by British and American readers, most of the Panda Books have had no impact among them. Only one book in the Great China Library was favored by foreign publishers and purchased copyright for publication, and the communication of most other books was not ideal. It is a misunderstanding that completing a qualified translation means that it will definitely be read and welcomed by readers of a different culture.

The introduction of Chinese culture through translation is not simple literal translation but communication, and the generation of translated text is only the beginning of communication. There are also issues such as the introduction, influence, reception and acceptance and so on. Bao Xiaoying holds that the key to the success of translation lies in whether the translated text meets the language requirements of target countries and whether the text content conforms to the mainstream ideology and poetics of target language, and more importantly, whether each link of translation communication is effective [13].

3.2 Analysis of the Present Communication Model and Corresponding Measures

Communication is the behavior and activity of human information sharing and exchanging. In the book *The Structure and Function of Communication in Society*, Harold Lasswell proposed the famous Lasswell Communication Model [14]. The communication process is made up of basic elements of the five words beginning with "w", that is, "Who says What in Which channel to Whom with What effect". Lasswell Communication Model lays down the five basic contents of communication research, namely, control analysis, content analysis, media analysis, recipient analysis, and effect analysis. Lasswell Communication Model is a linear model. Later communication researchers developed more comprehensive circular social system models, but most of them have retained the essential characteristics of Lasswell Communication Model.

If Lasswell Communication model is applied to the field of translation and introduction, it will be a translation and introduction model that includes five elements, namely, subject of translation, content of translation, channel, recipient, and influence. The factors involved in tourism classics translation correspond to the five elements. The subject of translation is the translator; the content of translation is the classic books; the channel is the media; the recipient is the reader; and the influence is the translation effect. When put into the Lasswell Communication Model "Who says What in Which channel to Whom with What effect", the present communication model is "Translator says Classic Books in Media to Readers with Effect".

In the present communication model, "Translator" is Chinese translators or foreign sinologists. "Classic Books" are mostly rigorous and academic translation of classic books. "Media" is traditional printed paper book. "Readers" are the translated book readers. "Effect" is the accepting of the translated books. Below the status quo in the communication of tourism classics is presented from the five factors respectively. The disadvantages of the present communication model are analyzed and corresponding improvement measures are provided.

3.2.1 Who—Collaborative Pattern

As the first link in the communication process, "Who" is the sender of the communication message. Presently relying on Chinese translators or relying on foreign sinologists is the mainstream translation mode. But for cultural classics, it is not proper to rely only on one side, because Chinese tourism classics are a complex combination of ancient Chinese and high-context culture. If the translator is a Chinese cultural scholar, he/she needs the assistance of foreign scholars in smoothing and polishing the text; while if the translator is a foreign sinologist, he/she needs the help of Chinese scholars to thoroughly understand the language expression and cultural implication of the original book. A good way to bring out their strengths and make up for their weaknesses can be a collaboration pattern. Typical examples of Chinese and Western collaborative translation are joint translation of *The Dream of Red mansions* 红楼梦 by Yang Xianyi and his wife Glaydis Yang, translation of Nobel prize winner Mo Yan's works by Howard Goldblatt and Sylvia Li-chun Lin, and translation of classic books and poems such as *Water Margin* 水浒传 and *Journey to the West* 西游记 by Goran Malmqvist, one of the 18 lifetime judges for the Nobel Prize in Literature, and his Chinese wife. The English version of the novels *Three Kingdoms* 三国演义 and *Journey to the West* 西游记 by the Foreign Language Publishing House is translated by English native speakers with Chinese translators. These are a few successful examples of the collaborative pattern and apparently this pattern is reasonable and valid.

Collaborative pattern focuses on the selection of translators. It makes the best of the both Chinese translators and translators of other languages. Collaborative pattern can ensure the correct interpretation of the original text and the accurate expression of the translation to the greatest extent.

3.2.2 What—Classical Pattern and Common Pattern

In the communication process, "What" is the communication message. The translation of classic books can be used for deep cultural research by research readers, and the study of classic books can also directly promote the development of research tourism. Egypt, for example, started the world's earliest research tourism, reaching its peak during the Ptolemaic Dynasty (305BC–30BC). At that time the city Alexandria was a city of rich cultural facilities. According to Peng Shunsheng, the Library of Alexandria was the first large library in the world, containing half a million volumes of manuscripts of all kinds, including almost all the ancient Greek works and some of the Eastern classics. Scholars often came here, engaged in the collating, annotating and revising of literature, and this was the place where the Old Testament was translated into Greek [15]. The attraction of classic works and the environment advocating academic research attracted many scholars to study. Furthermore, the scientific and cultural activities of many researchers and scholars enhanced the tourism attraction of this Greek cultural center. The same is true with Chinese classics. Their translation versions appeal to many scholars and researchers, consequently increasing the attraction of the traditional culture in Chinese tourism. The translation of the tourism classics can be rigorous and academic. Therefore, the classical pattern is applicable in this case.

Classical pattern focuses on the content of translation and introduction. It puts emphasis on the faithful and in-depth translation of the original classics to the greatest extent.

Tourism classics of mountains and rivers conform to the worldwide cultural expectation of exploring nature, which makes it convenient to arouse the interest of readers from different cultures. The readers of Classical pattern translations are mostly teachers and students in universities and researchers who are interested in Chinese culture. However, Classical pattern translations are of little interest to the general or common readers. They read the translations not for academic research, but for common knowledge, general ideas or just for interesting stories. It is necessary to meet the needs of multiple readers and launch universal and diversified translation versions, to improve the influence of translation in the context of the different reader groups. We can adopt the common/ popular pattern. The common or popular translation versions can be the select version, simplified version, popular science version, pocket book version and so on. For example, the book *The Travels of Marco Polo*, known as one of the wonder books in the world, boasts more than 140 transcripts and 150 translations versions. On Amazon, there are about 100 seller links for *The Travels of Marco Polo*. The translation of this book comes in various different versions for the needs of different readers. Moreover, there are many other related books. The related books provide background knowledge about *The Travels of Marco Polo*, covering the adventures of Marco Polo, the travels of Marco Polo, the travel maps of Marco Polo and so on. Thus it's not an exaggeration to say that the variety of translation versions, and the large number of related books help to construct a cultural context conducive to the book's communication.

Common/Popular pattern also focuses on the content of translation. This pattern puts emphasis on the various alteration translation versions of the original classics for the general or common readers, who constitute a large proportion of the reader population.

3.2.3 What Channel—Computerized Pattern and Convert Pattern

In the communication process, "What channel" refers to the way in which the message is communicated. The twenty-first century is a digital era, when a typical change in the field of communication is the popularity of new media. In the new digital era, the high degree of being computerized or digital can also be seen as a proof of the high demand among the audience. Digital reading on the Internet is the main way of reading for current readers. The readers' reading shows a tendency of "fragmentation", "superficiality", and "visualization"[3] [16]. In the present communication model, Chinese classics translations in pure text form will hardly attract overseas readers who have grown up in the digital new media environment, so a computerized or digital communication pattern is necessary. The communication of tourism classics needs to change the traditional mode with pictures and words as the main media, and adopt digital methods integrating pictures, words, sounds and videos and other media for better communication.

Computerized/Digital pattern is based on the transformation of the translation and introduction channel, the media. The presentation mode of cultural elements can adopt a multimedia complex, such as texts, pictures, audios, videos and so on.

As the cultural elements contained in tourism classics are all-embracing, the ways of artistic presentation of culture should be multi-dimensional. The culture message can be animated or converted into other art forms. For instance, *Shan Hai Jing/The Classic of Mountains and Seas* is both a geographical work and a collection of myths and legends. It records more than 400 supernatural beings and strange beasts, and it is the archetypal source of many traditional Chinese cultural images. *The Dictionary of Chinese Myths and Legends* [17] by Yuan Ke, mainly quotes the original texts of ancient books, including the mythological legends of people, gods and things and ancient reference books on myths. Among the 3,275 lexical items in the dictionary, 756 are directly quoted from the original texts of *Shan Hai Jing/ The Classic of Mountains and Seas*. For example, the legend animal Nine-tailed Fox was a symbol of witchcraft before Qin dynasty, and a symbol of auspiciousness in Han dynasty, indicating the good luck of having many children or the good fortune of becoming an emperor. But after Tang dynasty, the Nine-tailed Fox evolved into a negative image, indecent and seductive vixen. In Ming dynasty, the novel *Feng Shen Yan Yi* 封神演义*/ Creation of the Gods* depicted a main character Daji as a bewitching woman vixen who brought calamity to the country and the people. This ancient Chinese cultural element, with complex connotations, is always connected with mysterious culture, spreading to Japan, Korea, Vietnam, and other countries. It has been communicated in many forms of art and entertainment, such as games, plays, television series, films, cartons and so on. Moreover, rituals, ceremonies, customs and festivals recorded in tourism classics can also be converted and animated into many different art forms to present the traditional culture in active styles.

Convert/Animate pattern is also based on the transformation of the translation and introduction channel. The culture elements can be converted into other art forms, such as games, plays, television series, films, cartons and so on.

---

[3] "Fragmentation" means that people use tablet computers, smart phones and e-readers to read incompletely and intermittently. "Superficiality" means that in the age of fast pace of life and the explosion of information, readers don't like to read big books and are reluctant to read in depth. "Visualization" means that readers are more willing to accept the visual image, and picture reading mode has become a popular way of reading.

3.2.4 Whom—Corresponding Pattern

In the communication process, "Whom" is the culture message accepter. Here message accepter rather than message receiver is used because receiving a message does not necessarily mean accepting a message. Irrelevant messages can be invalid. Message communication which meets the demand of the receivers can be efficient. In other words, corresponding pattern of communication is suitable in the introduction of traditional Chinese culture. One example is the communication of a famous Chinese philosophy classic, *Dao De Jing* 道德经/*Tao te Ching* in Germany. Germany is known as a nation of philosophers. In Germany there are 104 German translation versions of *Dao De Jing*. Some of Lao-zi's thought, "Tao 道", "Wu-wei 无为", and some other concepts related to Taoism, "Fengshui 风水", "Yinyang 阴阳", "Taiji 太极" have been very popular among German readers. German Chancellor Gerhard Schroder once called on every family to buy a copy of *Tao Te Ching*. Apparently the communication of *Tao Te Ching* meets the demand and expectation of the German readers. Another good example is *Da Tang Xi Yu Ji* 大唐西域记. In the *twelfth* century, Buddhism in India suffered catastrophic destruction, almost all buddhist holy places including the famous Nalanda Temple, and buddhist texts were destroyed. Fortunately, an eminent monk in the Tang dynasty, Master Xuanzang, kept a detailed record of his journey, including the location, distance and direction of each Buddhist holy place in the book *Da Tang Xi Yu Ji*. The translation and introduction of this book was welcomed. On the basis of the record in this book, archaeological work and excavation of Buddhist sites in India helped to restore the ancient Indian Buddhist shrines. Thanks to this book, the scattered pieces of Indian Buddhism history like a puzzle finally locked together successfully. More importantly, it also summarized the geographical situation, climate, products, politics, economy, culture, custom and so on in the country. It can even be said that the translation of *Da Tang Xi Yu Ji* has restored the history of India. The translation and communication of this book undoubtedly enjoyed popularity.

Corresponding pattern is based on meeting the needs of the recipients, getting the right works for the readers in need. Corresponding pattern aims to realize the efficient communication of classical books through customized translation and introduction.

3.2.5 What Effect—Codependent Pattern

The world culture system is like an ecosystem. There are three main types of symbiotic relationships: parasitism, commensalism, and mutualism. Parasitism is a relationship in which one organism derives its food at the expense of its symbiotic associate, the host. Commensalism is a relationship, in contrast to parasitism, in which one partner benefits without significantly affecting the other. Mutualism is a relationship which benefits both partners. The communication of traditional Chinese tourism classics aims at mutualism. The introduction of fine traditional Chinese culture with its unique Oriental charm contributes to the cultural diversity of the world. And the reverse is also true. The communication helps Chinese culture to learn from other cultures and thus brings forth fresh ideas from the traditional culture. The effect of the communication is codependent development.

Codependent pattern seeks the ideal communication effect, mutualism and reciprocity for different cultures.

4 The 7C-Communication-Model for Tourism Classics

Focusing on the five elements of the communication translation model, there are many ways to optimize the communication of tourism classics. As has been suggested in the previous part, 7 patterns can be adopted, including Collaborative Pattern, Classical Pattern, Common/Popular Pattern, Computerized/Digital Pattern, Convert/Animate Pattern, Corresponding Pattern, and Codependent Pattern. With different focuses, but at the same time closely linked, the seven communication patterns form the 7C-Communication-Model, which serves as a three-dimensional and diverse model of communication for tourism classics (Fig. 1).

This 7C-Communication-Model for Tourism Classics is different from the present single threading communication model. It is a multi-layered and three-dimensional model. The Collaborative Pattern here means the collaboration of Chinese translators and foreign sinologists. They work together to thoroughly understand the cultural implication of the original classic books and translate them into other languages

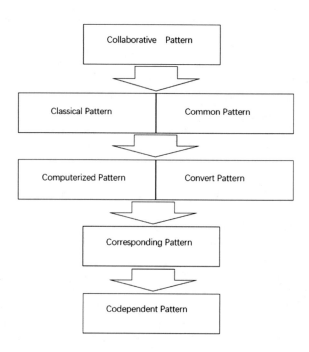

Fig. 1 The 7C-communication-model for tourism classics

with authentic and smooth expressions. The Classical Pattern here means translating the classic books into rigorous and academic versions. The Common/Popular Pattern in this model means translating the classic books into common or popular version, such as select version, simplified version, popular science version, pocket book version and so on. The Computerized/Digital Pattern here focuses on the digital methods integrating pictures, words, sounds, videos and other media for e-reading. The Convert/Animate Pattern here focuses on presenting the traditional culture in different art forms, such as games, plays, television series, films, cartons and so on. The Corresponding Pattern in this model stresses meeting the needs of the recipients, customizing the right translation works for the readers in need. The Codependent Pattern here emphasizes the reciprocity and mutual benefit of different cultures. It pursues an ideal effect, not two sides losing, or one side benefiting while one side losing, or only one side benefiting, but two sides winning.

In dealing with the challenge of the COVID-19 pandemic, many prominent problems and shortcomings have been exposed. Firstly, some industries operate in a single mode, which makes the emergency capacity particularly weak. Secondly, there is a problem of formalism in the integrative development among culture, tourism and technology. Thirdly, the combination of cultural and tourism industry is loose, so the construction quality of smart culture and tourism need to be greatly improved [18]. This severe global public health crisis provides extensive implications. As far as culture communication is concerned, it is necessary that the communication model should be reconstructed. The reconstructed model is based on the integration of culture and tourism, the transboundary innovative expression among different art fields, and the infusing of science and technology application.

The integration of culture and tourism promotes high-quality tourism development. As important carriers of traditional Chinese culture, tourism classics display deep-rooted culture genes. These culture genes generate the core appeal for tourists, thus benefiting sustainable and promising tourism development.

The transboundary innovative expression among different art fields is also an inevitable trend. The communication of culture is no longer confined to translation among different languages in literature. Instead, the culture genes in literature can be expressed in forms of painting, sculpture, architecture, music, dance, drama, film and so on.

The infusing of science and technology application is pushed by the general trend of digitalization and information. While the traditional cultural and tourism industry has been suffering a major impact in this major global health crisis, the emerging digital cultural and tourism industry has prominent advantages due to the characteristics of online consumption. New life styles such as electronic reading and VR travel help tourists enjoy immersive experience without actually being there. If science and technology are applied in more flexible and extensive ways in culture communication, they will become an essential part within the tourism industry for the long term.

The 7C-Communication-Model for Tourism Classics is developed against the background of global health crisis, but it has extensive application value in the future. This model consists of seven patterns, each pattern focusing on one element of the process of "Who says What in Which channel to Whom with What effect". This 7C-Communication-Model for Tourism Classics is a comprehensive model which maximizes the potential of culture gene, the transboundary innovative expressions of art forms and application of science and technology. Briefly, in the communication process, collaborative translators translates classic books into classical versions or common versions in computerized media or converted art forms to corresponding readers with codependent effect.

5 Conclusion

The law of cultural development shows that the development of culture cannot break away from the existing cultural traditions to create a new culture, but accumulates and progresses on the basis of inheriting traditions. Traditional culture takes tourism development as an opportunity to realize vertical inheritance from ancient times to the present times, and horizontal communication from one nation to the outside world. At the same time, tourism development also strengthens its deep core competitiveness and realizes sustainable development by virtue of cultural communication. Integration of culture and tourism helps to achieve a win–win situation of culture heritage protection and tourism development. In the context of globalization, communication of traditional cultures is beneficial for the world as a whole.

As one of the ancient and modern cultures, Chinese culture has been benefiting from world culture communication. It has rich cultural resources, such as the Chinese classics in tourism which are time-honored records of the traditional Chinese culture. The translation and introduction of Chinese classics have been active but the communication does not achieve the desired effect. The present stereotyped communication model is hindering smooth communication. We create the 7C-Communication-Model consisting of 7 communication patterns to help improve the communication of the Chinese classics. The integrated comprehensive communication model is hoped to better the introduction of culture classics. The Chinese culture communication is conducive to the vitality of Chinese culture, the diversity of world culture and the sustainable development in tourism.

References

1. Ji, X.: Ji Xianlin On Translation. Contemporary China Publishing House, Beijing (2007)
2. Jinah, P., Wu, B.: An integrated analysis of international tourism research patterns for the period of 2003–2012. Tour. Trib. **7**, 112 (2015)
3. Bao, J.: Tourism ideology-tourism development and cultural heritage protection. Tour. Res. **8**, 1 (2016)
4. Zhao, D.: Traditional Chinese Culture in Tourism. Tourism Education Press, Beijing (2015)
5. Yong, R.: Simplified Annotated Catalogue of the Si Ku Quan Shu. Shanghai Classics Publishing House, Shanghai (1964)

6. Ma, Z., Ren, R.: History of World's Translations of Chinese Writing. Hubei Education Press, Wuhan (1997)
7. Zhang, X.: Research in translation out of ancient Chinese classics across cultures. J. Xinjiang Normal Univ. (Philos. Soc. Sci.) **2**, 106–108 (2015)
8. Lin, G., Wang, Y., Shao, X.: Research on overseas communication of Chinese science and technology classics and construction of communication path. Hubei Soc. Sci. **2**, 154–157 (2020)
9. Xie, T.: Chinese literature and culture going global: theory and practice. Soochow Lecture Hall **2**, 49–52 (2013)
10. Hu, G.: Eco-translatology: research Foci and theoretical tenets. Chin. Transl. J. **2**, 5–9 (2011)
11. Hall, E.T.: Beyond Culture. Shanghai Culture Publishing House, Shanghai (1988)
12. Lin, Y.: Re-casting "collective textual context": problems in translating Chinese classics in the era of fragmentation reading. Shanghai J. Transl. **1**, 20–26 (2015)
13. Bao, X.: Exploration on the translation mode of Chinese culture going-out. Chin. Transl. J. **5**, 62 (2013)
14. Lasswell, H.: The Structure and Function of Communication in Society. Communication University of China Press, Beijing (2013)
15. Peng, S.: Development History of World Tourism. China Travel and Tourism Press, Beijing (2006)
16. Long, M.: Innovative retranslation of Chinese classics in the digital age. J. Foreign Lang. **2**, 121–128 (2020)
17. Yuan, K.: Dictionary of Chinese Myths and Legends. Shanghai Lexicographical Publishing House, Shanghai (1985)
18. Zhou, Z., Liu, S.: Research on the cultural and tourism industries' responses to Covid-19 and its follow-up effects of China. China Anc City **3**, 25 (2021)

Relationship Between Emotional Intelligence, Job Burnout and Turnover Intention of Hotel Staff

Xueying Lu, Jiajue Wang, and Limin Zhao

Abstract Emotional intelligence is a mental ability affecting perception and attitude, ultimately affecting behavioral intention. Based on the questionnaire survey of 312 hotel employees, this paper makes an empirical study on the relationship between hotel employees' emotional intelligence, job burnout and turnover intention. This study concluded a negative correlation between emotional intelligence and turnover intention, a positive correlation between job burnout and turnover intention and moderating effects of job burnout in the process of turnover decision-making. By verifying theoretical assumptions, in response to the plight of the hotel industry after the outbreak of COVID 19, this paper highlights relevant empirical strategies to improve employees' emotional intelligence, reduce their job burnout, finally it may reduce the turnover rate of employees in the hotel industry.

Keywords Emotional intelligence · Job burnout · Turnover intention · Hotel staff

1 Introduction

The high turnover rate of hotel staff has been a substantial challenge to the hospitality industry. The hospitality industry stakeholders should comprehend and predict the employees' turnover intention and lower their turnover rate. Mobley [1] highlighted that the predicted turnover behavior could be measured through the direct antecedent variable of turnover intention. Numerous academics have studied the turnover behavior of employees by exploring the influence mechanism and path

X. Lu (✉)
Xiamen University of Technology, Ligong Road 600 Jimei District, Xiamen, People's Republic of China
e-mail: xylu@xmut.edu.cn

J. Wang
China Jiliang University, 258 Xueyuan Street, Qiantang District, Hangzhou, Zhejiang, People's Republic of China

L. Zhao
Beijing Hetai Zhiyan Management Consulting Co., Ltd., Gaohe 208, Xinjiekou, No. 3, Xinjiekou North Street, Xicheng District, Beijing, People's Republic of China

of turnover intention. The turnover behavior of hotel staff is influenced by internal, external, organization, and individual factors. Previous studies regarding the turnover intention of the hotel staff mainly focused on the influence of work-related factors, such as working pressure, job satisfaction and burnout [2, 3]. Few studies have delved into the influence mechanism of turnover intention from the perspective of the emotional management of employees. In the 1970s, scholars began to consider the employee's emotion management. The Hospitality industry is very peculiar as it serves the public directly and the general mood of the hotel staff will directly affect customer experience. Therefore, the emotional factors of hotel staff on their work have been considered by academics, including the influence on turnover intention [4]. Moreover, due to the particularity of hotel work, hotel staff are more prone to job burnout. In the process of long-term customer service, hotel staff's emotional and work pressure cannot be relieved, thereby leading to related physiological and psychological problems that impact their job performance making them prone to leave their jobs. Li [5] argued that job burnout is an antecedent variable of turnover intention and also an essential mediating mechanism affecting turnover intention. Due to the considerable impacts of COVID-19 in early 2020, the overall performance of the hotel industry is sharply declining in the number of staff due to the lack of confidence in the business and industry, resulting in an unprecedented turnover rate.

Aiming at the above problem, this article has analyzed the relationship between the dimensions of emotional intelligence and turnover intention. It has also delved into the moderating effect of the dimensions of job burnout in the relationship between the two. This study aims to help hotels predict employees' turnover behavior and provide established references for human resources management in hotels.

2 Literature Review and Theoretical Hypothesis

2.1 Emotional Intelligence

The research on emotion management has emerged in the 1970s. The concept of emotional intelligence is first coined by American psychologists Mayer, Caruso, and Salovey [6] in 1990. They believe that emotional intelligence is a part of social intelligence, including the ability to understand our feelings and understanding the feelings of others, and the ability to recognize emotions thereby guiding thinking and behavior based on emotional information. Prosser et al. [7] believe that emotional intelligence is an accurate tool in the prediction of human behavior. Nikolaou and Tsaousis in [8] have proposed the theoretical framework of emotional intelligence and used it to study the ways in which employees control their emotions and deal with their working pressure. According to previous literature, numerous studies have been conducted regarding the influence of emotional intelligence on employees' way of controlling their emotions and dealing with working pressure [9–11]. However, few studies have delved into predicting the relationship between emotional intelligence and employees' individual behavior. Moreover, its influence on the turnover behavior of employees has rarely been studied from the perspective of emotional intelligence.

Scholars hold varying views regarding the structure of emotional intelligence. The most widely accepted theory in academia is the four-dimensional model of emotional intelligence proposed by Mayer et al. [6] in 1999, including self-emotional appraisal (SEA), others' emotional appraisal (OEA), use of emotion (UOE) and regulation of emotion (ROE). On this basis, they have developed multiple emotional Intelligence scales, which have been extensively applied in emotional intelligence research.

2.2 Job Burnout

Job burnout is a negative syndrome caused by the inability to deal with stress due to chronic working pressure. Maslach and Jackson in [12] have defined job burnout as a response of individuals to long-term emotional and interpersonal tension in the occupations that deal with the public. It is mainly manifested in the forms of emotional exhaustion, depersonalization, and reduced personal accomplishment amongst other symptoms. Therefore, Mastach and Jackson have developed the Maslash Burnout Inventory (MBI), a scale for job burnout, involving three dimensions of emotional exhaustion, depersonalization, and reduced personal accomplishment. It has become a trend to research the implication, influencing factors, and measurement dimensions of job burnout in recent years. The negative relationship between emotional intelligence and job burnout has been studied to some extent [13–16].

The hospitality industry is a service industry. The hotel staff have been plagued with physical and mental pressure due to labor shortage in recent years. In particular, front-line employees need to put in many emotions and receive a lot of negative emotions in face-to-face contact with guests. Members of staff are likely to foster a negative state, feel a sense of job burnout and thereby lead to an increase in turnover rate if they are devoid of a proper outlet. Existing studies have discussed the relationship between hotel employees' Job Burnout and turnover intention [17–19]. Their research has concluded that job burnout has a significant positive explanatory effect on turnover intention.

2.3 Turnover Intention

Turnover intention refers to the idea of employees to leave the organization. Mobley in [20] highlighted that turnover intention is the direct prediction factor of turnover behavior. Domestic and foreign scholars have conducted multidisciplinary studies on turnover intention. It is found from studies that personal factors [21], work and career development factors [3], organizational environment [22], external environment and other factors are the leading factors influencing the turnover intention of the hotel staff. In the analysis of turnover intention using the emotional theory framework, Lv et al. in [4] concluded that emotional factors exerted influence in predicting the turnover intention of hotel staff. In contrast, emotional intelligence is somewhat negatively correlated with turnover intention.

2.4 Research Review

Employees' turnover intention is influenced by both enterprise factors and micro individual factors [23, 24]. This study focuses on the influence of individual factors on turnover intention. It is inferred from the literature review those individual variables affecting the turnover intention of hotel staff include essential demographic characteristics such as gender, age, marital status, work department, an education level [25, 26]. Mayer and Salovey in [27] defined emotional intelligence as a mental ability in recognizing the emotions of oneself and others, distinguish the emotions of oneself and others, and use this information to shepherd thinking and take actions. Other scholars, such as Wong and Law [28], Wu et al. [29], Liu and Zhang [30], and Chen [31], have concluded through empirical studies that emotional intelligence is significantly correlated with job burnout, in which emotional intelligence can play a significant role in regulating all dimensions of job burnout. Therefore, this study proposes the hypothesis that emotional intelligence is negatively correlated with job burnout and that emotional intelligence has a conspicuous explanatory effect on job burnout. On the other hand, Wang [32] believe that emotional intelligence can significantly predict the turnover intention of the staff and that employees with low emotional intelligence tend to have high turnover intention. Therefore, a hypothesis is proposed in this paper arguing that emotional intelligence is negatively correlated with the turnover intention of the staff and that all dimensions of emotional intelligence can delineate turnover intention.

The above literature review indicates that there is still no consensus on the measurement dimension of job burnout in academic circles. However, the scale of job burnout built by Schaufeli and Enzmann in [33] on the basis of the original MBI scale applies to all professions. It includes three dimensions of exhaustion, cynicism and reduced personal accomplishment. In their research on the teachers' profession, Maslach and Jackson in [34] highlighted that formal turnover behavior is highly correlated with the dimension of exhaustion among the three dimensions of job burnout. Currently, most Chinese studies consider the global aspect of job burnout as a whole, overlooking the detailed analysis of the relationship between the three dimensions of job burnout and related variables. Therefore, it is assumed in this paper that job burnout is positively correlated with turnover intention in the hospitality industry and that each dimension of job burnout can explain the turnover intention.

The literature review concluded that emotional intelligence affects turnover intention and job burnout in different ways, which is a complex psychological process. The influencing mechanism and factors involved are also complex. This study mainly proves the main effect of emotional intelligence on turnover intention. It explores the moderating mechanism of job burnout affecting employees' emotional intelligence in the hospitality industry. To sum up, the hypotheses are proposed as below:

Hypothesis 1: Employees' emotional intelligence is negatively correlated to their turnover intention.

Hypothesis 2: All dimensions of emotional intelligence of employees have a significant ability to explain the turnover intention.

Hypothesis 2-a: Recognizing our own feelings has a significant ability to explain the turnover intention.

Hypothesis 2-b: Recognizing the feelings of others has a significant ability to explain the turnover intention.

Hypothesis 2-c: Emotion regulation has a significant ability to explain the turnover intention.

Hypothesis 2-d: Self-motivation has a significant ability to explain the turnover intention.

Hypothesis 3: Job burnout is positively correlated with turnover intention.

Hypothesis 4: All dimensions of job burnout have a significant ability to explain the turnover intention.

Hypothesis 4-a: Exhaustion has a significant ability to explain the turnover intention.

Hypothesis 4-b: Cynicism has a significant ability to explain the turnover intention.

Hypothesis 4-c: Reduced personal accomplishment has a significant ability to explain the turnover intention.

Hypothesis 5: Job burnout plays a regulating role in the decision making of employees' turnover intention.

Hypothesis 6: Job burnout plays a significant role in regulating the relationship between each dimension of employees' emotion regulation and turnover intention (Fig. 1).

3 Empirical Study

3.1 Research Scale

The emotional intelligence scale adopts the WLEIS (Wong and Law Emotional Intelligence Scale) with four dimensions to measure employees' emotional intelligence. WLEIS is found to have high reliability and validity. WLEIS is evaluated by using the five-point Likert scale, with positive scores. The job burnout scale uses the MBI-GS

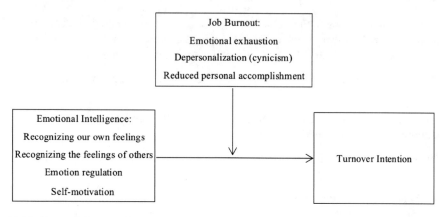

Fig. 1 Research framework

three-dimensional scale revised by Li Chaoping et al., to measure employees' job burnout. The five-point Likert scale is used in the job burnout scale, in which the first two dimensions are scored positively, while the third dimension is scored oppositely. The turnover intention scale adopts the turnover intention scale designed by Mobley [1], involving four questions. The five-point Likert scale is adopted as the scoring standard, in which the first two questions are scored in a positive way, whereas the last two questions are scored in the opposite way.

3.2 Overall Descriptive Analysis of Research Objects

In April 2017, this study distributed electronic questionnaires through the website (www.wjx.cn). 312 questionnaires are distributed, 312 are recovered, 312 are deemed valid, and the effective recovery rate is 100%. The basic descriptive analysis of the samples is carried out. Among them, 146 are under the age of 25, accounting for 46.8%. There are 91 employees over 36 years old, accounting for only 28.83%. There are 134 married respondents, accounting for 42.9%, and 178 unmarried respondents, accounting for 57. 1%. These figures indicate that the employees in the hospitality industry tend to be young and unmarried. In terms of education level, a total of 275 respondents have had a bachelor's degree or below, accounting for 88.2%. In terms of working years, the number of respondents working for less than one year or one to two years accounted for the largest proportion, totaling 51.6%. However, only 21.8% of the employees worked in the industry for more than 11 years. The total number of respondents in the front-line departments (including lobby, guest room or butler, public relations or marketing, catering, recreation and other departments) is 275, accounting for 88. 1%. The number of respondents working in second-line departments (including general office, human resources, finance, engineering, security and other departments) totaled 37, accounting for 11.9%.

3.3 Reliability and Validity Analysis

Reliability refers to the consistency degree of the results yield through the using of identical methods when measuring the same object repeatedly. The reliability of this study's emotional intelligence scale and job burnout scale is high, and the coefficients are 0.892 and 0.910, respectively. It bears testimony to the reliability and stability of the results. The turnover intention scale comprises four questions and is a single-dimensional variable. The Cronbach's α value is 0.886, indicating the high reliability of the results.

Validity is also referred to as correctness. The feasibility test of factor analysis is performed on the data prior to factor analysis. In this paper, factor analysis is conducted out on the items of emotional intelligence, job burnout and turnover intention. The principal component analysis is used to extract factors, The results show that the KMO value of job turnout is 0.885, and the approximate Chi-square of Bartlett's test is 2,550.536, with probability P equal to 0, less than the significance level of 0.05. The KMO value of turnover intention is 0.818, and the approximate Chi-square of Bartlett's test is 693.818, with probability P equal to 0, less than the significance level of 0.05. Both dimensions reject the null hypothesis of Bartlett's test are deemed suitable for factor analysis. The KMO value of emotional intelligence is 0.917, and the approximate Chi-square of Bartlett's test is 1,812.879, with probability P equal to 0, less than the significance level of 0.05. The above indicates that many common factors relate variables, which are very suitable for factor analysis. Therefore, all variables of this questionnaire are deemed highly valid and boost the reliability of the questionnaire.

3.4 Factor Analysis

Factor Analysis of Emotional Intelligence. The original questionnaire of emotional intelligence comprises 12 items, and each item of the original questionnaire is an effective indicator of the corresponding dimension. In factor extraction, the Principal Components Analysis is used to analyze the items in the emotional intelligence scale. Four factors with eigenvalues exceeding one are extracted. According to the analysis result, E1, E2 and E3 can be classified as the first factor to recognize our own feelings. E4 and E5, E6 can be classified as the second factor, named recognizing the feelings of others. E7, E8 and E9 can be grouped into the third factor, named emotion regulation. E10, E11 and E12 can be grouped into the fourth factor, named self-motivation. The 12 measurement items of emotional intelligence have been divided into four factors, and each item is assigned to the factor with the maximum load.

Factor Analysis of Job Burnout. The original questionnaire of job burnout comprises 15 items, and each item of the original questionnaire is an effective indicator of the corresponding dimension. Three factors with an eigenvalue greater than one are extracted by using principal component analysis. In the extraction of factors, according to the original variable correlation coefficient matrix, the principal component analysis method is used to extract factors, and the characteristic roots with an eigenvalue greater than one are selected. The first five items, S1, S2, S3, S4 and S5, can be grouped into one factor and named emotional exhaustion. The middle four items S6, S7, S8 and S9, can be classified as the second factor and named as cynicism. The last six items S10, S11, S12, S13, S14 and S15, can be classified as the third factor and named as a reduced personal accomplishment. The 15 measurement items of job burnout are divided into three factors, and each item is assigned to the factor with the maximum load. According to the result analysis, the contribution of the first three factors accounts for the total variance, and the load value of each factor exceeded the standard of 0.55. Therefore, it is believed that the job burnout scale possesses high structural validity.

3.5 Correlation Analysis

Correlation analysis is required before conducting the regression analysis of variables. Since the measurement scales of variables in this study are in the form of a Likert scale and the data are of fixed distance, Pearson simple correlation coefficient is adopted to measure the correlation between the variables of a fixed distance. Since the turnover intention scale involves a single dimension, the arithmetic mean of the three items is considered the variable for analysis. The correlation between variables is listed in Table 1.

It can be inferred from the above table that the turnover intention is significantly positively correlated with each dimension of job burnout at the level of 0.01 (bilateral). It shows that job burnout is directly proportional to turnover intention. The absolute values of the correlation coefficients between turnover intention and three dimensions of job burnout of emotional exhaustion, cynicism and reduced personal accomplishment are 0.410, 0.494 and 0.318, respectively, indicating that the turnover intention is moderately correlated with these three dimensions. At the level of 0.01 (bilateral), there is a significant negative correlation between turnover intention and each dimension of emotional intelligence. Emotional intelligence is shown to be inversely proportional to turnover intention. However, the correlation coefficients between turnover intention and the dimensions of emotional intelligence are less than 0.3, indicating that the two variables are weakly correlated. The results of correlation analysis support the hypothesis. Regression analysis will be used to verify each hypothesis further later in the article.

Table 1 Correlation coefficient table

	Variable	Mean	Variance	1	2	3	4	5	6	7	8
1	Turnover intention	2.99	1.10	1							
2	Emotional exhaustion	2.78	0.89	0.41**	1						
3	Depersonalization	2.52	0.97	0.49**	67**	1					
4	Reduced personal accomplishment	2.09	0.68	0.32**	24**	0.36**	1				
5	Recognizing our own feelings	3.88	0.71	−.19**	−0.20**	−0.29*	−0.65**	1			
6	Recognizing the feelings of others	3.83	0.66	−0.22**	−.6**	−0.20**	−0.67**	−0.66**	1		
7	Emotion regulation	3.80	0.75	−.19**	−.11**	−0.25**	−0.62**	0.69**	0.71**	1	
8	Self-motivation	3.79	0.69	−.17**	−.15**	−0.24**	−0.57**	0.63**	−0.69**	65**	1

Notes n = 312, * indicates $p < 0.05$; ** indicates $p < 0.01$

3.6 Regression Analysis

The above analysis establishes a general understanding of the relationship between emotional intelligence, turnover intention, and job burnout. Next, a stepwise regression analysis will be used to further analyze the relationship between variables.

According to the purpose of this study, the stepwise regression method is used to judge the explanation and significance degree of the increase of variance variation of dependent variables for each independent variable, and the variables are introduced into the model. The regression analysis results are listed in Table 2.

The first step is to introduce the demographic characteristic variables into the model as control variables. It can be inferred from Table 2 that the adjusted R^2 is 0.134, which means that the population factor of the control variable explains 13.4% of the variance of turnover intention. Meanwhile, the F value is 7.899, and the probability of F statistic value is below the significance level of 0.01, indicating the significance of the regression model.

Table 2 Summary of regression analysis results

Independent variable dependent variable	Turnover intention		
	Model 1	Model 2	Model 3
Step 1: Control variables			
1. Gender	−0.121	−0.113***	−0.121***
2. Age	−0.121	−0.123***	−0.145***
3. Marital status	−0.147	0.161***	−0.048
4. Education level	−0.059	0.080***	0.062***
5. Position	−0.193	−0.168***	−0.105***
6. Working years	−0.091	−0.075***	−0.110***
7. Department	−0.126	−0.171***	−0.213***
Step 2: Explanatory variables			
8. Recognizing our own feelings		−0.038***	−0.091***
9. Recognizing the feelings of others		−0.047**	−0.056***
10. Emotion regulation		−0.025*	−0.002
11. Self-motivation		−0.087***	0.001
Step 3: Moderator variables			
Emotional exhaustion			0.123***
Cynicism			0.404***
Reduced personal accomplishment			0.103***
F value	7.899	1926.431	817.536
R^2 value	0.154	0.986	0.975
Adjusted R^2 value	0.134	0.986	0.974

Notes Sample size N = 312; * indicates that the significance level p < 0.1, **indicates that the significance level p < 0.05, ***indicates that the significance level p < 0.01

The second step is to put the explanatory variables, namely, the dimensions of emotional intelligence, into the regression equation. The analysis results are used to test Hypothesis H1 and H2. As inferred from Table 2, the adjusted R^2 is 0.986, an increase of 85.2% compared with Model 1. It indicates that the interpretation ability of the model for the variance of turnover intention has significantly enhanced. The β value of the item of recognizing our own feelings is $-0.038***$, and that of self-motivation is $-0.087***$, showing that both recognizing our own feelings and self-motivation have a significant ability to explain the turnover intention. Therefore, it verifies the Hypotheses 2-a and 2-d. The β value of the item of recognizing the feelings of others is $0.047**$, and that of emotion regulation is $-0.025*$, showing that the Hypothesis 2-b and 2-c are verified. The above hypotheses help to explain the hypothesis H2.

The third step is to put each dimension of job burnout into the regression equation, respectively, for testing Hypothesis H3 and H4. As can be seen from Table 2, the adjusted R^2 is 0.974, a reduction of 1.2% compared with Model 2. Among the dimensions, emotion regulation and self-motivation no longer possess significant explanatory ability, indicating that the variable's ability to explain employees' turnover intention has slightly decreased. At the same time, the F value is 817.536, and the probability of F statistic value is below the significance level of 0.01. Among them, emotional exhaustion ($\beta = 0.123***$), cynicism ($\beta = 0.404***$) and reduced personal accomplishment ($\beta = 0.103***$) have a significant ability to explain the turnover intention; thus validating Hypotheses H3 and H4.

Regression analysis in SPSS is used to test the main effect and the moderating effect. The results of the regression analysis are shown in Table 2.

3.7 Analysis of the Moderating Effect

Job burnout has three dimensions, and emotional intelligence has four dimensions. Therefore, to simplify the analysis, this paper takes job burnout as a whole variable to test the moderating effect of job burnout on each dimension of emotional intelligence.

This section uses the weighted average synthesis method to calculate the overall job burnout. The specific calculation formula is as follows.

Job burnout = (Score of emotional exhaustion × Eigenvalue of emotional exhaustion + Score of cynicism × Eigenvalue of cynicism + Score of reduced personal accomplishment × Eigenvalue of reduced personal accomplishment) ÷ (Eigenvalue of emotional exhaustion + Eigenvalue of cynicism + Eigenvalue of reduced personal accomplishment) = (3.407 × Score of emotional exhaustion + 2.874 × Score of cynicism + 3.555 × Score of reduced personal accomplishment) ÷ 9.836.

The fourth step of this study is to put the interactive products of job burnout and four dimensions of emotional intelligence into the regression equation and test Hypothesis H5 and H6 to assess the presence of the regulatory effect of job burnout. The stepwise regression method for regression analysis is employed accordingly.

The validation results are yielded through the analysis of SPSS 22. The comparison of the third and fourth steps results is shown in Table 3. The results show that the adjusted R^2 value of Model 4 is 0.322, and that of Model 5 is 0.704, and the difference between them is the Δ adjusted R^2 value at 0.382. Moreover, the overall significance test F value of Model 5 is 7.826, which is significant at the 1% level. It shows that introducing job burnout significantly increases the model's explanatory power of employee turnover intention by 38.2%. In other words, the job burnout variable can significantly increase the explanatory power of 38.2% to the turnover intention after

Table 3 The regression analysis results of the moderating effect

	Turnover intention	
	Model 4	Model 5
Step 1: Control variables		
1. Gender	−0.246**	−0.316**
2. Age	−0.016*	−0.054
3. Marital status	0.194	0.269
4 Education level	0.139**	0.025*
5. Position	0.145	0.139
6. Working years	−0.127**	−0.164***
7. Department	−0.622***	−0.924***
Step 2: Explanatory variables		
8. Recognizing our own feelings	−0.015**	−0.179**
9. Recognizing the feelings of others	−0.040*	−0.223***
10. Emotion regulation	−0.164**	−0.196***
11. Self-motivation	0.052**	0.015
Step 3: Moderator variables		
Job burnout	0.372***	0.259***
Step 4: Analysis of the moderating effect		
Job burnout* Recognizing our own feelings		0.05
Job burnout* Recognizing the feelings of others		0.497***
Job burnout* Emotion regulation		0.233*
Job burnout* Self-motivation		0.217*
F value	6.742***	7.826***
R^2 value	0.378	0.807
ΔR^2 value		0.429
Adjusted R^2 value	0.322	0.704
Δ Adjusted R^2 value		0.382

Notes Sample size N = 312; * indicates that the significance level $p < 0.1$, ** indicates that the significance level $p < 0.05$, *** indicates that the significance level $p < 0.01$

the elimination of the influence of other variables and job burnout itself. Thus, it indicates that job burnout has a moderating effect, thereby verifying the Hypothesis.

Moreover, in the process of testing, it is found that in the cross items of job burnout variable and the dimensions of employee's emotional intelligence, the cross item of job burning out and recognizing our own feelings has no significant effect on turnover intention. However, the other three cross items (Job burnout* Recognizing the feelings of others, Job burnout* Emotion regulation, and Job burnout* Self-motivation) have a significant effect, verifying hypothesis H6.

3.8 Summary of Empirical Results

Based on these hypotheses, all the hypotheses and their test results are listed in Table 4. The results of these analyses are discussed further in the next chapter.

Table 4 Summary of empirical results (N = 312)

No	Hypothesis	Verification result
H1	Employees' emotional intelligence is negatively correlated to their turnover intention	Valid
H2	All dimensions of emotional intelligence of employees have a significant ability to explain the turnover intention	Valid
H2-a	Recognizing our own feelings has a significant ability to explain the turnover intention	Valid
H2-b	Recognizing the feelings of others has a significant ability to explain the turnover intention	Valid
H2-c	Emotion regulation has a significant ability to explain the turnover intention	Valid
H2-d	Self-motivation has a significant ability to explain the turnover intention	Valid
H3	Job burnout is positively correlated with turnover intention	Valid
H4	All dimensions of job burnout have a significant ability to explain the turnover intention	Valid
H4-a	Exhaustion has a significant ability to explain the turnover intention	Valid
H4-b	Cynicism has a significant ability to explain the turnover intention	Valid
H4-c	Reduced personal accomplishment has a significant ability to explain the turnover intention	Valid
H5	Job burnout plays a regulating role in the decision making of employees' turnover intention	Valid
H6	Job burnout plays a significant role in regulating the relationship between each dimension of employees' emotion regulation and turnover intention	Partially valid

4 Conclusion and Enlightenment

4.1 Conclusion and Discussion

In this paper, 312 employees at different positions from the hotels of different scales in various regions are studied through questionnaires. SPSS 22 is used to conduct factor analysis, correlation analysis and regression analysis on the collected data. The relationship between emotional intelligence, job burnout and turnover intention is discussed in combination with relevant literature and discussion and analysis of empirical research results. Finally, the following conclusions and practical significance are drawn:

The emotional intelligence of employees has a significant reverse effect on turnover intention. Emotional intelligence is shown to be inversely proportional to turnover intention. According to the results, hotel management should acknowledge the influence of emotional intelligence on management practices, and fully consider the current situation and development of employees' emotional intelligence. In particular, in early 2020, after the outbreak of COVID-19, the overall performance of the hotel industry is currently experiencing sharp decline. The lack of confidence in the industry has led to a more severe turnover. In the communication with peers in the past two years, the author has concluded that employees with high emotional intelligence still hold the industry in high regard. Furthermore, they also actively face adversity, enhance their personal and hotel competitiveness by constantly improving themselves and improving hotel products, and achieve the goal of overcoming difficulties and growing together with the hotel. On the one hand, this phenomenon not only reflects the findings of current study that employees' emotional intelligence has a significant reverse effect on turnover intention, but also puts forward practical suggestions for the hotel human resources department to consider the evaluation results of employees' emotional intelligence as a benchmark in personnel employment and promotion.

Job burnout can explain the turnover intention of hotel staff significantly. Job burnout is directly proportional to turnover intention, and vice versa. Based on this conclusion, hotel managers should consider employees' psychological state and emotional performance, identify problems in time, and take prompt action to eliminate their job burnout and improve their job satisfaction. On the one hand, the management should take personalized incentive measures for employees of different ages and different backgrounds. They should explore the potential needs of different types of employees and allocate corresponding positive incentive methods to alleviate their burnout and enhance job attractiveness. On the other hand, the hotel can give play to the role of the training system. Through different forms of training activities in various themes, they can strengthen employees' cognition of hotel corporate culture, reduce their job burnout and improve their professional identity. Furthermore, they can also enrich the work and life of employees through various activities beneficial to their physical and mental health to enhance the freshness of work and the employees' loyalty to the hotel. Especially in the context of the crisis brought by

COVID-19, hotels should actively assume social responsibilities, provide resources support for employees, help employees cope with setbacks and difficulties, and overcome difficulties.

Job burnout has a moderating effect on the relationship between emotional intelligence and turnover intention. From the cross items of regression analysis, the job burnout variable can significantly increase the explanatory power of 38.2% to the turnover intention, excluding the influence of other variables and job burnout itself. The conclusion states that job burnout tends to trigger their turnover intention in the hospitality industry, whether employees have high or low emotional intelligence. Therefore, in addition to the measures that hotel management should take to reduce employees' job burnout proposed in the preceding paragraph, hotels can also take more professional and targeted actions in consideration of the significant moderating effect of job burnout on turnover intention. The management can regularly gauge the job burnout of employees, implement EAP (Employee Assistance Program) for the employees at all levels in different stages, and open up the dual promotion channels for management and technical posts, to clearly understand the situation of employee job burnout and take corresponding measures. In this way, scientific methods can be used to minimize the job burnout of employees and reduce the turnover rate of employees.

4.2 Limitations and Prospects

Being bound by limited theoretical knowledge and research level, this study has encountered some limitations, which are mainly reflected in the following aspects:

In terms of research content, this study merely takes into account the impact of personal factors, such as emotional intelligence and job burnout on turnover intention. It overlooks the impact of external factors such as salary and welfare, organizational emotion and leadership, on turnover intention. Therefore, there are some limitations in the integrity and structure of the research.

This study has adopted the convenience sampling method. The researchers obtained the sample by asking hotel executives to hand out questionnaires rather than by random sampling which might affect the completeness and objectivity of the research results.

Only the hotel staff in Guangzhou, Beijing, Hangzhou, Shenzhen, Shantou, Huizhou and Xiamen are selected as respondents in this study. Whether the survey results of the subjects are universally representative remains to be further studied and verified.

Based on the above summary and drawbacks of this study, it is believed that the follow-up research should be further improved and perfected from the following aspects: In this paper, a simplified turnover intention model is adopted, but other variables that may affect the turnover intention of the hotel staff have not been introduced, such as employee salary, corporate image, work collaboration and job satisfaction. In this regard, some mediating variables or other regulating variables can be added in the future, or some of them can be controlled to enrich the research model and improve the integrity of the research.

Researchers should collect as much foreign literature as possible on the relationship between interaction, emotional intelligence, job burnout and turnover intention to solidify the theoretical basis of this study, and to boost the validity of the hypotheses. The three scales of emotional intelligence, job burnout and turnover intention involved in this paper are obtained from the relevant scales developed by Western scholars. Because of this, researchers can consider the cultural background factors of the hospitality industry in China and the personality characteristics of Chinese tourists in the preparation process of the relevant scale in the follow-up study, to make the scale more apt at addressing the measurement needs of hotel staff in China.

References

1. Mobley, W.H.: Intermediate linkages in the relationship between job satisfaction and employee turnover. J. Appl. Psychol. **62**(2), 237–240 (1977)
2. Lv, Y.: An empirical study of relationship between job burnout and turnover intention of hotel frontline employees. J. Xi'an Univ. Finance Econ. **27**(3), 23–27 (2014)
3. Ding, X.C., Zheng, F.H.: A study on the impact of emotional labor on turnover intent-based on job satisfaction mediating effect model. East China Econ. Manage. **30**(6), 144–151 (2016)
4. Lv, Q., Wu, Y.H., Dong, S.P.: A research on the effects of hotel employees' subjective wellbeing, emotional intelligence and emotional labor strategies towards turnover intention: a panel model on mediation and maderation. Hum. Resour. Dev. China **2**, 43–51 (2016)
5. Li, H.L.: A study on the relationship among job stress, job burnout and turnover intention of hotel employees. Master's thesis, Zhejiang University, Hangzhou (2009)
6. Mayer, J.D., Caruso, D.R., Salovey, P.: Emotional intelligence meets traditional standards for an intelligence. Intelligence **27**(4), 267–298 (1999)
7. Prosser, D., Johnson, S., Kuipers, E., Dunn, G., Szmukler, G., Reid, Y., Bebbington, P., Thornicroft, G.: Mental health, "burnout" and job satisfaction in a longitudinal study of mental health staff. Soc. Psychiatry Psychiatr. Epidemiol. **34**(6), 295–300 (1999)
8. Nikolaou, I., Tsaousis, I.: Emotional intelligence in the workplace: exploring its effects on occupational stress and organizational commitment. Int. J. Organ. Anal. **10**(4), 327–342 (2002)
9. Totterdell, P., Holman, D.: Emotion regulation in customer service roles: testing a model of emotional labor. J. Occup. Health Psychol. **8**(1), 55–73 (2003)
10. Qin, H., Chen, Y.Z., Meng, M.: The relationship between emotional labor, emotional intelligence and job burnout. Psychol. Res. **4**(1), 49–54 (2011)
11. Ning, L.C., Zhou, L., Cai, T.S.: Intermediary role of cope styles in the process of job burnout impacted by emotional intelligence. Acad. J. Gunagzhou Med. Univ. **42**(4), 147–150 (2014)
12. Maslach, C., Jackson, S.E.: The role of sex and family variables in burnout. Sex Roles **12**(7), 837–851 (1985)
13. Li, Y.X., Hou, Y.: Burnout, stress and depression. Psychol. Sci. **28**(4), 972–974 (2005)
14. Gerits, L., Derksen, J.J., Verbruggen, A.B., Katzko, M.: Emotional intelligence profiles of nurses caring for people with severe behaviour problems. Pers. Indiv. Differ. **38**(1), 33–43 (2005)
15. Reilly, N.P.: Exploring a paradox: commitment as a moderator of the stressor-burnout relationship. J. Appl. Soc. Psychol. **24**(5), 397–414 (1994)
16. Durán, A., Extremera, N., Rey, L.: Self-reported emotional intelligence, burnout and engagement among staff in services for people with intellectual disabilities. Psychol. Rep. **95**(2), 386–390 (2004)

17. Xu, L.: Job burnout of front-line staff in hotels. Hotel Modern. **2**, 60–63 (2010)
18. Liu, Y.J.: Research on job burnout of front-line employees in high-star hotels. J. Southwest China Agric. Univ. (Soc. Sci. Ed.). **10**(9), 5–8 (2012)
19. Niu, J.G.: A research on work pressure and job burnout of hotel staff. Master's thesis, Xiamen University, Xiamen (2009)
20. Mobley, W.H.: Employee turnover: causes, consequences, and control. Addison-Wesley, Reading (1982)
21. Peng, Y.F., Cao, S.W.: An empirical study on the relationship between work-family conflict and turnover intention of female employees in the hotel industry. J. Guangxi Vocat. Norm. Univ. **28**(4), 35–40 (2016)
22. Yang, K.J., Xu, R.R.: The relationship between emotion management and turnover intention of employees: a case study on the mediating effect of job satisfaction. Enterp. Econ. **35**(2), 158–162 (2016)
23. Muchinsky, P.M., Morrow, P.C.: The applicability of middle range theories to the study of organizational effectiveness. In: Pinder, C.C., Moore, L.F. (eds.) Middle range theory and the study of organizations, pp. 304–314. Springer, Dordrecht (1980)
24. Zeffane, R.: Job satisfaction and work redesign: findings from Australia. Int. J. of Comp. Sociol. **35**(1–2), 137–141 (1994)
25. Mobley, W.H., Griffeth, R.W., Hand, H.H., Meglino, B.M.: Review and conceptual analysis of the employee turnover process. Psychol. Bull. **86**(3), 493–522 (1979)
26. Igbaria, M., Greenhaus, J.H.: The career advancement prospects of managers and professionals: are MIS employees unique? Decis. Sci. **23**(2), 478–499 (1992)
27. Mayer, J.D., Salovey, P.: The intelligence of emotional intelligence. Intelligence **17**(4), 433–442 (1993)
28. Wong, C.S., Law, K.S.: The effects of leader and follower emotional intelligence on performance and attitude: an exploratory study. Leader. Q. **13**(3), 243–274 (2002)
29. Wu, W.K., Yu, T.L., Song, J.W.: An empirical study of the impacts of emotional intelligence on job burnout. J. Tsinghua Univ. (Philos. Soc. Sci.). **23**(S2), 122–133 (2008)
30. Liu, X.Y., Zhang, K.: The effects of emotional intelligence on job burn-out: an analysis of the work stress as a mediator. J. Southwest China Norm. Univ. (Nat. Sci. Ed.). **33**(3), 148–154 (2008)
31. Chen, W.J.: Research on job burnout of knowledge workers from the perspective of emotion. Master' thesis, Wuhan University of Technology, Wuhan (2009)
32. Wang, F.Z.: Empirical research on the relationship between emotional intelligence and organizational commitment of knowledge workers based on survey data of private enterprises in Huaining Industrial Park. Master' thesis, Anhui University, Heifei (2010)
33. Schaufeli, W., Enzmann, D.: The burnout companion to study and practice: a critical analysis. CRC Press, New York (1998)
34. Maslach, C., Jackson, S.E.: Maslach burnout inventory manual, 2nd edn. Consulting Psychologists Press, Palo Alto (1986)

Informal Tourism Employment for Poverty Alleviation Under the Covid-19 Pandemic: Research Advances and Novel Challenges

Muchun Li and Xingnan Wu

Abstract Employment to alleviate poverty is the most effective and direct way to sustainably alleviate poverty. The poverty alleviation effect of informal employment, especially informal tourism employment, deserves more attention. This study aims to investigate relevant research domains on employment poverty alleviation, informal employment and informal tourism employment. The findings showed that the means and methods of employment poverty alleviation, the characteristics of informal employment, the influencing factors and the impact on the relevant groups engaged in informal employment, and the social effects of informal tourism employment are the focus. This paper proposed a new conceptual framework for employment poverty alleviation, informal employment poverty alleviation and informal tourism employment poverty alleviation, discusses possible directions for research on informal employment in tourism under the influence of major public health events.

Keywords Targeted poverty alleviation · Employment poverty alleviation · Informal employment · Informal tourism employment · The COVID-19 pandemic

1 Introduction

Poverty is a universal problem of human development and has become a huge obstacle to China's sustainable development. The Chinese government proposed a precise poverty alleviation strategy in 2013 and achieved a comprehensive victory in the battle against poverty by the end of 2020, completing the arduous task of eliminating absolute poverty. However, the policy of precise poverty alleviation attaches more importance to the input of external resources, and to a certain extent it is difficult

M. Li · X. Wu (✉)
Guangdong Tourism Strategy and Policy Research Center, Key Laboratory of Digital Village and Sustainable Development of Culture and Tourism Industry, Department Tourism Management Institute of Tourism Development, South China University of Technology, Guangzhou, Guangdong, People's Republic of China
e-mail: wxn1324@163.com

M. Li
e-mail: limch@scut.edu.cn

to mobilize the development desire and development ability of the poor themselves, and there is a risk that the effect of poverty alleviation is not sustainable.

Poverty alleviation through employment is an effective way to solve the problem of intergenerational poverty transmission. The ongoing industrialization and urbanization in China has contributed to a change in the employment structure, with informal employment becoming one of the employment pathways [1]. The greatest gains in tourism to address employment are not in the formal sector, but in the pull to informal employment, and in turn address structural unemployment and alleviate the incidence of poverty [2]. Although studies have focused on the group and spatial characteristics [3, 4], influencing factors and multidimensional benefits brought by informal tourism employment [5, 6], the number of studies is limited and the research areas are scattered, and a "complete picture" depicting the focus, hot spots and the inner logical connections of the studies has not been formed. At the same time, in the dual context of the comprehensive opening of the rural revitalization strategy and the huge impact brought by the COVID-19 Pandemic, there is insufficient grasp of the characteristics and advantages of informal tourism employment and its inherent poverty alleviation mechanism, and the practical guidance is limited. Therefore, this paper attempts to clarify the content logic of informal tourism employment research by sorting out the relevant research topics and methods of informal tourism employment poverty alleviation and taking the relevant studies on employment poverty alleviation, informal employment poverty alleviation and informal tourism employment poverty alleviation as the entry point; on this basis, it explores the impact of the COVID-19 pandemic and macro policy changes on informal tourism employment poverty alleviation research, and explores the impact of the major public health events under In this regard, we explore the impact of the COVID-19 Pandemic and macro policy changes on informal tourism employment poverty alleviation research, and explore the turn of informal tourism employment research under major public health events.

2 Research Topics

2.1 The Solution to the Dilemma of Precise Poverty Alleviation: Employment to Alleviate Poverty

Employment is the biggest welfare of people's livelihood and one of the important ways to eliminate poverty. Employment poverty alleviation is aimed at People in poverty with employability and employment aspirations, and a variety of measures are taken to help them find full and stable employment or start their own business in order to improve their own income and achieve long-term poverty alleviation [7, 8].

In terms of the purpose of employment poverty alleviation, employment is not only the greatest livelihood benefit, but also one of the important ways to eliminate poverty [9]. Its overall task is to provide employment opportunities for every poor family that is willing to be employed and eligible for employment [10]. According to the focus of research, it can be divided into the economic effect theory, which focuses on the construction of anti-poverty system [8, 9], the labor force enhancement theory, which focuses on the quality improvement and stable employment of poor labor force, and the transfer employment theory [11, 12]. Therefore, the purpose of employment poverty alleviation is to achieve sustainable poverty alleviation for the poor, build a lasting and stable anti-poverty system, and help poor laborers achieve stable employment and multidimensional poverty alleviation.

Therefore, how to unfold employment poverty alleviation has become the focus of research. Because employment poverty alleviation is highly local in practice, most of the relevant studies adopt a "central-local" narrative framework, describing specific practices in each province based on interpreting the requirements of government documents.

In general, employment poverty alleviation mainly achieves the goal of precise poverty alleviation through precise information, precise subjects, precise funds on the government side and precise skills training on the poor household side. For example, Zunyi City launched a recruitment information release platform and built a management information system for precise employment and poverty alleviation, drew a "map of employment demand" and "map of job supply", and implemented map work [5]; the four southern Xinjiang prefectures combined employment poverty alleviation with industrial poverty alleviation and labor export, and actively explored "satellite factories". The four southern Xinjiang prefectures combine employment and poverty alleviation with industrial poverty alleviation and labor export, and actively explore poverty alleviation models such as "satellite factories", "poverty alleviation workshops" and "township factories" to absorb employment [4]; Shanxi Province, by coordinating various training resources, has provided training for 60,000 workers in 36 counties. In Shanxi Province, by coordinating various training resources, 60,000 People in poverty in 36 counties have been trained for free to realize the link between training and employment [13].

2.2 The Special Form of Employment Poverty Alleviation: Informal Employment Poverty Alleviation

Informal employment originated from the concept of informal sector introduced by the International Labor Organization (ILO). Its theoretical basis is the theory of poverty employment and the dualistic segmentation of the labor market [14]. Despite the specific description of informal sector by ILO, the development of informal employment in different countries is influenced by factors such as social system, ideology and economic development status, and the country-specific characteristics are obvious. As we can see, it is still very difficult to define and measure "informal employment" precisely [15]. Guo Wei et al. suggest that the core of informal employment includes the absence of tax supervision, lack of social security system, and

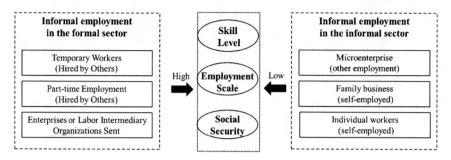

Fig. 1 Composition of informal employment in China

unregulated and unstable labor relations [3]. Therefore, informal employment exists in both the formal and informal sectors, and the composition of informal employment in China is shown in Fig. 1 below.

The forms and sectors of informal employment determine the distinctive features of informal employment that are very different from formal employment: first, the forms of operation are mainly self-employment, family enterprises and small, medium and micro enterprises; second, the production and service activities of these units are not strictly separated from the living and consumption activities of households; third, there are no independent operating accounts and no legal rights of independent legal entities; fourth, the production and operation Fourth, the production and operation behaviors are not recorded by the business sector [16]. Analysis of the structural characteristics of informal employment from a meso perspective shows that the unbalanced distribution of informal employment in terms of industries and regions has become the main driving force for the large-scale entry of migrant workers into cities and towns [1]. The basic form of compensation in informal employment is hourly wages [17], and the main employees are rural households [18]. These characteristics indicate that informally employed people are at a relatively low level in terms of social status, employment treatment, and working environment.

From the 1798 documents retrieved by CNKI with "informal employment" as the keyword, the frequency of "informal employment group" is as high as 9 times among the top 40 keywords. At present, scholars have done a lot of research on informal employment groups. The main focus is on migrant workers, college students, urban laborers and women. The research focuses on the factors influencing the choice of informal employment and the influence on each group, including demographic characteristics (age, marital status and household registration status), human capital (education level) and family characteristics (whether to support the elderly, number of children and elderly, family voice). discussed. Therefore, the existing studies have formed a roadmap of "antecedent-thematic-consequence" with informal employment as the central topic, and the inherent logic of the study is clear. For more details, see Tables 1 and 2.

Informal employment is one of the important forms of employment, which not only alleviates the structural unemployment problem in China to some extent, but

Table 1 Influencing factors of research on informal employment groups in China

Influencing factors	Specific dimensions	Views support
Demographic characteristics	Age	Ding Yu et al. concluded from a study in Xiamen that urban women's informal employment in the new era is characterized by youthfulness [19]
	Marriage and childbirth	Liu, Sanming et al. argue that married women are prone to work-family conflict and their likelihood of engaging in informal employment is higher [20]
	The household registration	Through the analysis of CGSS data, Zhang Shubo et al. concluded that there is invisible status discrimination in the household registration system, and that there is a 13% influence of household registration discrimination in the choice between formal and informal employment [21]
Human capital	Education level	Hou, Haibo et al. argue that informal employment is an effective way of employment for some socially disadvantaged groups [22]
Family characteristics	Children and old people	Liu Yan et al. argue that children and the elderly promote women's choice of informal employment [23]
	Whether to support the elderly	Yanhua Wu et al. argue that family elder care increases the likelihood that women will engage in informal employment [24]
	Family discourse power	Guo Wei et al. argues that there is an interaction between family discourse and the income of informal employment or the personality of the practitioner [5]

also has a symbiotic relationship with urban development [27]. When the level of economic development exceeds a certain stage, workers' wage level and employment security can be improved, and the labor market will be formalized automatically [28]. However, China's economic development is still at an upward stage at this stage, and the marginal social status of the poor, their low skill level, and their mostly rural

Table 2 The impact of informal employment on various groups

Level	Specific dimensions	Views support
The society level	The spatial distribution	Lin Minhui et al. analyzed the clustering characteristics of informal employment in different types of tourism Spaces in cities, and believed that the functions, locations, management blind spots and consumer markets affected their clustering patterns [4]
The individual level	Occupational mobility	Yang Fan et al. found that informal employment not only directly promoted the their willingness to work, but also indirectly increased their willingness to work mobility through influencing their work characteristics [13]
	Job satisfaction	Liu Cuihua et al. used CLDS data to quantitatively test the impact of informal employment on residents' job satisfaction, found that informal employment had a negative impact on it [25]
	Quality of life perception	Liang Zengxian et al. discussed the life quality composition of urban tourism informal workers, concluded that the composition of it was unique, and the social demographic characteristics and employment status had little impact on it [26]
	Improving poverty	Guo Wei et al. believe that informal employment, especially informal tourism employment, is an effective means to increase the income of Tibetans through the investigation of employment of Tibetans around Qinghai Lake [6]

household registration are all realistic factors that limit their chances of obtaining employment in the formal sector. At this stage, informal employment has an important role in urban job creation, transfer of surplus rural labor and poverty alleviation [29], and informal employment has a significant effect on poverty alleviation for the group of migrant workers in cities [30].

2.3 *Informal Tourism Employment and Employment Poverty Alleviation*

Tourism informal employment is a special manifestation of informal employment, which is both informal employment and has its own characteristics of the tourism industry. In terms of legality, tourism informal employment is not equal to illegal employment, but is a flexible and viable form of employment, with characteristics such as mobility and instability [31]. In terms of basic size, any business unit with a size of less than 20 people that contributes to tourism in a direct or indirect way can be defined as tourism informal employment [32]. In terms of type, hawkers selling tourist souvenirs, small street craftsmen, rickshaw drivers, homestays without business licenses, unlicensed tour guides and roadside food stalls near scenic spots all belong to tourism informal employment [33].

From the perspective of influencing factors, Guo Wei takes the poor's family as the basic unit of analysis, points out that family size and family discourse personality can significantly influence family income, and argues that tourism informal employment can indirectly improve the individual's discourse in the family through the interaction of personal income or personality [5]; Liang Zengxian et al. cut from the perspective of tourism informal employment's income level, pointing out investment capital, motivation to work, external support and innovation ability are the main factors influencing the income level of tourism informal employment, and emphasize that the benefits of tourism informal employment require the joint efforts of the government, market and practitioners, and should not be limited to the practitioners themselves [34]. Yuan Chao et al.'s focus on "villager guides" provides strong evidence for this view. They argue that the emergence of "villagers' tour guides" is closely related to external factors, such as the local nature of villages, the insufficient supply of formal tour guides by tourism companies, the single source of income of village collective economy, and the doubtful social justice of tourism distribution system, which shape this tourism informal employment subject [33]. In terms of the impact on practitioners, Liang Zengxian and Xie Chunhong found that tourism informal employment can provide practitioners with more career outlets and is a career pathway for low-level workers to shift to high-level urban employment, effectively responding to the debate between informal employment as a last resort strategy to escape involuntary unemployment or as a voluntary choice based on income or utility maximization [35]. However, at the same time, due to the specificity of informal employment, tourism informal job seekers are likely to encounter many practical challenges. Zhang Ruoyang et al. pointed out that informally employed groups in rural tourism often face multidimensional exclusion including economic exclusion, political participation exclusion, career development exclusion, social relationship exclusion, and identity exclusion [36], thus failing to effectively share the fruits of tourism development; Meng Wei, on the other hand, argued that in the practice of tourism informal employment, tourists, residents, formally employed people, and government workers can have a negative impact on tourism informally employed people form dynamic stigmatizing narratives and influence the logic of action of tourism informally employed people [37]. In terms of overall effects, one of the important social effects of tourism informal employment is its ability to affect the livelihoods of the poor due to the specificity of tourism informal employment and the convergence of employment group characteristics. Through a series of articles, Guo Wei and his team elucidated the poverty alleviation effect of tourism informal employment from the perspective of the overall pull effect of employment, the growth of household discourse, and the increase of individual income level, and argued that tourism informal employment can be an important tool for precise poverty alleviation [2, 5, 6].

In general, most of the studies on tourism informal employment emerged after 2010, and the overall number of studies is small, and the relevant research topics focus on the influencing factors of tourism informal employment, the impact on practitioners and the pull effect. From the perspective of research regions, most studies on tourism informal employment still focus on cities, resort centers and seaside, and not enough attention is paid to rural areas. From the perspective of influencing factors, the research on tourism informal employment has gradually expanded from focusing on the factors of the workers themselves to a comprehensive consideration of the external environment, presenting a "subject perspective" around one or more of the tourism informal workers, the market and the government, trying to present the complexity, heterogeneity and The complexity, heterogeneity and differences of the tourism informal sector [2]. However, there is a lack of a systematic and relational perspective on tourism informal employment, and the influencing factors and formation logic of informal employment and governance measures are still under debate [33]. From a macro context, there is a relative lack of attention to the development, operational mechanisms and group characteristics of tourism informal employment in the context of the global public health event of the COVID-19 pandemic, and more cutting-edge research results have not yet been produced.

2.4 Informal Tourism Employment in the Context of COVID-19 Pandemic: Can It Have a Pro-Poor Effect?

The global and enormous scale, multidimensional and interrelated impact of COVID-19 Pandemic challenges current values and systems and leads to worldwide recession and depression [38]. As an environmentally sensitive industry, the global pandemic of the COVID-19 pandemic has confronted the tourism industry with unprecedented dilemmas and has had a tremendous impact on tourism practitioners, with tourism becoming the center of international public opinion.

In terms of established research findings, the topic of relevant studies has focused on the impact of the COVID-19 pandemic on tourism and tourism research. At the level of theoretical research, the current discussion under COVID-19 Pandemic shows a paradigm-shifting self-consciousness, with Marianna Sigala shifting the research focus to challenge, reset and refute institutional logics, systems and assumptions as a way of examining and challenge and help us deconstruct and challenge the mechanisms and systems that sustain harmful and unsustainable tourism development [38, 39]. This critical paradigm emphasizes that tourism research should move away from an excessive focus on crisis management and economic efficiency and return to the 'human' side of tourism activity, focusing on the 'paradox' of tourism research in the context of the new coronary pneumonia [38], and providing an opportunity to raise the importance of the tourism informal worker in tourism research.

Freya Higgins-Desbiolles, on the other hand, calls for a community-centered value orientation that places tourism in the social context in which it occurs, emphasizing the need to redefine and reorient tourism according to the rights and interests of local communities and local people, and to use tourism to promote the empowerment and well-being of local communities in order to counter neoliberal injustices and exploitation that have emerged among the tourism industry [39]. And at the empirical research level, Colin Charles Williams discusses the interaction between tourism informal workers and government departments under the impact of the COVID-19 pandemic and points out the vulnerability of tourism informal workers in accessing temporary financial support and proposes the practice of voluntary disclosure initiatives [40]. Tom Baum and Nguyen Thi Thanh Hai, through A "real time" assessment of the impact of the COVID-19 pandemic on the right to participate in hospitality and tourism suggests that the right to gainful employment in the hospitality and tourism industries may continue to be denied in whole or in part in parts of Asia, Europe and North America in the context of restricted mobility [41]. In addition, the ILO's promotion of the right to decent work for all has been challenged by the consequences of the economic turmoil triggered by COVID-19, and social protection and employment rights for those in informal employment are limited or non-existent in developing countries worldwide [42].

3 Research Methods

3.1 Qualitative Analysis

For the study of informal tourism employment in China, the focus is on the influencing factors and outcomes in the selection process of informal tourism employment, such as investigating the impact of workers' income and quality of life, and their data collection is based on structured or semi-structured interviews, observations, and objective analysis. Since the aim of these papers is to construct different explanatory perceptions of the behavior and meaning of informal tourism employment, qualitative analysis methods are more common. In terms of data collection methods, questionnaires and in-depth interviews are dominant [2, 3, 6]. In terms of data analysis methods, grounded theory is widely applied [43, 44].

3.2 Quantitative Analysis

3.2.1 Data Analysis Method

The main topic of quantitative analysis has focused on the micro level, discussing the impact of informal employment and informal tourism employment on some characteristics of the groups involved [26, 45, 46]. Scholars have tried to develop econometric analysis models that depict the relationship models between different factors through regression analysis. Since the dependent variables involved in the relational models are mainly ordered discrete binary variables, ordered Probit models and binary logistic models are widely used.

For example, Liu Cuihua et al. examined the effect of the core explanatory variable informal employment and related variables such as gender, age, and years of education on residents' job satisfaction through an ordered Probit model [25]. First, descriptive statistical analysis was conducted on the relevant samples and regressions were performed on the full sample to report the results of the marginal effects of informal employment on residents' job satisfaction when the mean of each explanatory variable was taken; second, differential analyses were conducted for heterogeneous groups such as different genders and different years of education; third, the instrumental variables approach was applied, and provincial pension insurance coverage was used as an instrumental variable to address the relationship between informal employment and Fourth, the relationship between informal employment and job satisfaction is re-estimated using the propensity score matching method (PSM) using stata software to exclude the endogeneity problem due to "self-selection bias".

3.2.2 Methods of Data Quality Inspection

Data quality testing methods are used throughout the empirical analysis process, and different data properties determine different data quality testing methods, so testing methods must be chosen carefully. For data obtained through questionnaires, interviews, and other forms, scholars often use tools to conduct reliability and validity tests before modeling. For example, Liang Zengxian et al. used Cronbach's coefficients from the traditional SPSS statistical tool to test the reliability of the subjective well-being and overall life evaluation scales of informally employed urban tourism workers, and interpreted the validity of the questionnaire through KMO values and Bartlett's sphericity test [26, 35]. Other data sources in some literature are large-scale comprehensive social surveys such as CGSS, CHNS and CLDS, whose data have been tested for reliability and validity before presenting the findings. The endogeneity of the modeling is crucial in determining the value of the study. Therefore, scholars have focused on robustness testing after model modeling. In the literature on USES linear regression modeling, most scholars use the instrumental variables approach and two-stage maximum likelihood estimation to avoid the endogeneity problems associated with ordinary least square (OLS) linear regression [45–47]. By some scholars, they prefer value-weighted analysis, also called preferential value point matching method (PSM) to control the selection bias that may occur during sample selection. For example, Wang Qingfang used the PSM method to analyze the income gap between urban informally employed workers and formal workers to determine the net effect of informal employment decisions on workers' income [48].

4 The Relational Model of the Employment Poverty Alleviation, Informal Employment and Informal Tourism Employment

From the above literature review, it can be seen that there is a relationship between employment poverty alleviation, informal employment and informal tourism employment. Employment poverty alleviation is an effective way to solve the practical problems of "blood transfusion" poverty alleviation deviation and serious poverty return in targeted poverty alleviation. One of its core objects of concern is the poor population. The characteristics of these People in poverty in terms of demographic characteristics, human capital and family characteristics make them often choose informal employment in reality. In reality, a considerable part of tourism employment is manifested as informal employment in both towns and villages, and thus, informal tourism employment is an important form of informal employment. Since informal employment is one of the important ways for People in poverty to obtain employment income, according to scholars' studies, informal employment, especially informal tourism employment, has an important role in poverty alleviation and poverty reduction, and becomes an effective embodiment of employment poverty alleviation. Based on the above analysis, this paper tries to construct the relationship model of employment poverty alleviation, informal employment and informal tourism employment, as shown in Fig. 2 below.

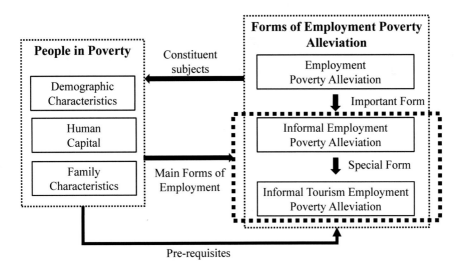

Fig. 2 Relation model of employment poverty alleviation, informal employment and informal tourism employment

5 Conclusions

At present, China's targeted poverty alleviation work has made decisive achievements, and the overall poverty problem in the region has basically been solved. Now it has come to the stage of attacking the city. This paper comprehensively composes the research contents and research methods of employment poverty alleviation, informal employment and informal tourism employment in China from the perspective of targeted poverty alleviation, and tries to clarify the previous concerns and research results on related issues. The results show that. In terms of research content, the concepts, characteristics and influencing factors of poverty alleviation, informal employment and informal tourism employment are the focus of attention; in terms of research methods, the studies are mainly based on quantitative analysis, and linear regression Probit models are widely used; the qualitative analysis methods mainly rely on grounded theory to explore the relationship patterns between informal tourism employment and various factors.

And the global pandemic of COVID-19 has pushed tourism research to think about the paradigm shift in research and research topics. Overall, tourism in the context of COVID-19 Pandemic has become the focus of tourism research, though. Critiques of neoliberalism in theoretical studies have highlighted the social attributes of tourism, and reflections on established paradigms in tourism research have brought into sharper focus the critical role of people and communities; while empirical studies devoted to tourism informal employment have emphasized the fluidity of the pandemic and tourism itself, placing the discussion on tourism practitioners who are in vulnerable situations. However, few studies have paid attention to poverty alleviation in tourism informal employment under the COVID-19 pandemic, both in theoretical and empirical studies. Therefore, it is difficult to explain whether tourism informal employment can function properly in a complex and vulnerable external environment, whether there are new interactions between relevant influencing factors, and whether new changes in group characteristics arise under the pandemic, thus preventing a discussion of how the occurrence of a major public health event acts on the interrelationship between tourism informal employment and poverty.

References

1. Hu, A.G., Yang, Y.X.: Employment pattern transformation: From formal to the regularization, informal employment in cities and towns in China. Manage. World **2**, 69–78 (2001)
2. Guo, W., Li, X.J., Xu, K.: The neglected true power: Informal tourism employment and its pull effects. Tour. Trib. **29**(8), 70–79 (2014)
3. Guo, W., Qin, Y., Wang, L.: On the group features of tourism informal employment and industrial satisfaction: taking the survey of tourism informal departments in Qingdao and Yantai as an example. Tour. Trib. **27**(7), 81–90 (2012)
4. Lin, M.H., Huang, L.Y., Zheng, J.J.: A study on informal employment agglomeration in urban tourism space: a case study of Guangzhou. Tour. Sci. **33**(4), 13–31 (2019)

5. Guo, W., Tian, J. W.: Poverty, family discourse power and informal tourism employment: an investigation on informal tourism workers of Qingdao. Tour. Sci. **32**(3), 39–50, 62 (2018)
6. Guo, W., Huang, W. D., Kou, M.: The road to prosperity: informal employment of Tibetans in tourism—a survey on the employment of Tibetans around Qinghai Lake **1**(3), 39–50, 121 (2017)
7. Zhang, L.B.: Accurate theoretical research for poverty alleviation of employment. China Labour **3**, 4–14 (2018)
8. Li, P.: Poverty alleviation in the context of precision poverty alleviation: policy analysis, problem annotation and governance path. J. Guangxi Univ. Financ. Eco-Nomics **30**(6), 5–12 (2017)
9. Sun, Z.Q.: Accurate theoretical research for poverty alleviation of employment. Hum. Resour. Dev. **2**, 29–30 (2019)
10. Pan, H.: Problems and countermeasures of poverty alleviation by employment in four prefectures in southern Xinjiang. Trib. Soc. Sci. Xinjiang **2**, 30–35 (2019)
11. Yuan, L.J.: The practice of employment in our country poverty alleviation achievements, problems and countermeasure analysis. Mod. Manag. Sci. **9**, 109–111 (2018)
12. Zhang, L.B.: Policies and implementation of poverty alleviation through employment in China. Shandong Hum. Resour. Soc. Secur. **4**, 10–14 (2019)
13. Yang, F., Pan, Y.: Effects of informal employment on occupational mobility intentions of migrant workers. Population Res. **43**(4), 97–112 (2019)
14. Zhang, H.C.: Informal employment: Development status quo and policy measures. Manage. World **11**, 57–62 (2002)
15. Cai, F.: Informal employment: give play to the role of labor market in allocating resources. The Front **5**, 17–19 (2005)
16. Cai, F., Wang, M.Y.: Informal employment and the development of labor market—on the growth of urban employment in China. Econ. Inf. **2**, 24–28 (2004)
17. Tian, F., Sun, B.: Under the background of the "double gen" informal employment microscopic analysis of the impact of labor market—based on Marx's labor value theory perspective. Tianjin Econ. **2**, 32–36 (2016)
18. Hu, Q.W.: The development and urbanization effect of informal employment in Chinese cities. New Econ. **11**, 26–31 (2017)
19. Ding, Y., Shi, H.M.: Informal employment of young urban women in the new era. Popul. Soc. **32**(2), 32–38 (2016)
20. Liu, S.M., Ma, H.Y., Kang, S.J.: A review of foreign studies on gender-based differences in work-family conflict. Collect. Women's Stud. **5**, 116–121 (2013)
21. Zhang, S.B., Cao, X.B.: Research on the household discrimination between the formal and informal employment: based on propensity score matching. J. Nanjing Univ. Financ. Eco-Nomics **1**, 72–80 (2017)
22. Hou, H.B., Liu, Y.H.: Analysis of heterogeneity of educational return rate of informal employment. World Surv. Res. **10**, 36–41 (2018)
23. Liu, Y., Li, Y.Y.: An analysis of gender differences in informal employment of migrant rural labor—a case study of Nanjing city. Chin. Rural. Econ. **12**, 20–27 (2007)
24. Wu, Y. H., Li, J. C., Liu, B.: The impact of informal care on women's informal employment. J. Bus. Econ. **3**, 47–57, 86 (2018)
25. Liu, C.H., Ding, S.L.: The impact of informal employment on residents' job satisfaction—the experience analysis of the China labor-force dynamics survey. Contemp. Econ. Manag. **40**(11), 70–79 (2018)
26. Liang, Z.X., Li, J.Y., Wen, T.: Tourism and quality of life perceptions among urban tourism informal employees: a case study of Guangzhou city. Tour. Trib. **30**(9), 72–81 (2015)
27. Zhang, Y.J., Zhang, L., Wu, L.Y.: Manufacturing spatial restructuring from the perspective of informal employment: an empirical study on prefecture—level cities in 2000 and 2010. Econ. Geogr. **35**(8), 142–148 (2015)
28. Wu, Y.W.: The destination of informal employment. Econ. Res. J. **44**(7), 91–106 (2009)

29. Xue, J.J., Gao, W.S.: Informal employment in urban China: Its size, features and earning disparity. Comp. Econ. Soc. Syst. **6**, 59–69 (2012)
30. Du, Y., Wan, G.H.: Informal employment in the urban labour market and its role in poverty reduction. Econ. Perspect. **9**, 88–97 (2014)
31. Li, Z.F., Yu, Z.: Informal tourism employment: Multi-dimensional comparison between China and foreign countries. J. Wuhan Commer. Serv. Coll. **32**(2), 5–10 (2018)
32. Wang, L., Guo, W., Chen, Z.: Literature review of tourism informal sector and employment—self-employment. J. Beijing Int. Stud. Univ. **32**(9), 41–48,27 (2010)
33. Yuan, C., Kong, X., Chen, P.Y., et al.: Informal rural tour guides: willing or reluctant participants? Tour. Trib. **36**(1), 87–98 (2021)
34. Liang, Z. X., Zhao, Z., Xiao, Y, Y., et al.: The influencing factors on income level of informal tourism employees. Tour. Forum **9**(5), 62–69 (2016)
35. Liang, Z.X., Xie, C.H.: Informal tourism employment: the end to a career or a channel for career development? Tour. Trib. **31**(01), 102–110 (2016)
36. Zhang, R.Y., Fu, X.X., Zhang, M., et al.: Investigating the social exclusion perception of the informally employed group in Chinese rural tourism: a case study of Zhuji ancient alley. Tour. Trib. **34**(5), 26–36 (2019)
37. Meng, W.: Stigmatization of informal tourism employees. Tour. Trib. **35**(6), 66–77 (2020)
38. Sigala, M.: Tourism and COVID-19: Impacts and implications for advancing and resetting industry and research. J. Bus. Res. **117**, 312–321 (2020)
39. Higgins-Desbiolles, F.: Socialising tourism for social and ecological justice after COVID-19. Tour. Geogr. **22**(3), 610–623 (2020)
40. Colin, C., W.: Impacts of the coronavirus pandemic on Europe's tourism industry: Addressing tourism enterprises and workers in the undeclared economy. J. Tour. Res. **23**, 79–88 (2021)
41. Baun, T., Nguyen, T.T.H.: Hospitality, tourism, human rights and the impact of COVID-19. Int. J. Contemp. Hosp. Manag. **32**(7), 2397–2407 (2020)
42. International Labour Organisation, http://www.ilo.org/wcmsp5/groups/public/%96dgreports/%96dcomm/documents/briefingnote/wcms%5F740877.pdf
43. Zou, Z.H., Guo, W., Liao, S.F.: Employment discrimination, social identity and informal tourism employment groups. Tour. Forum **9**(1), 55–62 (2016)
44. Xu, Y.W., Gan, Q.L.: The growth path of tourism informal sector based on grounded theory: a case of Xidi ancient village in Anhui. Hum. Geogr. **151**(5), 99–105 (2016)
45. Zhang, K.S., Ding, S.L., Liu, C.H.: The impact of informal employment on residents' social justice cognition——The experience analysis of the Chinese general social survey. Mod. Financ. Econ.-J. Tianjin Univ. Financ. Econ. **37**(9), 65–76 (2017)
46. Zhang, K.S., Ding, S.L., Liu, C.H.: A study on the impact of informal employment on social integration of residents——based on empirical analysis of the survey of dynamic labor market in China. Economist **12**, 20–29 (2016)
47. Fei, X. X., Dong, Y., Peng, X. M.: Research on the influence of informal employment on workers' subjective well-being. J. Qiqihar Univ. (Philos. Soc. Sci. Ed.) **8**, 44–49,61 (2019)
48. Zhang, Y.J., Qin, B.: Spatial agglomeration of informal employment and its co-location with formal employment—based on empirical study of manufacturing and customer services. Econ. Geogr. **35**(8), 142–148 (2015)

Predicting Green Hotel Visit Intention of College Students Using the Adjusted Theory of Planned Behavior

Yiwei Zhang, Aiping Xu, and Lin Gu

Abstract Due to the COVID-19 pandemic, to promote the green consumption has become one of the important marketing strategies for tourism and hotel industry. It is crucial for green hotels to predict customers' visit intention. The present study tries to identify the factors that affect the college students' green hotel visit intention using the theory of planned behavior (TPB). An online survey is employed to gather data from 260 college students. A subsequent analysis is then applied to the data using a moderated-mediation model. The findings show that a student's attitude, subjective norm, and perceived behavior control can positively and significantly influence the intention for a student's green hotel visit. Particularly, the attitude plays the greatest role. Moreover, our moderated-mediation model analysis shows that a student's attitude towards green hotels mediates the relationship between subjective norm and the visit intention. A student's perceived behavior control moderates the attitude on the intention. We believe that our study provides some new insights for the customers' visit intention towards green hotels. We highlight the important and new roles of attitude and perceived control behavior in the formation of intention.

Keywords Green hotel · Visit intention · College students · TPB

1 Introduction

The outbreak and spread of COVID-19 has caused severe damage to the global economy [1], and shocked the global tourism industry due to travel restrictions. According to the statistics of the United Nations World Tourism Organization, the

Y. Zhang · L. Gu
Shanghai Sanda University, Shanghai, China
e-mail: zyw9001@126.com

L. Gu
e-mail: mikaela98@126.com

A. Xu (✉)
Shanghai Polytechnic University, Shanghai, China
e-mail: xuaiping_2008@163.com

number of international tourists in 2020 dropped by 74%, and the loss of international tourism revenue was 1.3 trillion US dollars. Although the tourism industry has suffered considerable stagnation, COVID-19 has forced people to rethink the relationship between humans and ecosystems and become more aware of the importance of the environment [2]. Due to COVID-19, green marketing has become one of the important marketing strategies of tourism and hotel industry [3].

Green hotels are defined as "environmentally friendly property whose managers are eager to institute programs that save water, save energy, and reduce solid waste-while saving money-to help protect our one and only earth" [4]. Green hotels can not only help protect the environment, but also help reduce operating costs and increase revenue by reducing energy consumption [5]. However, the success of green hotels depends on consumers' green habits and behaviors. Therefore, understanding consumers' attitudes and intentions towards green hotels is very important for hotels to gain a competitive advantage in the accommodation market.

A wide range of literature has identified consumers' green hotel visit intentions and behaviors. However, few studies have focused on college students' intention to visit green hotels. Students are current/potential customers of the hotel. Understanding their intentions can not only help hotels understand their customers, especially future customers, but also help them adjust their marketing strategies.

This paper uses the theory of planned behavior to study the intention of college students to visit green hotels in the COVID-19 pandemic. We found that green consumption attitudes, subjective norms, and perceived behavior control all have a significant positive impact on green hotel visit intentions. Among them, the role of attitude is the most important. At the same time, we adjusted the traditional model of TPB and discovered the mediating role of attitudes in the relationship between subjective norms and students' willingness to consume green hotels, and the mediating role of perceived behavior control in the relationship between attitudes and students' visit intentions.

The rest of this article is organized as follows. In the next section, we discuss relevant literature and provide theoretical arguments related to green hotel visit intentions. Next, we introduce our methods and data. After that we show and discuss the results. Finally, we outline the conclusions and some directions for future research.

2 Conceptual Framework

2.1 Theory of Planned Behavior (TPB)

Consumer behavior is affected by psychological factors, social factors, and economic factors. Various theories of consumer behavior have been put forward [6]. The theory of planned behavior (TPB) is widely used to explain consumer's behavior in many fields, such as health behaviors [7], leisure choice [8], internet using [9], as well as green behaviors [10].

TPB is the extension of the theory of Reasoned Action (TRA). TRA assumes that people are rational, and the behavior is mainly determined by intention. When people believe that the behavior will result in a specific outcome, they will take or not take action [11]. The intention is the core concept in TRA, which is a function of attitude and subjective norm. However, TRA addresses a high degree of volitional control in the decision-making process [12], and ignores the non-motivational factors such as requisite opportunities and resources [11]. So TPB extends the boundary of conditions of TRA and incorporates perceived behavior control as one of the important factors determining an individual's behavior intention [6]. Thus, TPB has wider applicability than TRA and allows us to analyze an individual's intention and behavior under the circumstance of non-volitional control [12].

2.2 Hypothesis Development

2.2.1 Attitude

Attitude plays a central role in understanding individual behavior. Attitude refers to "degree to which a person has a favorable or unfavorable evaluation of the behavior in question" [6]. As a measurable psychological component, attitude is believed to be rooted in significant behavioral beliefs and outcome assessments [13]. Ajzen [6] believes that people will form a favorable attitude towards behaviors related to desirable outcomes, and vice versa. Generally speaking, attitudes can guide, influence, shape or predict the actual behavior of an individual [14]. The stronger and more stable the attitude, the more predictable one's behavior.

In the context of green consumption, with the rise of environmentalism, consumers' environmental attitudes will have a positive impact on his/her decision to choose green hotels [10, 15, 16]. In the TPB model, attitude is considered to be the most important factor predicting consumers' intentions to visit green hotels [10]. Kang et al. [15] even found that consumers with higher environmental attitudes will pay a premium for green hotels in the United States due to social recognition. Hence, we put forward that:

H1: Attitude has a significant and positive influence on the student's green hotel visit intention.

2.2.2 Subjective Norm

In the model of TPB, the subjective norm is defined as "the perceived social pressure to perform or not to perform the behavior" [11]. People are embedded in social networks [17], so they must follow the norms [18]. Other people, especially those who are important to the individual, such as family, relatives, friends, colleagues, and neighbors, can influence his/her decision-making [10, 13].

When consumers make green hotel choices, subjective norm is an important determinant. For decades, people have realized the importance of environmental protection. Environmental protection has gradually become a social norm and has an important impact on green consumption. More and more people are beginning to change their consumption habits and needs, and try to buy environmentally friendly products [19, 20]. Other people's views on environmental protection will affect consumers' green hotel visit decisions. Han and Kim [13], Verma and Chandra [10] found that subjective norms have a significant positive impact on consumers' intentions to visit/revisit green hotels. The stronger the personal subjective norm, the higher the intention to visit green hotels. Therefore, we put forward our hypothesis:

H2: Subjective norm has a significant and positive influence on student's green hotel visit intention.

2.2.3 Perceived Behavior Control

Consumers' behavior is affected by non-motivational factors, such as resources and opportunities, which represent people's actual control over their behaviors [6]. However, it is more important to study perceived control from the perspective of psychology. Ajzen [6] proposed the concept of perceived behavior control, which is defined as "people's perception of the ease or difficulty of performing the behavior of interest". When an individual thinks that the more resources and opportunities he has, the fewer obstacles he expects, the stronger his control of perceived behavior will be. Many studies have shown that there is a positive correlation between perceived behavior control and consumer's intention, as is research on green hotel visit [10, 13, 21]. For example, a recent study by Verna and Chandra [10] verified a positive correlation between perceived behavior control and green hotel visit intentions through a structural model. Hence, we hypothesize:

H3: Perceived behavior control significantly and positively influences the student's intention to visit green hotel.

2.2.4 Adjusted Relationship Among Attitude, Subjective Norm and Perceived Behavior Control

TPB pointed out that attitude, subjective norm, and perceived behavior control all affect consumers' behavioral intentions. These three factors are parallel and influence each other. But we argued that student's green hotel attitude is affected by subjective norm. Attitude is affected by various factors. Han, Hsu, and Sheu [12], Han and Kim [13] found that subjective norm has a significant and positive impact on attitude toward intention of visiting green hotel. It means that significant others (such as family, friends, and so on) can influence an individual's attitude formation through social pressure [13, 22].

The influence of student attitudes on the intentions to visit green hotels is also moderated by perceived behavioral control. Green products usually cost more than ordinary products, and consumers should pay more for these products [23, 24]. Not all consumers are willing to pay a premium for green products [25], especially those low-income students, which will reduce their positive attitudes and intentions towards green hotels. In China, although most green hotels do not require premium prices, they do not provide personal toiletries, which is actually more costly for students. Students' perceived behavior control can reduce the influence of attitude on intention. If a student feels more control over taking certain actions (such as sufficient resources), even though he/she has low attitude toward green hotel, he/she still has intention to visit a green hotel [12].

Hence, based on the discussion above, we hypothesize:

H4: Attitude is significantly and positively influenced by the student's subjective norm.

H5: Perceived behavior control can weaken the effect of the student's green hotel visit attitude on intention.

3 Methodology

3.1 Measures

The questionnaire in this article consists of three parts: The first part is the description of the questionnaire, which mainly explains the purpose of the questionnaire and the requirements for answering the questionnaire. The second part is a survey of personal information, including the student's gender, grade, major and monthly living expenses. The third part is the construction of the TPB model, including the construction of predictors (attitude, subjective norms and perceived behavior control) and student's intention to visit green hotel. There is no standard TPB questionnaire [13]. Therefore, we adopted a verified questionnaire and adjusted it according to research needs and China's national conditions. These items are all measured using Likert's five-level scale, from 1 for "strongly disagree" to 5 for "strongly agree".

3.2 Data Collection

The subjects of this study are college students. Internet-based questionnaires are considered to be an effective survey method [26], so we publish questionnaires via the Internet. From January 29 to February 6, 2020, a total of 281 questionnaires were received. 26 questionnaires were considered invalid because the completion time was too short or there was no choice to change. In the end, 260 valid questionnaires were obtained, with an effective rate of 92.5%. The demographic characteristics of the respondents are shown in Table 1.

Table 1 Demographic characteristics distribution table

Variables	Frequency	Percentage (%)
Gender		
Male	119	45.8
Female	141	54.2
Grade		
Freshman	23	8.8
Sophomore	42	16.2
Junior	60	23.1
Senior	109	41.9
Master and above	26	10.0
Major		
Science and Engineering (MajorSE)	64	24.6
Economy and Business (MajorEB)	86	33.1
Literature, History and Philosophy (MajorLHP)	70	26.9
Others	40	15.4
Monthly living expenses (LivingEx)		
Below 1000 RMB	37	14.2
1000–1500RMB	108	41.5
1501–2000 RMB	69	26.5
Above 2001 RMB	46	17.7

Reliability analysis is used to test whether the data collected by the questionnaire is consistent. The most commonly used method is Cronbach's α. It is generally believed that Cronbach's α between 0.6 and 0.7 is acceptable, and greater than 0.7 is the best. The higher the α, the higher the reliability of the questionnaire. Cronbach's α in this study is 0.850, which is greater than 0.7, indicating that the overall reliability of the questionnaire is relatively high. Table 2 is the summary statistics of the variables, and Table 3 is the correlation matrix between all independent variables.

4 Result

4.1 Effect of Attitude, Subjective Norm and Perceived Behavior Control

We tested the impact of student's attitude, subjective norm, and perceived behavior control on their intention to visit green hotel. We use OLS regression to estimate the coefficients. Table 4 shows the results. In Model 1, we estimate the basic specifications including the control variables. Coefficient estimates indicate that there is no

Table 2 Summary statistics of variables

Variables	n	Mean	sd	Median	Min	Max
Gender	260	0.542	0.499	1	0	1
Grade	260	3.281	1.123	4	1	5
MajorSE	260	0.246	0.432	0	0	1
MajorEB	260	0.331	0.471	0	0	1
MajorLHP	260	0.269	0.444	0	0	1
LivingEx	260	2.477	0.944	2	1	4
AT	260	3.924	0.741	4	1.2	5
SN	260	3.960	0.727	4	1	5
PBC	260	3.744	0.872	4	1.25	5
Intent	260	4.099	0.604	4.25	2	5

Note AT = attitude, SN = subjective norm, PBC = perceived behavior control, Intent = Intention

significant relationship between demographic characteristics and green hotel visit intention. In Model 2, we estimate the coefficients of the core independent variables. In Model 3, we estimate the specification that includes both control variables and independent variables. The coefficients of attitude, subjective norm and perceived behavior control in Model 3 are 0.286 (p = 0.000), 0.231 (p = 0.000) and 0.104 (p = 0.006), respectively. The results show that student's attitude, subjective norm and perceived behavior control have a positive and significant impact on green hotel visit intention. H1, H2 and H3 are verified. In addition, we found that attitude has a greater influence than subjective norm and perceived behavior control. This result is consistent with previous studies [10, 12].

4.2 The Mediation Effect of Attitude

In this part, we use the causal process to examine the mediating role of attitude between subjective norm and intention [27, 28]. We test the relationship between the independent variable and the dependent variable first. We then test the relationship between the independent variables and the mediating variables. Finally, the relationship between the mediator and the dependent variables are tested. The results are shown in Table 5. Model 1 shows subjective norm has a significant impact on student's intention to visit green hotel ($\beta = 0.373$, p = 0.000). Model 2 shows subjective norm also has a significant impact on student's attitude ($\beta = 0.360$, p = 0.000). In Model 3, attitude has a significant impact on student's intention ($\beta = 0.310$, p = 0.000). Although the coefficient of subjective norm is still significant (p = 0.000), it is smaller than that in Model 1 ($\beta = 0.262 < \beta = 0.373$). The result shows that attitude has a partial mediation effect between subjective norm and green hotel visit intention. H4 is verified.

Table 3 Correlation matrix

	Gender	Grade	MajorSE	MajorEB	MajorLHP	LivingEx	AT	SN	PBC
Gender	1.000								
Grade	0.320***	1.000							
MajorSE	−0.031	−0.071	1.000						
MajorEB	−0.010	0.006	−0.402***	1.000					
MajorLHP	0.123*	0.034	−0.347***	−0.427***	1.000				
LivingEx	0.072	0.095	−0.052	−0.113	0.042	1.000			
AT	0.010	−0.029	−0.132*	0.044	0.044	−0.04	1.000		
SN	−0.070	−0.123*	−0.064	0.090	−0.107	0.023	0.351***	1.000	
PBC	0.005	0.016	−0.027	−0.007	−0.088	0.001	0.280***	0.318***	1.000

Note $*p < 0.05; **p < 0.01; ***p < 0.001$

Table 4 TPB model

Variables	Model 1		Model 2		Model 3	
	Estimate	t value	Estimate	t value	Estimate	t value
Gender	0.127	1.590			0.118	1.806*
Grade	−0.050	−1.402			−0.023	−0.804
MajorSE	−0.218	−1.769*			−0.046	−0.449
MajorEB	−0.105	−0.891			−0.041	−0.425
MajorLHP	−0.202	−1.666*			−0.079	−0.790
LivingEx	−0.045	−1.121			−0.038	−1.151
AT			0.289	6.484***	0.286	6.333***
SN			0.231	5.028***	0.231	4.927***
PBC			0.108	2.887***	0.104	2.755***
Constant	4.320	22.320***	1.649	7.860***	1.708	6.157***
R2	0.030		0.355		0.367	
Adjusted R2	0.007		0.347		0.344	
F	1.292		46.89		16.08	

Note $*p < 0.10$; $**p < 0.05$; $***p < 0.01$

Table 5 The mediation effect of attitude

Variables	Model 1		Mode 2		Model 3	
	Intention		Attitude		Intention	
	Estimate	t value	Estimate	t value	Estimate	t value
Gender	0.136	1.898*	0.046	0.495	0.122	1.850*
Grade	−0.019	−0.604	0.001	0.025	−0.020	−0.668
MajorSE	−0.128	−1.157	−0.192	−1.343	−0.069	−0.673
MajorEB	−0.085	−0.809	−0.042	−0.310	−0.072	−0.746
MajorLHP	−0.101	−0.922	0.050	0.353	−0.116	−1.157
LivingEx	−0.054	−1.499	−0.047	−1.005	−0.040	−1.193
SN	0.373	7.932***	0.360	5.929***	0.262	5.675***
AT					0.310	6.902***
Constant	2.697	10.050***	2.590	7.483***	1.895	6.953***
R2	0.224		0.14		0.347	
Adjusted R2	0.202		0.12		0.327	
F	10.37		5.94		16.7	

Note $*p < 0.10$; $**p < 0.05$; $***p < 0.01$

Table 6 The mediation effect of attitude with mediation package

	Estimate	P	Estimate bootstrap10000	P
ACME	0.0995	0.000	0.104	0.000
ADE	0.2537	0.000	0.233	0.000
Total effect	0.3532	0.000	0.337	0.000
Prop. Mediated	0.2820	0.000	0.308	0.000

To further illustrate the mediation effect, we use the mediation package in R to test the effect [29]. Both non-bootstrap and bootstrap are used to estimate the average causal mediating effect (ACME) and the average direct effect (ADE). The results are shown in Table 6. We found that the estimated ACME and ADE are significantly different from zero within the 95% confidence interval, which indicates that attitude plays a mediating role between subjective norm and intention. The moderating effect accounted for 30.8% of the total effect.

4.3 Moderating Effect of Perceived Behavior Control

In this part, we estimate the moderating effect of perceived behavior control on student's attitude and intention. Figure 1 depicts the moderating effect of perceived behavior control. Table 7 lists the regression results. The estimated coefficient of the moderating effect is negative and significantly different from zero ($\beta = -0.093$, p $= 0.030$ in model 3). This means that perceptual behavior control can weaken the influence of student's attitude on intention of visiting green hotel. So H5 is verified.

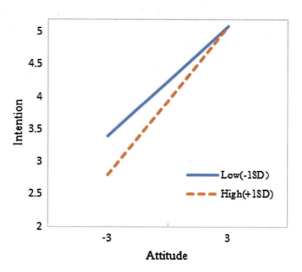

Fig. 1 Figure of moderating effect

Table 7 Moderating effect of perceived behavior control

Variables	Model 1		Model 2		Model 3	
	Estimate	t value	Estimate	t value	Estimate	t value
Gender	0.112	1.609	0.119	1.755*	0.130	1.999**
Grade	−0.038	−1.241	−0.034	−1.130	−0.016	−0.563
MajorSE	−0.107	−0.987	−0.081	−0.771	−0.060	−0.597
MajorEB	−0.080	−0.784	−0.061	−0.601	−0.068	−0.711
MajorLHP	−0.183	−1.729	−0.144	−1.378	−0.105	−1.052
LivingEx	−0.030	−0.851	−0.023	−0.660	−0.031	−0.953
AT	0.399	8.949***	0.353	7.848	0.288	6.434***
SN			0.140	3.627	0.094	2.490***
PBC					0.233	5.011***
AT*PBC			−0.089	−1.985**	−0.093	−2.189**
Control	2.664	10.628***	4.178	25.427***	3.189	12.654***
R2	0.264		0.316		0.379	
Adjusted R2	0.243		0.291		0.354	
F	12.89		12.83		15.17	

Note $*p < 0.10$; $**p < 0.05$; $***p < 0.01$

5 Conclusion and Discussion

5.1 Conclusion

In this study we verified the traditional model of TPB and found that attitude, subjective norm and perceived behavior control have a significant positive impact on student's intention to visit green hotel. We also found that attitude plays the most important role in the student's decision-making process of visiting green hotel. These results are consistent with previous studies.

In addition, we found that attitude has a mediating role in the relationship between subjective norm and intention. Subjective norm not only directly affects the student's intention, but also indirectly affects the intention to visit green hotel through attitude. At the same time, we found that perceived behavior control has a moderating role in the relationship between attitude and intention. Perceived behavior control can weaken the role of attitude.

Although some studies have found demographic differences in consumer intentions [19, 30]. For example, female customers are more likely to purchase green accommodation products [19]. There is little evidence that demographic characteristics have a significant influence on student's intention in our study.

5.2 Implication

College students are future customers, and their green hotel visit intentions are of great significance to the environmental protection and sustainable development of the future society. Since attitude is one of the most important factors that determine personal intention, colleges and universities should develop green education to improve students' attitudes towards green consumption. In particular, schools should advocate the concept of green consumption on campus and promote it as a social norm.

In order to encourage green consumption, hotels should strive to reduce costs, provide a variety of options, and improve customers' perception and behavior control capabilities. At the same time, hotels also need to continuously improve service quality so that customers can feel the value of green consumption.

5.3 Future Research

Green hotel visit intention is an interesting topic. Although we have discovered the mediating role of attitude and the moderating role of perceived behavior control, there are still some limitations that deserve further study. First, we should expand the survey sample to further verify our hypothesis. Secondly, more mediators and moderator factors should be found in the study of green hotel visit intention. Third, we should extend our model to other green products, not just green hotels.

References

1. Gössling, S., Scott, D., Hall, C.M.: Pandemics, tourism and global change: a rapid assessment of COVID-19. J. Sustain. Tour. **29**(1), 1–20 (2020)
2. Zhou, P., Yang, X. L., Wang, X. G., Hu, B., Zhang, L., Zhang, W., ... Shi, Z. L.: pneumonia outbreak associated with a new coronavirus of probable bat origin. Nature **579**(7798), 270–273 (2020)
3. Jiang, Y., Wen, J.: Effects of covid-19 on hotel marketing and management: a perspective article. Int. J. Contemp. Hosp. Manag. **32**(8), 2563–2573 (2020)
4. Green Hotels Association: what are green hotels?. (2014). Retrieved from http://www.greenhotels.com, 27 July, 2020
5. Manaktola, K., Jauhari, V.: Exploring consumer attitude and behaviour towards green practices in the lodging industry in India. Int. J. Contemp. Hosp. Manag. **19**(5), 364–377 (2007)
6. Ajzen, I.: The theory of planned behavior. Organ. Behav. Hum. Decis. Process **50**(2), 179–211 (1991)
7. Conner, M., Norman, P., Bell, R.: The theory of planned behavior and healthy eating. Health Psychol. **21**(2), 194–201 (2002)
8. Hrubes, D., Ajzen, I., Daigle, J.: Predicting hunting intentions and behavior: an application of the theory of planned behavior. Leis. Sci. **23**(3), 165–178 (2001)
9. Pavlou, P.A., Fygenson, M.: Understanding and predicting electronic commerce adoption: An extension of the theory of planned behavior. MIS Q., 115–143 (2006)

10. Verma, V.K., Chandra, B.: An application of theory of planned behavior to predict young Indian consumers' green hotel visit intention. J. Clean. Prod. **172**, 1152–1162 (2018)
11. Madden, T.J., Ellen, P.S., Ajzen, I.: A comparison of the theory of planned behavior and the theory of reasoned action. Pers. Soc. Psychol. Bull. **18**(1), 3–9 (1992)
12. Han, H., Hsu, L.T.J., Sheu, C.: Application of the theory of planned behavior to green hotel choice: Testing the effect of environmental friendly activities. Tour. Manag. **31**(3), 325–334 (2010)
13. Han, H., Kim, Y.: An investigation of green hotel customers' decision formation: developing an extended model of the theory of planned behavior. Int. J. Hosp. Manag. **29**(4), 659–668 (2010)
14. Kraus, S.J.: Attitudes and the prediction of behavior: A meta-analysis of the empirical literature. Pers. Soc. Psychol. Bull. **21**(1), 58–75 (1995)
15. Kang, K., Stein, L., Heo, C.Y., Lee, S.: Consumers' willingness to pay for green initiatives of the hotel industry. Int. J. Hosp. Manag. **31**(2), 564–572 (2012)
16. Han, H., Hsu, L.T., Lee, J.S.: Empirical investigation of the roles of attitudes toward green behaviors, overall image, gender, and age in hotel customers' eco-friendly decision-making process. Int. J. Hosp. Manag. **28**(4), 519–528 (2009)
17. Lin, N.: Building a network theory of social capital. Connections **22**(1), 28–51 (1999)
18. Burt, R.S.: The network structure of social capital. Res. Organ. Behav. **22**, 345–423 (2000)
19. Han, H., Hsu, L.T.J., Lee, J.S., Sheu, C.: Are lodging customers ready to go green? An examination of attitudes, demographics, and eco-friendly intentions. Int. J. Hosp. Manag. **30**(2), 345–355 (2011)
20. Roberts, J.A.: Green consumers in the 1990s: Profile and implications for advertising. J. Bus. Res. **36**, 217–231 (1996)
21. Chen, M.F., Tung, P.J.: Developing an extended theory of planned behavior model to predict consumers' intention to visit green hotels. Int. J. Hosp. Manag. **36**, 221–230 (2014)
22. Ryu, K., Jang, S.: Intention to experience local cuisine in a travel destination: the modified theory of reasoned action. J. Hosp. Tour. Res. **30**(4), 507–516 (2006)
23. Chia-Jung, C., Pei-Chun, C.: Preferences and willingness to pay for green hotel attributes in tourist choice behavior: the case of Taiwan. J. Travel. Tour. Mark. **31**(8), 937–957 (2014)
24. Haws, K.L., Winterich, K.P., Naylor, R.W.: Seeing the world through GREEN-tinted glasses: Green consumption values and responses to environmentally friendly products. J. Consum. Psychol. **24**(3), 336–354 (2014)
25. Millar, M., Baloglu, S.: Hotel guests' preferences for green guest room attributes. Cornell Hosp. Q. **52**, 302–311 (2011)
26. Kim, S.: E-mail survey response rates: A review. J. Comput. Mediat. Comm. **6**(2), 1–20 (2001)
27. Baron, R.M., Kenny, D.A.: The moderator-mediator variable distinction in social psychological research: conceptual, strategic, and statistical considerations. J. Pers. Soc. Psychol. **51**(6), 1173–1182 (1986)
28. Judd, C.M., Kenny, D.A.: Process analysis: Estimating mediation in treatment evaluations. Eval. Rev. **5**(5), 602–619 (1981)
29. Tingley, D., Yamamoto, T., Hirose, K., Keele, L., Imai, K.: Mediation: R package for causal mediation analysis. J. Stat. Softw. **59**(5), 1–38 (2014)
30. Han, H., Ryu, K.: Moderating role of personal characteristics in forming restaurant customers' behavioral intentions: an upscale restaurant setting. J. Leis. Mark. **15**(4), 25–53 (2006)

Tourism Research on National Parks and Protected Areas

Donghui Lu, Xiaoyu Wang, and Hongxi Zhang

Abstract By visualizing bibliometric data, this work tries to describe the scholarly landscape of the tourism research field on national parks and protected areas. Data of 930 specific documents published between 1996 and 2020 were collected from Web of Science, using VOSviewer and CiteSpace to employ collaboration analysis, co-citation analysis, and co-occurrence analysis. The results show that national parks and protected areas have been good study samples for 12 tourism forms like wildlife tourism, community-based tourism, etc. The discussions of this field focus on environment conservation, visitor experience, community development, and climate change, and the best solutions to achieve the state of the art of them are provided. It was examined that 9 topics like recreation and outdoor recreation, resilience, etc. are the key hotspots. World Tourism Oganization should take national parks and protected areas as the KPI to assess the sustainable development of each country since the importance disgussed in this paper. There should be greater communication among the scholars and practitioners from different fields or departments due to the cross-diciplines social networks. This research provides clear empirical evidence for literature reviews from diverse perspectives, as well as for improving national park and protected area development and research.

Keywords National parks · Protected areas · Bibliometric analysis · CiteSpace · VOSviewer · COVID-19

D. Lu
Guangdong Technology College, Zhaoqing, Guangdong, People's Republic of China

X. Wang (✉)
Tourism Management Department, Management School of Jinan University, 601 West Huangpu Avenue, Tianhe District, Guangzhou, People's Republic of China

Jinan University, Guangzhou, Guangdong, People's Republic of China

H. Zhang
South China University of Technology, Guangzhou, Guangdong, People's Republic of China
e-mail: hongxizh@gzmu.edu.cn

Guizhou Minzu Unversity, Guiyang, Guizhou, People's Republic of China

© The Author(s), under exclusive license to Springer Nature Singapore Pte Ltd. 2022
Y. Luo et al. (eds.), *Tourism, Aviation and Hospitality Development During the COVID-19 Pandemic*, https://doi.org/10.1007/978-981-19-1661-8_14

1 Introduction

There has been an increase in the volume of study on national parks and protected areas in recent years, and systematic reviews or scientific maps are needed to assist researchers and practitioners in fully comprehending this topic. Previous reviews or bibliometric analyses limited their discussion to research samples, areas, or management, for example; however, this study uses bibliometric analysis to examine systemetically exclusively from the standpoint of tourism. National parks and protected areas are the best solutions for managing sustainable tourism [1]. International Union for Conservation of Nature (IUCN), and its World Commission on Protected Areas (WCPA), has defined "National Park" in Category II as large natural or near natural areas set aside to protect large-scale ecological processes, along with the complement of species and ecosystems characteristic of the area, which also provide a foundation for environmentally and culturally compatible spiritual, scientific, educational, recreational and visitor opportunities [2]. In other words, "national park" is one of the protected areas categories. While IUCN defined distinguished features and criteria for national parks, many protected areas in many countries are called national parks even when they correspond to other categories of the IUCN Protected Area Management Definition [3]. Searching "national park*" but not "Parkinson" in the Web of Science database got 60,879 results (Date: August 21, 2020), which suggested that the research on national parks and protected areas are well documented, there is enough data for bibliometric analysis, and no prior study using this approach to analyze the data only in the category of tourism of Web of Science. Some massive visitors traveled to national parks or protected areas every year for sight-seeing or outdoor recreation all over the world, the present study aims to discuss national parks and protected areas that can contribute to the local economy through tourism, and try to map out the tourism research progress of national park and protected areas.

2 Material and Methodology

2.1 Data Collection

All the data of the current study were collected from ISI Web of Science Core Collection and made sure the data contained full records and could be employed co-citation analysis. Data of 930 pieces of literature that included 658 articles, 259 proceeding papers, 23 reviews, and 22 early accesses published between 1996 and 2020 were collected by topic searching of "national park*" or "protected area*" refined in the category of "hospitality leisure sport tourism", by the time of 21:29, July 25th, 2020. Proceeding papers show their importance when the unrefined search results were ranked by cited frequencies, and should not be excluded from the sample data.

2.2 Methodologies

The current study employed bibliometric analysis with VOSviewer and CiteSpace software packages, both of them have a powerful function in co-occurrence analysis and co-citation analysis [4, 5]. A science map from the bibliometric analysis can represent the discipline situation and development status [6]. Hall [7] classifies evaluative metrics into three groups. The first group includes productivity measures. The second includes impact measures. The third consists of hybrid metrics. Relational techniques explore relationships among the research fields, the emergence of new research themes and methods, or co-citation and co-authorship patterns [8]. Relational techniques can be divided into four categories: co-citation analysis, co-word analysis, co-authorship analysis, and bibliographic coupling and implemented in CiteSpace or VOSviewer software packages.

3 Results

3.1 The Annual Trends of Publications and Cited Times

Figure 1 shows that the counts (curved line) and cited times (bars) of the publications. 930 documents accumulated 6639 citations. As the inclusion in SSCI of *Tourism Management (TM)* and *Annal of Tourism Research (ATR)* began in 2006, that of *Journal of Travel Research (JTR)* and *Journal of Sustainable Tourism (JOST)* began from 2008, the annual statistic is senseless before 2006. Both the publication numbers and their cited times increased sharply from 2014, implying the importance of the research in this field. Added trendline for the period between 2006 and 2019 for the curve and the bars, returned with two regression lines and their R^2. $Y_p = 8.4088X - 16860$ ($R_p^2 = 0.9746$) for publications and $Y_c = 90.699X - 182117$ ($R_c^2 = 0.9015$) for the cited times. Table 1 shows that research articles were published in *JOST* and

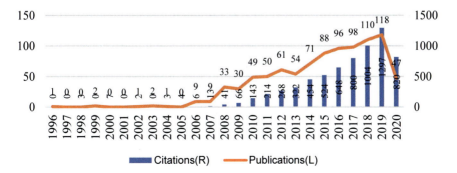

Fig. 1 Publications and citations (1996–2020)

Table 1 Top 5 Journals (1996–2020)

Journal	Records	% of 930
Journal of Sustainable Tourism	174	18.71
Tourism Management	100	10.75
Journal of Outdoor Recreation and Tourism Research Planning and Management	45	4.84
Tourism Management Perspectives	37	3.98
Current Issues in Tourism	35	3.76

TM. Added trendline to the annual publication curve of JOST and returned with $Y_{st} = 7.556X - 15,138$ ($R^2 = 0.8738$), similar to Y_p, which suggests previous research of this topic is mainly contributed by key tourism journals and play an important role in sustainable tourism research.

3.2 Contributed Authors and Their Collaborative Networks

Authors of scientific literature are the subject of scientific research activities. 2037 authors were examined and 510 of them earned 0 citations. 460 of them collaborated with other authors no more than 1 time. Most of the citations were distributed to a few core authors. Table 2 lists the authors by documents ranking, citation ranking, co-authorship ranking, coupling ranking, and co-citation ranking. The most productive authors with their articles numbers are Gyan P. Nyaupane (11), Betty Weiler (10), Susan A. Moore (10), Melville Saayman(8), Jie Zhang (7), Kate Rodger (7), Peter Fredman (7) and Petra Hlavackova (7). The most influential authors with their citations are Susan A. Moore (503), Betty Weiler (498), Ramkissoon Haywantee (472), Liam David Graham Smith (445), and Ralf Buckley (436). The core authors are leading the research orientation of the discipline.

Ralf Buckley, C.M. Hall, P.F.J. Eagles, D.B. Weaver, C. Ryan, D. Scott, S. Gosling, Bill Bramwell, RE Manning, Ajzen I, S. Becken, G. Brown, R, Sharpley, Gyan P. Nyaupane, and Lee T.H. were mostly co-cited by the other authors, most of them are the editorial board member of *JOST* or the core authors of sustainable tourism study [1]. Some of them won over 100 citations only with 1 document. The research in this field is established on their contributions.

The co-authorship link strength in Table 2 explains the frequency of collaborative networks. The stronger the strength is, the more collaborative the author is. Figure 2 visualizes the authors' collaborative network. There isn't enough universal collaboration but separated into many small groups. The authors from China have stronger co-authorship link strength, as well as stronger coupling strength, which suggests that the more collaboration, the more coupling, especially for authors endowed with

Table 2 Top 15 Authors Ranking (1996–2020)

No	By documents (counts)	By citations (counts)	By coauthorship (links)	By coupling (links)	By co-citation (TLS)
1	Nyaupane, Gyan P. (11)	Moore, Susan A. (503)	Newman, Peter (29)	Weiler, Betty (10,005)	Buckley, R. (16,702)
2	Moore, Susan A. (10)	Weiler, Betty (498)	Weiler, Betty (31)	Moore, Susan A. (8985)	Hall, C.M. (14,391)
3	Weiler, Betty (10)	Ramkissoon, H. (472)	Zhang, Jie (26)	Zhang, Jie (6675)	Eagles, P.F.J. (11,507)
4	Saayman, Melville (7)	Smith, L. Graham (445)	Moore, Susan A. (22)	Ramkissoon, H. (6396)	Weaver, D.B. (11,268)
5	Fredman, Peter (7)	Buckley, Ralf (436)	Zhang, Honglei (21)	Nyaupane, G. P. (6128)	Ryan, C. (9954)
6	Rodger, Kate (7)	Ham, Sam H. (308)	Rodger, Kate (17)	Wolf, Isabelle D. (5699)	Scott, D. (9379)
7	Zhang, Jie (7)	Nyaupane, Gyan P. (275)	Brownlee, M. T. J. (17)	Rodger, Kate (5210)	Gossling, S. (8408)
8	Jakubis, Matus (7)	Deng, Jinyang (253)	Zheng, Chunhui (17)	Smith, L. D. G. (5183)	Bramwell, B. (8301)
9	Hlavackova, Petra (7)	Powell, Robert B. (246)	Deng, Jinyang (16)	Haukeland, Jan V. (4957)	Manning, RE. (7331)
10	Wolf, Isabelle D. (6)	Lepp, Andrew (213)	Saayman, Melville (16)	Zheng, Chunhui (4787)	Ajzen, I. (7108)
11	Haukeland, Jan V. (6)	Thapa, Brijesh (211)	Xiao, Xiao (16)	Zhang, Honglei (4774)	Becken, S. (6589)
12	Newman, Peter (6)	Tonge, Joanna (207)	Dawson, Jackie (16)	Moyle, Brent D. (4691)	Brown, G. (6543)
13	Brownlee, M. T. J. (6)	Kim, Hyounggon (193)	Moyle, Brent D. (16)	Newman, Peter (4357)	Sharpley, R (6471)
14	Wang, Erda (6)	Fredman, Peter (188)	Banerjee, Onil (16)	Fredman, Peter (4235)	Nyaupane, G.P (6453)
15	Banas, Marek (6)	Scott, Daniel (186)	Lal, Pankaj (16)	Saayman, M. (4199)	Lee, TH (6385)

TLS: Total Link Strength

different resources. There are 3 collaboration streams and 4 national or international clusters among the authors from China. Employed the authors overlay visualization results that research team in China are freshly active, this may lead to productive research output.

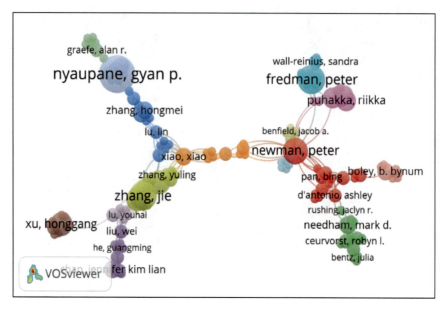

Fig. 2 Co-authorship collaborative networks (1996–2020)

3.3 Collaboration and Contribution of Organizations and Their Countries

There are 824 organizations examined and 576 of them contributed no more than 1 document, 165 of them have not been cited, 391 of them collaborated with the other organizations no more than once, and the top 20 of them contributed 34.1% of the total citations. The coupling analysis defined the most inferential organizations with their link strength are Griffith University (14,479), Clemson University (8222), Murdoch University (8130), Monash University (6747), University of Waterloo (5916), Arizona State University (5590), University of Johannesburg (5336), Sun Yat-Sen University (5301), University of Queensland (5234), Hong Kong Polytechnic University (4749), Norwegian Univ Life Sci (4573) and Nanjing University (4411).

Table 3 lists the top 15 organizations ranking of this research topic. The most productive organizations with their counts are Griffith University (31), Clemson University (21), Murdoch University (21), University of Johannesburg (15), and Sun Yat-Sen University (15). The contributions of Mendel University in Brno (41) and Technical University of Zvolen (16) are less comparative as most of them are book sections of the Public Recreation and Landscape Protection series. Tourism research on national parks and protected areas are an exactly nature-based study given that Surrey University and Hong Kong Polytechnic University, the leading organization in tourism and hospitality research, are absent from Table 3. The most actively collaborative organizations with their link strength are Clemson University (30), Griffith University (26), National Park Service in the USA (25), Pennsylvania

Table 3 Top15 Organization rankings (1996–2020)

No.	Documents (counts)	Citations (counts)	Collaborations (links)
1.	Mendel U brno (41)	Griffith univ (1228)	Clemson univ (30)
2.	Griffith univ (31)	Monash univ (801)	Griffith univ (26)
3.	Clemson univ (21)	Murdoch univ (627)	Natl pk serv (25)
4.	Murdoch univ (21)	So cross univ (502)	Penn state univ (24)
5.	Tech univ zvolen (16)	Univ waterloo (481)	Univ waterloo (21)
6.	Univ Johansbrg (15)	Texas a&m univ (442)	Murdoch univ (20)
7.	Sun yat sen univ (15)	Univ queensland (403)	Univ Johannsbrg (20)
8.	Univ waterloo (14)	Colorado s univ (370)	Arizona s univ (19)
9.	Arizona state univ (14)	Clemson univ (364)	Colorado s univ (19)
10.	Univ queensland (14)	Univ idaho (364)	Univ queenslnd (18)
11.	Penn state univ (13)	W virginia univ (305)	Sun yat sn univ (16)
12.	Colorado s univ(13)	Arizona s univ (282)	Univ oulu (16)
13.	Natl pk serv (12)	Sun yat-sen univ (275)	Utah state univ (16)
14.	North west univ (12)	Wageningen univ (246)	Auburn univ (15)
15.	Utah state univ (11)	Univ Wollongong (230)	Chinese acad sci (15)

State University (24), University of Waterloo (21), Murdoch University (20), University of Johannesburg (20), Arizona State University (19), Colorado State University (19), University Queensland (18), Sun Yat-Sen University (16), University of Oulu (16), Utah State University (16), Auburn University (15) and Chinese Academy of Science (15). The organizations in USA, Australia, and China are more comparatively open than the others. Figure 3 visualized the collaborative networks and clusters of organizations with their countries and regions.

15 clusters were examined. The collaboration led by the organizations of the USA focused on outdoor recreation, the collaboration led by the organizations of China focused on world heritage site destination and tourist's leisure participation. The collaboration led by Norway and New Zealand focused on the marine protected area. Outdoor recreation valued national parks and protected areas tourism from sightseeing pro-environmentally.

Table 4 lists 88 countries and regions examined by VOSveiwer, 27 of them contributed no more than 1 document, 36 of them collaborated without other countries no more than once. The most productive countries with their counts are USA (213), Australia (144), China (122), Czech Republic (84), U.K. (54),Canada(49), Slovakia (48), South Africa (38), South Korea (26), Spain (26), New Zealand (25), Malaysia (22), Norway (20), Germany (19), Sweden (17), etc. 68.54% of the total citations distributed to Australia (4303), USA (4060), China (1609), Canada (1185) and UK (897). The coupling analysis also shows that the USA (32,594), Australia (28,938), China (23,067), Canada (10,548) and UK (10,300) are also the top 5 countries. These five countries are the most influential. The Czech Republic and Slovakia are productive but less influential in this research area.

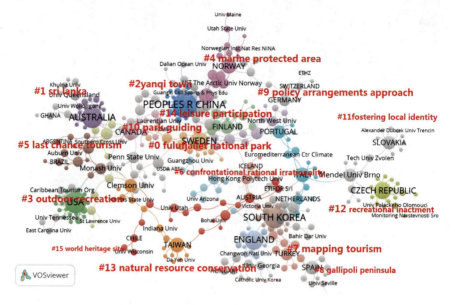

Fig. 3 Collaborative Network of Organizations (1996–2020). *Note* Generated and clustered by CiteSpace after finding path and merging network, visualized by VOSviewer

Table 4 Top10 Countries rankings (1996–2020)

No	Documents (counts)	Citations (counts)	Collaborations (links)	Coupling (TLS)
1	USA-213	Australia-4303	USA-90	USA-32594
2	Australia-144	USA-4060	Australia-62	Australia-28938
3	China-122	China-1609	China-55	China-23067
4	Czech R-84	Canada-1185	UK-35	Canada-10548
5	UK-54	UK-897	Canada-26	UK-10300
6	Canada-49	S Korea-484	S Africa-26	S Africa-7773
7	Slovakia-48	Spain-460	S Korea-24	S-Korea-6158
8	South Africa-38	N Zealand-449	N Zealand-21	Spain-5469
9	South Korea-26	Germany-385	Finland-15	Norway-5361
10	Spain-26	S Africa-382	Sweden-13	N Zealand-5127

TLS: total link strength

There are frequent collaborations among the USA and the members of commonwealth nations. 11 countries and regions were examined having co-authorship with P. R. China, the productive non-English speaking country, they are USA (11 links), Australia (7 links), New Zealand (7 links), Taiwan region (4 links), Canada (3 links), England (3 links), South Korea (2 links), Spain (1 link), South Africa (1 link) and

Austria (1 link), involving 5 native languages. Co-authorship is a good choice for non-English speaking countries and regions.

3.4 Funding Agencies Statistic

Nation Natural Science Foundation of China ranked No. 1 of funding agencies, supported 26 publications and 367 references, far more than the second-place funding agency. Sustainable tourism is institutionally driven from political economy perspective, the funding returns of the Nation Natural Science Foundation of China suggest that P. R. China acknowledges the importance of research in sustainable tourism as well as that in national parks and protected areas, which may return with more high-quality results.

3.5 Sources and Source Co-citation Networks

Sources analysis would target the core academic resource of a specific discipline or topic. As listed in Table 1, most of the articles were published on *JOST*, *TM*, *ATR*, and *JTR*, the key tourism academic journals.

Source co-citation networks would define the core theories for a specific discipline or topic. Figure 4 shows the co-citation network of the source. There are mainly 6 kinds of journals that were co-cited. The research in this field is a cross-disciplinaries topic integrated tourism, leisure, environment science, marketing and business, heritage and landscape plan.

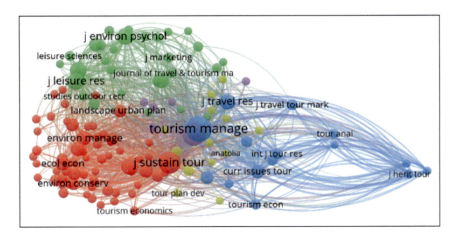

Fig. 4 Source co-citation network (1996–2020, $N_{citation} \geq 40$)

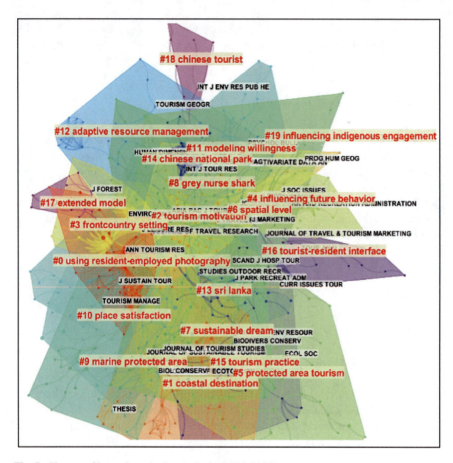

Fig. 5 Clusters of journal co-citation analysis (1996–2020)

Figure 5 shows the cluster analysis results of Journal co-citation. There are articles concerning tourism and tourist published in the journals beyond the WOS journal category of "hospitality leisure sport tourism". It is assumed that all authors cite while writing only essentially tourism-related references from non-tourism journals, the cluster labels will represent the mainstream topics. The clusters are resident-employed photography, coastal destination, tourism motivation, frontcountry, influencing future behaviour, protected area tourism, spatial level, sustainable dream, grey nurse shark, marine protected area, place satisfaction, modeling willingness, adaptive resource management, Sri Lanka, Chinese national park, tourism practice, tourist-resident interface, extended model, Chinese tourist, and influencing indigenous engagement.

3.6 Key Articles and Cited References

Table 5 lists the top 25 sample articles ranked by citations, and the citation networks are visualized in Fig. 6. Key articles implied the key theme of this specific topic. Buckley, Ralf (2012) published *Sustainable tourism: research and reality* on *Annual of Tourism Research* ranked the first place with 339 citations, followed by Ramkissoon with 215, then Powell et al. (2008) with 192 citations, and so on. As visualized by Fig. 6, the hot discussions are the authenticity, place attachment, pro-environmental behaviour, residents' attitudes, climate change, adaptive co-management, environmental motivation, protected area, tourists' satisfaction, visitor attraction management, tourists' travel, indigenous tourism, world heritage sites and nationalism.

Table 6 lists the top 24 co-cited references. The cited references co-citation analysis explains the base theories depended on, they shall be included in the literature reviews on this topic. There are 34,471 cited references detected. Focus on the visualization in Fig. 7, a few non-tourism articles published before 1990 are distinguished from most of the co-cited references published in tourism journals. Claes Fornell and David F. Larcker (1981) [9] published the article titled *Evaluating structural equation models with unobservable variables and measurement error* in the *Journal of Marketing Research*, proposed a more comprehensive testing system that based on measures of explanatory power (shared variance) for the (1) structural model, (2) measurement model, and (3) overall model. this article was cited 67,754 times in Microsoft Academic by Sept. 12, 2020. Besides, James C. Anderson et al. (1988) [10] also published the article titled *Structural equation modelling in practice: a review and recommended two-step approach* on *Psychological Bulletin*, discuss the comparative advantages of this approach over a one-step approach. Structural equation models have been a popular tool for social science research.

Icek Ajzen and Martin Fishbein [11] published the book titled *understanding attitudes and predicting social behavior* in 1979. The book is concerned with the prediction and understanding of human behaviour, explained the "theory and reasoned action" model, and then applied the model to various cases. It is cited 46,714 times in Microsoft Academic by Sept. 12, 2020. In 1991, Icek Ajzen [12] published the article titled *the theory of planned behavior* in *Organizational Behavior and Human Decision Processes*, the theory is acknowledged to be well supported by empirical evidence, that intentions to perform behaviors of different kinds can be predicted with high accuracy from attitudes toward the behavior, subjective norms, and perceived behavioural control. It was cited 79,914 times by Sept. 12, 2020, in Microsoft Academic. R. W. Butler [13] published the article titled *the concept of a tourist area cycle of evolution: implications for management of resources* on *Canadian Geographer* in 1980. All the references mentioned in this part implied that psychology and behavior science are the based theory stones for empirical studies to this topic, especially for the topic of environmental behaviours in tourism.

Table 5 Top25 cited articles (1996–2020)

No.	Title	Author	Journal	Year
1.	Sustainable tourism: research and reality	Buckley, Ralf	ATR	2012
2.	Testing the dimensionality of place attachment and its relationships with place satisfaction and…	Ramkissoon, H. et al.	TM	2013
3.	Can ecotourism interpretation really lead to pro-conservation knowledge, attitudes, and behaviour?…	Powell, R.B. et al.	JOST	2008
4.	Residents' attitudes towards tourism in Bigodi Village, Uganda	Lepp, Andrew	TM	2007
5.	Residents' perspectives of a world heritage site …	Nicholas, L.N. et al.	ATR	2009
6.	Implications of climate and environmental change for nature-based tourism in the Canadian Rocky…	Scott, D. et al	TM	2007
7..	Collaboration theory and tourism practice in protected areas…	Jamal, T. et al.	JOST	2009
8.	Importance-satisfaction analysis for marine-park hinterlands…	Tonge, J. et al.	TM	2007
9.	The New Environmental Paradigm and Nature-Based Tourism Motivation	Luo, Y.J. et al.	JTR	2008
10.	Segmentation by visitor motivation in three Kenyan national reserves	Beh, A. et al.	TM	2007
11.	Place attachment and pro-environmental behaviour in national parks: the development of a conceptual…	Ramkissoon, H. et al.	JOST	2012
12.	Using resilience concepts to investigate the impacts of protected area tourism on communities	Strickland-Munro et al.	ATR	2010
13.	Tourism and nationalism	Pretes, M.	ATR	2003
14.	Impacts of environmental values on tourism motivation: The case of FICA, Brazil	Kim, H. et al.	TM	2006
15.	Picking up litter: an application of theory-based communication to influence tourist behaviour in …	Brown, T.J. et al.	JOST	2010
16.	Community decision-making - Participation in development	Li, W.J.	ATR	2006
17.	A picture and 1000 words: Using resident-employed photography to understand attachment to…	Stedman, R. et al.	JLR	2004

(continued)

Table 5 (continued)

No.	Title	Author	Journal	Year
18.	Sustainable performance index for tourism policy development	Castellani, V. et al.	TM	2010
19.	Protected areas as attractions	Reinius, S.W. et al.	AT	2007
20.	Defining and characterizing team resilience in elite sport	Morgan, P.B.C. et al.	PSE	2013
21.	Exploring social representations of tourism planning: issues for governance	Moscardo, Gianna	JOST	2011
22.	Managing protected areas for sustainable tourism: prospects for adaptive co-management	Plummer, R. et al.	JOST	2009
23.	Sustainability Indicators for Tourism Destinations: A Complex Adaptive Systems Approach Using …	Schianetz, K et al	JOST	2008
24.	Relationships between place attachment, place satisfaction, and pro-environmental behaviour in…	Ramkissoon, H. et al.	JOST	2013
25.	Research priorities in park tourism	Eagles, Paul F.J.	JOST	2014

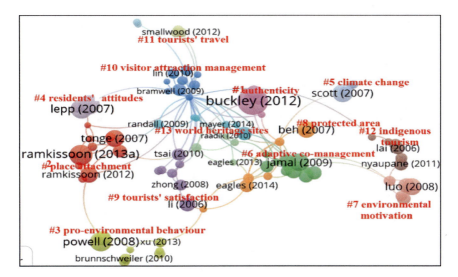

Fig. 6 Citation network of sample documents (1996–2020). $N_{citation} \geq 30$, cluster label ranked according to the citation of first articles of the group

Table 6 Top24 Co-citation references (1996–2020)

No.	References	CC	TLS
1.	fornell c, 1981, j marketing res, v18, p39, https://doi.org/10.2307/3151312	35	2924
2.	eagles pfj, 2014, j sustain tour, v22, p528, https://doi.org/10.1080/09669582.2013.785554	44	2807
3.	jamal t, 2009, j sustain tour, v17, p169, https://doi.org/10.1080/09669580802495741	32	2638
4.	ajzen i, 1991, organ behav hum dec, v50, p179, https://doi.org/10.1016/0749-5978(91)90020-t	33	2575
5.	eagles p., 2002, sustainable tourism	38	2480
6.	halpenny ea, 2010, j environ psychol, v30, p409, https://doi.org/10.1016/j.jenvp.2010.04.006	30	2384
7.	eagles p.f., 2002, tourism natl parks p	36	2259
8.	hair j. f., 2010, multivariate data an	25	2136
9.	manning r, 1999, studies outdoor recr	36	2108
10.	weaver db, 2007, tourism manage, v28, p1168, https://doi.org/10.1016/j.tourman.2007.03.004	20	2027
11.	manning re, 2011, studies outdoor recr	35	2019
12.	jamal tb, 1995, ann tourism res, v22, p186, https://doi.org/10.1016/0160-7383(94)00067-3	23	1960
13.	plummer r, 2009, j sustain tour, v17, p149, https://doi.org/10.1080/09669580802359301	25	1856
14.	eagles pfj, 2009, j sustain tour, v17, p231, https://doi.org/10.1080/09669580802495725	22	1824
15.	tosun c, 2000, tourism manage, v21, p613, https://doi.org/10.1016/s0261-5177(00)00009-1	20	1794
16.	saarinen j, 2006, ann tourism res, v33, p1121, https://doi.org/10.1016/j.annals.2006.06.007	22	1785
17.	scheyvens r, 1999, tourism manage, v20, p245, https://doi.org/10.1016/s0261-5177(98)00069-7	20	1754
18.	ramkissoon h, 2012, j sustain tour, v20, p257, https://doi.org/10.1080/09669582.2011.602194	16	1709
19.	kruger o, 2005, biodivers conserv, v14, p579, https://doi.org/10.1007/s10531-004-3917-4	17	1686
20.	balmford a, 2015, plos biol, v13, https://doi.org/10.1371/journal.pbio.1002074	27	1671
21.	whitelaw pa, 2014, j sustain tour, v22, p584, https://doi.org/10.1080/09669582.2013.873445	24	1668

(continued)

Table 6 (continued)

No.	References	CC	TLS
22.	dunlap re, 2000, j soc issues, v56, p425, https://doi.org/10.1111/0022-4537.00176	24	1660
23.	anderson jc, 1988, psychol bull, v103, p411, https://doi.org/10.1037/0033-2909.103.3.411	21	1645
24.	ballantyne r, 2009, tourism manage, v30, p658, https://doi.org/10.1016/j.tourman.2008.11.003	13	1626

CC: Co-Citations; TLS: total link strength

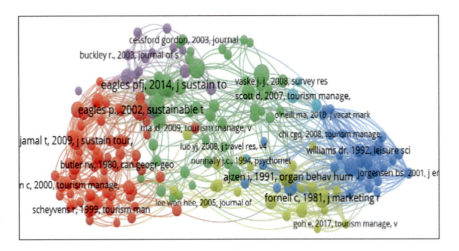

Fig. 7 Co-citation network of cited references (1996–2020). $N_{co\text{-}citation} \geq 10$

3.7 Co-occurrence of Keywords

Keywords snapshot the themes, samples, methodology, purpose, and even contents of an article, so the researcher can figure out the structure or map out the progress of the specific discipline through keywords co-occurrence analysis. Koseoglu et al. [14] categorized bibliometric analysis as theme-focused, method-focused, and sample-focus, as well as journal-focused and contributor-focused. Figure 8 shows the author's keywords co-occurrence network. Keywords with high co-occurrence frequency are national parks (243), protected areas (210), tourism (170), management (156), conservation (113), ecotourism (111), impacts (98), sustainable tourism (88), perceptions (73) and recreation (71). Sample-focused review studies focus on the samples which can be categorized into three groups: industry, people, and place. National parks and protected areas have been the popular study sample for ecotourism (111), nature-based tourism (57), wildlife tourism (21), community-based tourism (19), rural tourism (14), geo-tourism (10), heritage tourism (9), coastal tourism (6), cultural tourism (6), marine tourism (5), mountain tourism (5) and volunteer tourism (5). The

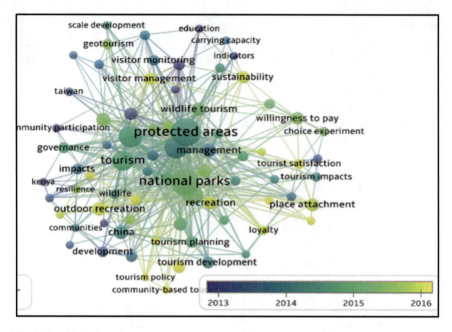

Fig. 8 Overlay keywords co-occurrence network (1996–2020). Full counting authors keywords, frequency ≥ 6

countries endowed resources of national parks and protected areas would be easier to improve their tourism research. For instance, the co-occurrence frequency of China is 24, which means China with its national parks and protected areas were chosen as the study samples of tourism research.

The high keyword co-occurrence frequency also reveals the aim, the challenge, the solution, and the tools for the research in the present topic. The aim is to achieve the stakeholders' better experiences (62) and satisfaction (58) by developing proper recreation (71) and outdoor recreation (36). Climate change (42) and biodiversity (39) are the key challenges for research on this topic. Willingness to pay (31) is the best solution for balancing financial performance and environment conservation. Methodology-focused review studies constituted articles directly focusing on how methodologies have evolved in the tourism literature. The theory of planned behavior(18) is a good tool of methodologies to understand and encourage more positive behaviours.

Theme-focused studies include articles discussing how one or more themes, such as climate change or biodiversity, have evolved in the entire discipline. As shown in Fig. 8, the yellow nodes are the tourism research hot themes in recent years. They are recreation and outdoor recreation, climate change, place attachment, sustainability, visitor management, rural tourism, tourist satisfaction, and loyalty and tourism policy. There are also some interesting themes like willingness to pay, pro-environmental

Tourism Research on National Parks and Protected Areas 235

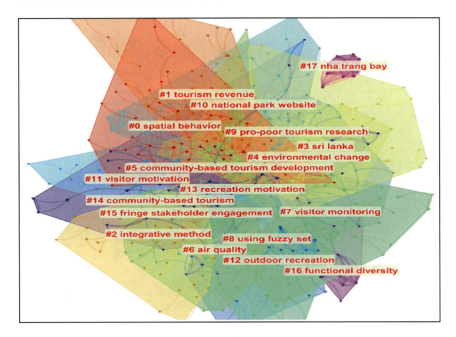

Fig. 9 Keywords co-occurrence clusters (1996–2020)

behaviour, and soundscape. The educational function of national parks and protected areas was hot since 2013 but less discussed after 2016.

Figure 9 visualizes 18 subjects defined by keywords co-occurrence network clustering. They are spatial behaviour, tourism revenue, Sri Lanka, environmental change, community-based tourism development, air quality, visitor monitoring, using fuzzy set, pro-poor tourism research, national park website, visitor motivation, outdoor recreation, recreation motivation, community-based tourism, fringe stakeholder engagement, functional diversity, and Nha Trang bay.

3.8 Terms Co-occurrence Analysis

Terms co-occurrence can identify the pattern of specific intellectual research evolutions, provide a piece of empirical evidence to support the literature review. Figure 10 visualizes the clusters of terms co-occurrence. The tourism research on national parks and protected areas concentrated on 4 macro clusters, which were community development (red group), visitors' experience (green group), environment conservation (blue group), and climate change (yellow group). Employed term clustering analysis with CiteSpace, generated Fig. 11 with micro subject clusters, including adaptive co-management, tourism stakeholders perception, Canadian rocky mountain, urban

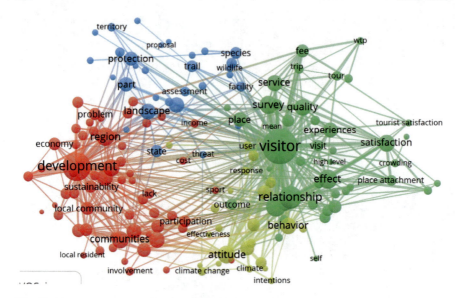

Fig. 10 Terms co-occurrence clusters (1996–2020). $N_{co-occurrence} \geq 20$

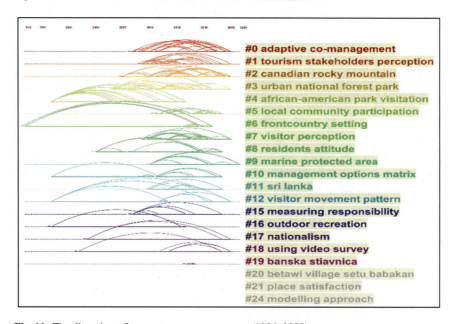

Fig. 11 Timeline view of term co-occurrence custers (1996–2020)

national forest park, African-American park visitation, local community participation, frontcountry setting, visitor perception, residents attitude, marine protected area, management option matrix, Sri Lanka, visitor movement pattern, measuring responsibility, outdoor recreation, nationalism, using video survey, Banska Stiavnica, Batawi village Setu Babakan, place satisfaction, and modeling approach. Table 7 lists the summary of micro research subjects from Figs. 3, 5, 6, 9, and 11. They are the empirical evidence for reviewing the literature.

(1) Community development

Tourism, various kinds of proper tourism are the best solution to achieve community development. Community-based tourism (CBT) has been widely considered to be a viable vehicle for development in rural and remote areas [15], that involves direct local participation in the development, management, and benefits of tourism activities that are integrated into the local economy [16]. Nature-based tourism and community-based ecotourism are suitable for the community endowing natural national parks and

Table 7 Summary of clusters and its categories (1996–2020)

	Cluster	Themes
1.	Community development	Adaptive co-management, tourism stakeholders' perception, local community participation, frontcountry setting, management option matrix, nationalism, tourism revenue, community-based tourism development, pro-poor tourism research, fringe stakeholder engagement, tourism practice, tourist-resident interface, influencing indigenous engagement. indigenous tourism, world heritage sites, residents' attitudes, Batawi village Setu Babakan, policy arrangement approach, Yanyi town, fostering local identity
2.	Visitors experience	visitor perception, using video survey, place satisfaction, modelling approach, spatial behaviour, national park website, visitor motivation, recreation motivation, Chinese tourist, extended model, visitor attraction management, tourists' travel, tourists' satisfaction, authenticity, place attachment, functional diversity, tourism motivation, leisure participation, recreational enactment, Sri Lanka, African-American park visitation, parking guiding
3.	Environment conservation	Measuring responsibility, visitor monitoring, visitor movement pattern, Nha Trang bay, using resident-employed photography, coastal destination, protected area tourism, spatial level, grey nurse shark, modelling willingness, adaptive resource management, Chinese national park, environmental motivation, protected area, pro-environmental behaviour, using fuzzy set, natural resource conservation, fulufjallet national park
4.	Climate change	environmental change, Canadian Rocky Mountain, outdoor recreation, air quality, climate change, influencing future behaviour, sustainable dream, marine protected area, last chance tourism

Sourced from Figs. 3, 5, 6, 9, and 11

protected nature areas. Pro-poor tourism is suitable for far less developing communities. Rural tourism is suitable for communities in developed countries. From the definition of CBT, local participation is crucially important, that many discussions focus on local people's participation in developing a plan, the perception of residents, and the interface between residents and visitors.

Adaptive co-management (ACM) has been advocated as one approach to improve the governance of protected areas [17] Ryan Plummer et al. [18] envisions the prospects of ACM) as an alternative approach to protected areas management for sustainable tourism. ACM reflects a substantial paradigmatic shift in pursuing and understanding protected area governance as well as sustainable tourism by multi-stakeholders. Islam et al. [19] regard ACM as a dynamic approach to governance whereby institutional arrangements and ecological knowledge are continually revised through a process of 'learning-by-doing', and proposed that incorporate governance, social learning, and multi-stakeholder engagement for future research of ACM.

Besides, the resilence of environment to the host community used to draw a lot of attention from the scholars and practitioners, but the COVID-19 pandemic ceased largely the tourism industry in March, 2020. All the discussion about resilence focus on the society and economic in the community [20]. Previous research on crises and disasters do show similar patterns and existing theories can often very well explain the current phenomena [21], local authorities and tourism organizations should take appropriate post-pandemic recovery actions with the other stakeholder in the host community [22]. Improving the infrastructure and offering e-tourism are some good ways to enhance the tourism resilience in the community [23].

(2) Visitor experience

Tourism destinations provide sightseeing and recreations experience for visitors. Visitors segments included Escapists, Learners, and Spiritualists, and understanding the differences in these visitor segments will help managers of the reserves better provide alternative activities and services to tourists [24]. Those who are more supportive of limits to growth and who are more concerned about eco-crisis tend to have a higher desire to be close to nature, to learn about nature, and to escape from routine and issues associated with cities. In addition, those whose motivations are oriented to develop skills and abilities or seek to experience new things, environments, and social contact tend to be more supportive of the notion of human over nature [25]. Recreationists with different experiences profiles have distinct setting preferences but are mixed regarding supporting a link between settings and experiences. setting management systems may function to change the rate at which experiences are produced rather than the intensity [26].

A good thematic interpretive guided tour makes a positive impact on visitor experiences, thus making training of tourism businesses' employees as park guides will be a good investment. Visitor experiences can be enhanced by using thematic interpretation in park guiding service [27]. Good experiences would result in place satisfaction and attachment [28, 29], loyalty [30], the effect of destination fascination on improving subjective well-being and destination attachment and shows the effects of subjective well-being and destination attachment on enhancing destination loyalty. Subjective well-being and destination attachment fully mediated effects from destination fascination to destination loyalty [31].

(3) Environment conservation

Though tourism was regarded as a clean industry, tourism entities and tourists' activities impact greatly the environment of national parks and protected areas. Sustainable tourism development needs natural resource protection, land trusts have proved economically viable and effective methods for protecting natural areas. Land trusts and tourism entities have convergent needs and goals regarding natural resource protection, possibly making them suitable partners to conserve natural resources [32]. Economic contributions of park tourism are rarely documented for individual parks in developing countries or made relevant to management or governance concerns. comparing economic contributions of member reserves while also attributing a range of values in financial, social, and political domains to different components of the system, thus enabling integration of results with resilience-oriented management frameworks and decision-making processes [33].

On the other hand, conducting individual pro-environmental behaviours of tourists is an important consensus. Visitors may change their attitude for place attachment [34] and place satisfaction [28], and perform more pro-environmental behaviour in national parks. The Theory of Planned Behaviour (TPB) helps to understand why the visitors behave or do not behave pro-environmentally, and the role of pro-environmental values is more suitable for predicting general environmental worldviews as compared to the TPB being more suitable for predicting specific behavioural intentions [35]. And visitors' pro-environmental behaviour can be fostered [36].

(4) Climate change and tourism

Tourists movements involve in climate change when pursuing outdoor recreation based on nature as a way of maintaining a healthy lifestyle. Scott et al. [37] developed a statistical model to examine how climate change may influence park tourism in the Rocky Mountain region by focusing on both the direct and indirect impacts of climate change on visitation. McEvoy et al. [38] advocated the discussion on how to maintain the quality of an environment that is under combined pressure from both visitor numbers and climate change. Focusing on two landscape types considered to be the most vulnerable to a changing climate, the coastal zone, and the uplands, presented 'downscaled' climate change scenarios, and provided an assessment of how a combination of climate and non-climate factors are likely to impact these vulnerable landscapes in the future. Leon et al. [39] modelled how tourists evaluated climate change risk and compared the differences between the monetary measures of willingness to accept and willingness to pay (WTP) for changes in climate change risk, discovered that tourists would like to pay for the high risk than lower risk. Seasonal weather sensitivity and climate change impact the national parks visitation, the temperature below 11degrees C and above 33 degrees C would barrier more tourists to visit the parks [40], not to mention the vulnerable park visitation under climate extremes conditions (Jedd et al. [41]). No matter imputing to tourism activities or other industries, climate change topic aroused an anxious tourism form, the last chance tourism. Travel to impact-sensitive destinations has been on the rise in recent years. Coined "last chance tourism" (LCT), visitors are increasingly coming to these destinations to see them before they are gone [42]. Studies concerning climate change and tourism will continually be integrative and critical in the future.

4 Conclusions and Discussions

The present study tries to visualize the intellectual network of tourism research on national parks and protected areas by integrating bibliometric analysis tools of VOSviewer and CiteSpace. The publication about this topic increased quickly after 2014, showing the importance of national parks and protected areas to tourism study. There are many small collaborative networks among the authors, suggesting that there shall be more international co-authorship in the research topic. The most productive authors are Gyan P. Nyaupane, Betty Weiler, Susan A. Moore, Melville Saayman, Jie Zhang, Kate Rodger, Peter Fredman, and Petra Hlavackova, but the most co-cited authors are Ralf Buckley, C.M. Hall, P.F.J. Eagles, D.B. Weaver, C. Ryan, D. Scott, S. Gosling, Bill Bramwell, RE Manning, Ajzen I, S. Becken, G. Brown, R, Sharpley, Gyan P. Nyaupane and Lee T.H., all of them are the core authors of sustainable tourism study. The most productive organizations are Griffith University, Clemson University, Murdoch University, University of Johannesburg, and Sun Yat-Sen University. The top 20 organizations contributed 34.1% of the total citations. The organizations in the USA, Australia, and China are more comparatively open in the research of this topic than the others. The discipline discourse is firmly in the dominant of the USA and British Commonwealth Countries, co-authorship is a good choice for the non-English countries like China or Spain.

National parks and protected areas have been the popular study sample for ecotourism, nature-based tourism, wildlife tourism, community-based tourism, rural tourism, geo-tourism, heritage tourism, coastal tourism, cultural tourism, marine tourism, mountain tourism, and volunteer tourism, suggesting that the tourism research on national parks and protected areas are all nature-resource based. The more national parks and protected areas resources the countries and regions endow, the more productive they are.

The 25 years of research on this topic focused on 4 discussions: community development, visitors experiences, environment conservation, and climate change. All the studies on this topic are tried to balance the state of arts that develop the local community and conserve the environment while providing visitor impressive experiences. The present study also defined recreation and outdoor recreation, climate change, place attachment, sustainability, visitor management, rural tourism, tourist satisfaction and loyalty, tourism policy, willingness to pay, pro-environmental behavior, soundscape, and the resilence from pandemic are the hotspots for current research in this topic. World Tourism Oganization should take national parks and protected areas as the KPI to assess the sustainable development of each country since the importance disgussed above. There should be greater communication among the scholars and practitioners from different fields or departments due to the cross-diciplines social networks.

This paper also presents more empirical evidence for Ph.D. candidates, researchers, group leaders, and policy-makers to review literature or develop collaborative strategies than the other similar research articles.

Acknowledgements This paper was supported by the funds of:

1. Study on measurement of development level of beautiful China and the influence on quality and quantity change of inbound tourism flow, supported by the National Social Science Fund of China, No. 19BJY207;

2. Innovation Project of Guangdong Polyethnic College, P. R. China (to Donghui Lu), No. 2019GKJSK001;

3. Philosophy and Social Science Federation Program of Zhaoqing, P. R. China (to Donghui Lu), No. 19ZC-42;

4. Study on the Mutual Benefit and Cooperation Mechanism of Cruise Tourism Promoting the Coordinated Development of Tourism in Guangdong-Hong Kong-Macao Greater Bay Area, supported by Guangzhou Philosophy and Social Science Project, China, 2018, No. 2018GZYB23;

5. Graduate Education Innovation Program "Exploring Research on the Teaching Reform of International Education for Graduate Students Majoring in Tourism Management", supported by Department of Education of Guangdong Province, China, 2017, No. 2017JGXM-ZD03;

6. Graduate English Course "Study comparatively between Chinese and international hospitality industry", supported by South China University of Technology, 2018.

References

1. Wei, W., Lu D., Xu, X., Wang, X., Zhang, H.: Bibliometric analysis and visualization for sustainable tourism products. Tour. Prod. Dev. China, Asian and European Countries. P1-23 (2019)
2. IUCN, https://www.iucn.org/theme/protected-areas/about/protected-areas-categories/category-ii-national-park (2016)
3. Gissibl, B., Höhler, S., Kupper, P.: Civilizing nature. National Parks in Global Historical Perspective. Berghahn, Oxford (2012)
4. Chen, C.: CiteSpace II: detecting and visualizing emerging trends and transient patterns in scientific literature. J. Am. Soc. Inform. Sci. Technol. **57**(3), 359–377 (2006)
5. Eck, N.J.V., Waltman, L.: Software survey: VOSviewer, a computer program for bibliometric mapping. Scientometrics. **84**, 523–538 (2010)
6. Garousi, V., Mantyla, M.V.: Citations, research topics and active countries in software engineering. Comput. Sci. Rev. **19**, 56–77 (2016)
7. Hall, C.M.: Publish and perish? Bibliometric analysis, journal ranking and the assessment of research qu ality in tourism. Tour. Manage. **32**, 16–27 (2011)
8. Benckendorff, P., Zehrer, A.: A network analysis of tourism research. Ann. Tour. Res. **43**, 121–149 (2013)
9. Fornell, C., Larcker. D.F.: Evaluating structural equation models with unobservable variables and measurement error. J. Mark. Res. **24**(2), 337–346 (1981)
10. Anderson, J.C., Gerbing, C.: Structural equation modeling in practice: a review and recommended two-step approach. Psychol. Bull. **27**(1), 5–24 (1988)
11. Ajzen, I.: Understanding attitudes and predicting social behavior. Prentice-Hall (1980)
12. Ajzen, I.: The theory of planned behavior. Organ. Behav. Hum. Decis. Process. **50**, 179–211 (1991)

13. Butler, R.W.: The concept of a tourist area cycle of evolution: implications for management of resources. Can. Geogr.. XXIV, 1 (1980)
14. Koseoglu, M.A., Rahimi, R., Okumus, F., Liu, J.Y.: Bibliometric studies in tourism. Ann. Tour. Res. **61**, 180–198 (2016)
15. Hall C.M.: Tourism: rethinking the social science of mobility. Prentice-Hall (2005)
16. Ruiz-Ballesteros, E., Caceres-Feria, R.: Community-building and amenity migration in community-based tourism development: an approach from southwest Spain. Tour. Manage. **54**, 513–523 (2016)
17. Islam, M.W., Ruhanen, L., Ritchie, B.W.: Tourism governance in protected areas: investigating the application of the adaptive co-management approach. J. Sustain. Tour. **26**(11), 1890–1908 (2019)
18. Plummer, R., Fennell, D.A.: Managing protected areas for sustainable tourism: prospects for adaptive co-management. J. Sustain. Tour. **17**(2), 149–168 (2009)
19. Islam, M.W., Ruhanen, L., Ritchie, B.W.: Adaptive co-management: A novel approach to tourism destination governance? J. Hosp. Tour. Manag. **37**, 97–106 (2017)
20. Gssling, S., Scott, D., Hall, C.M.: Pandemics, tourism and global change: a rapid assessment of COVID-19. J. Sustain. Tour. **29**(1), 1–20 (2021)
21. Zenker S., Kock F.: The coronavirus pandemic—a critical discussion of a tourism research agenda. Tour. Manag. **81**, 104164 (2020)
22. Qiu R., Park J., Li S., et al.: Social costs of tourism during the COVID-19 pandemic. Ann. Tour. Res. **84**, 102994 (2020).
23. Gretzel, U., Fuchs, M., Baggio, R., et al.: e-Tourism beyond COVID-19: a call for transformative research. Inf. Technol. Tour. **22**(2), 187–203 (2020)
24. Beh, A., Bruyere, B.L.: Managing protected areas for sustainable tourism: prospects for adaptive co-management. Tour. Manage. **28**(6), 1464–1471 (2007)
25. Luo, Y.J., Deng, J.Y.: The new environmental paradigm and nature-based tourism motivation. J. Travel Res. **46**(4), 392–402 (2008)
26. Blcklund, E.A., Stewart, W.P.: Effects of setting-based management on visitor experience outcomes: differences across a management continuum. J. Leis. Res. **44**(3), 392–415 (2012)
27. Amin, V.L., Yok, M.C.K., Omar, M.S.: Enhancing visitor experiences using thematic interpretation in park guiding service in sarawak national parks. In: 4th international conference on tourism research, vol. 12 (2014)
28. Ramkissoon, H., Smith, L.D.G., Weiler, B.: Relationships between place attachment, place satisfaction and pro-environmental behaviour in an Australian national park. J. Sustain. Tour. **21**(3), 434–457 (2013)
29. David, A.: Experiential places or places of experience? Place identity and place attachment as mechanisms for creating festival environment. Tour. Manag. **55**, 49–61 (2016)
30. Moore, S.A., Rodgger, K., Taplin, R.: Moving beyond visitor satisfaction to loyalty in nature-based tourism: a review and research agenda. Curr. Issue Tour. **18**(7), 667–683 (2015)
31. Wang, Y.C., Liu, C.R., Huang, W.S., Chen, S.P.: Destination fascination and destination loyalty: subjective well-being and destination attachment as mediators. J. Travel Res. **59**(3), 496–511 (2020)
32. Chancellor, C., Norman, W., Farmer, J., Coe, E.: Tourism organizations and land trusts: a sustainable approach to natural resource conservation? J. Sustain. Tour. **19**(7), 863–875 (2011)
33. Musavengane, R., Kloppers, R.: Social capital: An investment towards community resilience in the collaborative natural resources management of community-based tourism schemes. **34**, 15 (2020)
34. Ramkissoon, H., Weiler, B., Smith, L.D.G.: Place attachment and pro-environmental behaviour in national parks: the development of a conceptual framework. J. Sustain. Tour. **20**(2), 257–276 (2012)
35. Goh, E., Ritchie, B., Wang, J.: Non-compliance in national parks: An extension of the theory of planned behaviour model with pro-environmental values. Tour. Manag. **59**, 123–127 (2017)
36. Zhang, Y.C., Moyle, B.D., Jin, X.: Fostering visitors' pro-environmental behaviour in an urban park. Asia Pac. J. Tour. Res. **23**(7), 691–702 (2018)

37. Scott, D., Ones, B.J., Konopek, J.: Implications of climate and environmental change for nature-based tourism in the Canadian Rocky Mountains: a case study of Waterton Lakes National Park. Tour. Manag. **28**(2), 570–579 (2007)
38. McEvoy, D., Cavan, G., Handley, J., McMorrow, J., Lindley, S.: Changes to climate and visitor behaviour: Implications for vulnerable landscapes in the north west region of England. J. Sustain. Tour. **16**(1), 101–121 (2008)
39. Leon, C.J., Arana, J.E., Gonzalez, M., Leon, J.D.: Tourists' evaluation of climate change risks in the Canary Islands: a heterogeneous response modelling approach. Tour. Econ. **20**(4), 849–868 (2014)
40. Hewer, M., Scott, D., Fenech, A.: Seasonal weather sensitivity, temperature thresholds, and climate change im pacts for park visitation. Tour. Geogr. **18**(3), 297–321 (2016)
41. Jedd, T.M., Hayes, M.J., Carrillo, C.M., et al.: Measuring park visitation vulnerability to climate extremes in U.S. Rockies National Parks tourism. Tour. Geogr. **20**(2), 1–26 (2017)
42. Miller, L.B., Hallo, J.C., Dvorak, R.G., Feter, J.P., Peterson, B.A., Brownlee, M.T.J.: On the edge of the world: examining pro-environmental outcomes of last chance tourism in Kaktovik Alaska. J. Sustain. Tour. **28**(11), 1703–1722 (2020)

Research Hotspots on Inbound Tourism from the Perspective of Globalization

Wei Wei, Kehanfei Li, Sandy Chen, and Xin Xu

Abstract The COVID-19 pandemic presses the pause button for the global tourism industry, especially not only in the cross-border tourism industry, but also in cross-border tourism research. Using the research results from the many that have been published, this paper seeks to visualize the basic characteristics of articles and research hotspots on inbound tourism, to analyze and summarize the causes and background of these hotspots as well as their effects on the development of tourism. Based on a bibliometric analysis of 1,232 articles on the Web of Science database between 1997 and 2020, this paper shows results that (1) inbound tourism can be divided into three main research stages, among which the last four years witness the most fruitful results; (2) inbound tourism research is concentrated in a small number of countries/regions, and the research institutions and scholars in this field tend to be independent, resulting in a global academic community that has not yet formed; (3) the research hotspots could be summarized into two main directions and seven themes. Among them, studies related to COVID-19 focus on themes of macro aspects like "the influence of negative social factors on inbound tourism", while the micro perspectives received less attention. The findings could provide insights and suggestions for inbound tourism research in the post-demic period.

Keywords Globalization · Inbound tourism · Bibliometric analysis · CiteSpace · Research hotspots

---

W. Wei · K. Li (✉) · X. Xu
Department of Tourism Management, South China University of Technology, Guangzhou, Guangdong, People's Republic of China
e-mail: likehanfei_scut@163.com

W. Wei
e-mail: weiweitour@163.com

W. Wei
Guangzhou City University of Technology, Guangzhou, Guangdong, People's Republic of China

S. Chen
Department of Recreation, Sport Pedagogy & Consumer Sciences, Ohio University, Athens, OH, USA
e-mail: Chens5@ohio.edu

1 Introduction

Inbound tourism plays a key role in the development of a global tourism industry, which not only represents the image of each country or region but also reflects their comprehensive development level and competitiveness. In 2020, due to the impact of COVID-19, the global inbound tourism industry is facing distinct levels of threat, and the phenomenon of inbound tourism during the pandemic period has also attracted extensive attention. While cross-border tourism is becoming less and less, the future development of inbound tourism should be discussed on the globalization the pandemic as well as the global academic research. However, few scholars have systematically explored the current research situation of inbound tourism from the perspective of COVID-19.

Based on the 1,232 articles reviewed, this paper summarizes the basic characteristics of articles and research hotspots of inbound tourism. It helps formulate a comprehensive grasp of the current situation and pattern of global inbound tourism research and provides theoretical and practical inspiration for follow-up research in the post-pandemic era.

2 Methodology

2.1 Research Methods

This paper uses bibliometric analysis and knowledge graph analysis methods. Bibliometric analysis is a quantitative research method based on literature analysis, which is used to analyze various external characteristics of literature, including authors, journals, and citations [1]. In bibliometrics analysis, frequency analysis, co-occurrence analysis, co-citation analysis, and clustering analysis are often used [2].

The knowledge graph is a type of graphic representation, depicting the development of knowledge in a certain field and structural relationship [3]. The knowledge graph analysis is a method of mapping the networks through visual analysis software, which involves analysis of cooperative network graphs, co-occurrence network graphs, co-citation network graphs, and clustering network graphs. This paper uses CiteSpace software to draw knowledge graphs of articles on global inbound tourism. By describing the nodes, links, density, centrality, and other information in the graph networks, research distributions and hotspots are determined.

2.2 Data Sources

To ensure the authority and comprehensiveness of the sample, this paper takes the SCI and SSCI journals in the Web of Science (1997–2020) as the data source. Then searching the subject terms: 'inbound tourism', 'inbound travel', 'inbound visit', 'cross-border tourism', 'transnational tourism', and 'transnational travel'. From the 1,552 sources obtained, the type of literature was further refined to 'ARTICLE', resulting in 1,232 valid articles obtained.

3 Basic Characteristics of Articles

3.1 Trend of Publications

From Fig. 1, the number of research publications on inbound tourism between 1997 and 2020 has maintained an upward trend. According to the increase in publications, this whole period could be divided into three stages. The first stage (1997–2005) is the germination stage of inbound tourism research. As scholars initially explore the field of inbound tourism, the number of publications is relatively small and the overall trend is slow. In the second stage (2006–2016), inbound tourism is in the exploration stage of research, and the number of publications breaks through double digits, showing an increasing trend. The third stage (2017–2020) is the rapid development of inbound tourism research. Both the number of publications and the increase rate have significantly increased. In this stage, an average of 152 articles was published each year, showing a rapid growth trend. Despite the disruption by the pandemic in 2020, academic research related to inbound tourism continued to increase.

Fig. 1 The trend of the number of inbound tourism literature between 1997 and 2020

3.2 Distribution of Countries/Regions

As popular destinations for inbound tourism, the United States (282), England (166), China (165), and Australia (128) are also the main countries/regions that focus on inbound tourism, as shown in Table 1. Among them, the United States ranks first with 282 articles published and is the leading force in inbound tourism research. Overall, these countries and regions published 1,044 articles, accounting for 84.74% of the total. This shows that global inbound tourism research is highly concentrated in the hands of a few economically developed countries/regions.

Figure 2 reflects the research cooperation of major countries/regions on inbound tourism and represents the degree of globalization of inbound tourism research.

Table 1 Top Ten countries and regions of inbound tourism research

Frequency	Countries/Regions	Frequency	Countries/Regions
282	The United States	62	Germany
166	England	55	Spain
165	China	43	Taiwan, China
128	Australia	38	Italy
67	Canada	38	South Africa

Fig. 2 Cooperation network of countries and regions

According to the density of links, there are more links formed with the central nodes of the United States and England. The centrality of the two nodes is 0.35 and 0.25 respectively, indicating that they have engaged in research cooperation with other countries/regions. In general, the network density of the cooperation network is 0.0587, indicating that the overall research relevance is strong, with strong global research cooperation.

3.3 Main Research Institutions

Research institutions are the primary research sources concerning inbound tourism, integrating the wisdom and wealth of multiple scholars. Among them, ten research institutions have published twelve or more articles related to inbound tourism (Table 2), including Hong Kong Polytechnic University (34), University of London (31), and the University of California System (24). The number of publications of Hong Kong Polytechnic University far exceeds that of others, and it is the backbone of long-term research on inbound tourism, mainly focusing on 'behavior and experience of inbound tourists', 'inbound tourism demand and forecast', 'inbound health tourism', and other topics, covering a wide range of topics.

Figure 3 shows the research cooperation among various institutions. The largest network cluster in the graph is centered on the node of Hong Kong Polytechnic University. The node has formed many links outwards, which indicates that Hong Kong Polytechnic University has research cooperation with other universities, such as Bournemouth University, University of Surrey, and Sun Yat-Sen University. The density of the overall network is 0.0027, reflecting that the global cooperation among various institutions is not close, and they still mainly conduct related research independently.

Table 2 The top 10 research institutions of inbound tourism

Frequency	Institutions
34	Hong Kong Polytechnic University
31	University of London
24	University of California System
18	University of Texas System
17	Monash University
16	University of New South Wales Sydney
16	University of Surrey
13	Griffith University
13	Sun Yat-Sen University
12	University Of California Los Angeles

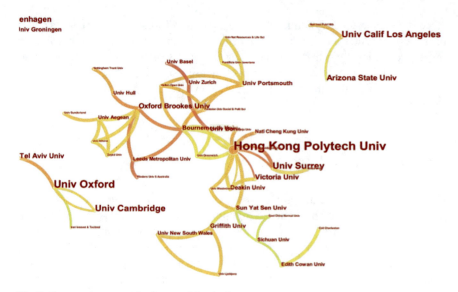

Fig. 3 Cooperation network of research institutions

3.4 Core Research Authors

As shown in Table 3, among authors in the field of inbound tourism, Ming-Hsiang Chen (11) and Valorie A. Crooks (10) have the highest number of publications, followed by Jeremy Snyder (9) and Larry Dwyer (8). They have created rich academic achievements in inbound tourism research and are representatives of the core research forces in this field.

According to Fig. 4, the whole network is loose and sporadic, where a few authors form network clusters, but fail to form a strong global academic research community.

Table 3 Main authors of inbound tourism research

Frequency	Main authors	Frequency	Main authors
11	Ming-Hsiang Chen	7	Yang Yang
10	Valorie A. Crooks	7	Khalid Zaman
9	Jeremy Snyder	6	Susan Frohlick
8	Larry Dwyer	6	Giray Gozgor
7	Gang Li	6	Haiyan Song

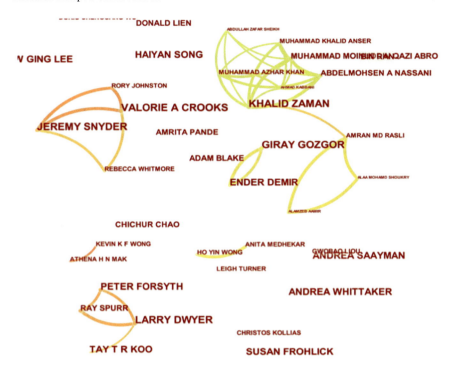

Fig. 4 Cooperation network of authors

4 Research Hotspots of Articles

Statistics and clustering of keywords or subject terms of articles could be used to summarize the research hotspots and help sort out the development of research hotspots.

4.1 Analysis of Keywords and Subject Terms

As significant words for retrieving articles, there are differences between keywords and subject terms. Keywords refer to words that appear frequently in the articles, usually identified by the authors themselves, while subject terms are a series of standardized professional words. To an extent, both could be used to analyze research hotspots, but there are differences in the clustering effects. Therefore, this paper will compare them through two indicators, frequency, and network correlation, to select the more appropriate one for cluster analysis. Through using CiteSpace, main keywords and main subject terms with the frequency of the top twenty are counted and filtered. Low-representation and low-relevance general words are excluded, resulting in the data in Table 4.

Table 5 presents the statistical results of the maximum frequency, minimum frequency, range, and average of keywords and subject terms. The larger the overall span of the words, the more obvious the cluster boundary forms, and the better the final clustering effect. The number of main keywords and main subject terms are not equal, and the range of keywords (34) is significantly higher than the range of subject terms (13), suggesting the effect of selecting keywords for cluster analysis is better. In addition, the frequency of words reflects the degree of activity in the research field. Generally, the higher the frequency, the more active the research field

Table 4 The top twenty keywords and subject terms of inbound tourism research

Frequency	Keywords	Frequency	Subject terms
48	Migration	23	Inbound tourists
38	Model	22	International tourism
37	Impact	21	Hong Kong
26	Gender	19	In-depth interviews
25	Transnational terrorism	18	Medical tourism
24	Politics	16	Tourism demand
23	Demand	15	South Africa
22	Identity	15	Global south
18	Policy	15	Tourism development
18	Governance	13	Terrorist attacks
17	Experience	13	National borders
17	Geography	12	North America
17	City	12	Global north
16	State	12	Transnational mobility
16	Migrant	12	Tourist arrivals
16	Destination	12	Transnational perspective
16	Mobility	11	Southeast Asia
15	Network	11	European union
14	Space	11	South Korea
14	Place	10	Economic growth

Table 5 The frequency, range, and average of the top twenty keywords and subject terms

	Keywords	Subject terms
Keywords	48	14
Subject terms	23	10
Maximum frequency	48	23
Minimum frequency	14	10
Range	34	13
Average	21.85	14.65

will be. Because the average value of keywords (21.85) is higher than that of subject terms (14.65), research hotspots of inbound tourism based on cluster analysis using keywords will be more active and typical.

To judge the suitability of keywords and subject terms to be used in the cluster analysis, it is also necessary to perform network correlation analysis. Figure 5 shows the co-occurrence network graphs of keywords and subject terms, which could be seen that the density of the co-occurrence network of keywords (Fig. 5a) is 0.0124, indicating that there is a strong correlation among keywords; the density of the network of subject terms (Fig. 5b) is 0.005, reflecting that network is relatively loose and the correlation among them is weak. Therefore, by comparing the network relevance of keywords and subject terms, keywords are more suitable for cluster analysis of research hotspots on inbound tourism.

In summary, comparing the two indicators of frequency and network relevance, keywords meet requirements better than subject terms. So this paper chooses keywords as the object of cluster analysis in the research hotspots.

a) Co-occurrence network of keywords   b) Co-occurrence network of subject terms

Fig. 5 Co-occurrence network of keywords and subject terms

4.2 Cluster Analysis of Research Hotspots

Clustering of keywords with strong relevance clearly reflects research hotspots. To further ensure the accuracy of the clustering effect, this paper uses a combination of two methods, which are automatic clustering with CiteSpace and artificial classification. First, applying clustering function of CiteSpace to automatically classify keywords through an algorithm, and then divides clusters of different topics according to the meaning of keywords, as shown in Fig. 6.

The clustering network shows the top fourteen clusters with the largest number of keywords, which represent fourteen research hotspots. In descending order of the number of keywords, the cluster labels of research hotspots in inbound tourism are: #0 ecotourism, #1 sex tourism, #2 air pollution, #3 tourism demand, #4 input–output mode, #5 happiness, #6 ethnography, #7 urban poverty, #8 service quality, #9 gmm estimators, #10 international political economy, #11 surrogacy, #12 neoliberalism, #13 gender. Considering that mentioned above clustering themes have a large deviation from inbound tourism obviously, the seven cluster themes with low representation and low relevance were eliminated: #1 sex tourism, #6 ethnography, #7 urban poverty, #9 gmm estimators, #11 surrogacy, #12 neoliberalism and #13

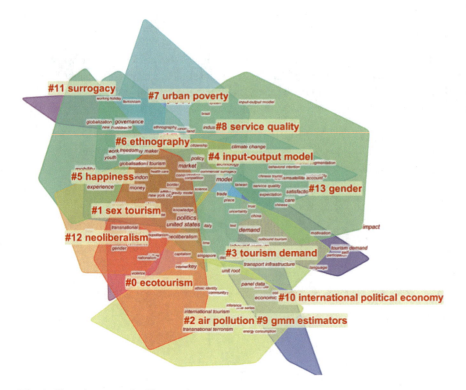

Fig. 6 Clustering network of keywords

gender. The remaining seven clusters and corresponding high-frequency keywords will be the focus of discussion and analysis.

4.3 Keywords Cleaning and Coding Classifications

When CiteSpace performs automatic clustering, the algorithm of the software may have problems, such as improper classification and fuzzy clustering boundary. Therefore, this paper firstly uses CiteSpace for automatic clustering; and then analyzes the correlation among keywords by reading the articles where keywords are located; finally to optimize and manually code the keywords in seven cluster plates. For the optimized main keywords, renaming clustering themes and constructing a classification coding table of keywords (Table 6). In addition, the clustering themes and keywords are divided into seven main classes and several subclasses.

4.4 Analysis of Research Hotspots on Inbound Tourism

4.4.1 Inbound Ecological and Medical Tourism

In the field of inbound tourism, some scholars have based their discussions on ecotourism and medical tourism. Among them, scholar Valorie Crooks, as the representative of this research field, has made an in-depth study of inbound medical tourism and published several articles. According to the related literature, the reason why scholars are keen to study this field is as follows: with the continuous transformation of concepts of life, production and consumption, people tend to seek better healthy and medical services in other countries. A negative consequence of this trend is that many global infectious diseases, such as the ongoing COVID-19 pandemic, are largely attributable to inbound tourism. As the control of pandemic has been normalized, people's awareness of environmental protection and health preservation is becoming a constraining factor to inbound tourism.

For the above reasons, global health, ecotourism, and medicine have gradually become the research hotspots in inbound tourism. The popularity of this field reflects that attention to global health has become a general trend. It is of great significance in strengthening the awareness of environmental protection and risk prevention of inbound tourists, as well as in formulating coping strategies.

4.4.2 Natural Environment of Inbound Tourism Destination

Keywords like greenhouse gas, air pollution, and carbon emission are highly related to the natural environment. Much of the research is from the perspective of interaction and influence between the natural environment and inbound tourism. Pintassilgo et al.

Table 6 Classification and coding table of research hotspots on inbound tourism

Code	Main class	Subclass
G1	Inbound ecological and medical tourism	ecotourism, ecoculture, culture of medicine, surgery, global health, conservation, health care delivery, cross-border healthcare, wildlife tourism
G2	Natural environment of inbound tourism destination	air pollution, greenhouse gas, carbon emission, water efficiency, carbon efficiency, natural resources, climate change, life-cycle assessment, nature, environmental extended input–output model, carbon footprint, water
G3	The influence of negative social factors on inbound tourism	terrorism, domestic terrorism, h1n1 flu, transnational terrorism, terrorist attacks, long-run impacts, short-run impacts, uncertainty, conflict, HIV, disruption, vulnerability
G4	Demand and forecast of inbound tourists	tourism demand, inbound tourism demand, tourist arrivals forecasting, airfare, shopping spending, transport cost, airline competition, prices, exchange rates, demand models, forecasting, price of substitutes, hotel room rates, relative domestic prices, price variables, behavioral intention
G5	Service and marketing of inbound tourism	service quality, technical efficiency, quantitative destination marketing, performance appraisal, production function, brand equity, destination marketing, online order batching, service gaps, tourism marketing, market segmentation, tourism promotion, brand image, brand awareness
G6	Consumption behavior and psychology of inbound tourists	revisit intention, customer satisfaction, brand loyalty, perceived value, satisfaction, perceived quality, dining experience, decision-making, tourist satisfaction, happiness, well-being, cultural intimacy, wellbeing, life satisfaction, emotion, trust, sense of community, happiness index
G7	Immigrants and cross-border tourists	Chinese outbound tourism, international second home retirement, transnational leisure, international tourism, immigrants, youth mobility, immigration, mobility, transnational migration, transnationalism, return migrants, international migration, Korean diaspora, racialized mobility

analyze the impact of climate change on the tourism industry of inbound countries [4]. Yang et al. show the effects of relative air quality on vacationers' perceived destination restorative qualities [5]. Research on the natural environment of China's inbound tourism mainly focuses on Beijing, where the haze phenomenon is frequent. Zhou et al., Dong et al., Tang et al. and Ruan et al. respectively describe the impact of air pollution in Beijing on the economic growth of inbound tourism [6–9].

The natural environment attracts so much attention in the field of inbound tourism because the image of the natural environment in inbound tourism destinations will influence the perception and evaluation of overseas tourists. When the destination's natural environment is seriously damaged, it will reduce its attraction to them. Therefore, relevant exploration from this perspective could provide some specific suggestions, such as the protection of the natural environment and the improvement of the air quality of destinations. At the same time, it provides ideas for tourism departments to expand the inbound tourist market.

4.4.3 The Influence of Negative Social Factors on Inbound Tourism

In the research on the influence of negative social factors on inbound tourism, terrorism, sudden diseases like COVID-19, and political instability have been concerned. Representative studies include the following: Drakos et al. focus on three countries with a high incidence of terrorism in the Mediterranean, and find that terrorism reduces the number of inbound tourists [10]. Saha et al. discuss the combined effects of political instability and terrorism on the development of inbound tourism [11]. Shi et al. evaluate how the outbreak of MERS affects Chinese tourists to South Korea [12].

The COVID-19 pandemic also belongs to a research hotspot in inbound tourism. Some scholars, such as Johan et al. and Zhang et al. have studied the impact of COVID-19 on inbound tourism and developed an imported risk index under the background of COVID-19 [13, 14]. Others, such as Sun et al., analyzed the main tourism factors causing the COVID-19 outbreak [15]. Based on the research conclusions, some scholars have put forward recommendations on pandemic prevention and control for inbound tourism. There is no doubt that COVID-19, as a serious negative factor, has had an impact on the global inbound tourism industry. Tourism academia might start from the actual needs and guide the practice through theoretical research, to put forward countermeasures for the development of inbound tourism in the post-pandemic period.

4.4.4 Demand and Forecast of Inbound Tourists

Predicting demands and motivations of inbound tourists through price, cost and other factors are always the topics of scholars' attention. They usually construct different demand models for analysis. Seetanah et al., Claveria et al., Kim et al., etc., start with various levels of international tourism demand and research tourist attraction and key demand factors [16–18]. In addition, Song et al. found that seasonal factors are a major focus of tourism demand analysis in their research [19]. Peng et al. explore the relationship between the accuracy of a tourism demand forecasting model, data characteristics and research characteristics [20].

In the era of globalization, the needs of inbound tourists are constantly changing and unpredictable. For each tourism enterprise, accurate prediction of inbound tourists' demand is the key to their sustainable development. Therefore, such a hot research area is worth exploring in any context, especially in the current situation of the normalization of pandemic prevention and control.

4.4.5 Service and Marketing of Inbound Tourism

As marketing strategies and service contents adopted by tourism destinations are different, the impact on inbound tourists will also be diverse. Some scholars, for example, Kim et al., have conducted relevant surveys based on this field [21]. They investigate the factors affecting the brand image of inbound tourism destinations of Korea, finding that marketing strategies such as price, word of mouth, and advertising have positive impacts on the shaping of destination brands. Chen et al. put forward the shortcomings of services around three major service contents of group tourism in their research [22]. Their research takes inbound group tourists from mainland China to Macau as their research object and investigates the shortcomings of services received by these tourists. Shapoval et al. use a data mining tool to analyze the behavior of inbound tourists to better develop effective destination marketing strategies in the future [23].

Overall, although many inbound tourism marketing strategies and tools have been designed and applied, there is still a lack of research on services and marketing in the context of COVID-19. Thus, they may need to become the focus of scholars' attention in the future.

4.4.6 Consumption Behavior and Psychology of Inbound Tourists

Satisfaction, loyalty, well-being, dining experience are keywords that belong to tourists' consumption behavior and psychology. With the widespread appearance of these keywords, studies on individual travel consumers are gaining more and more attention. Musa et al. conducted an in-depth survey on medical service satisfaction of inbound tourists visiting Kuala Lumpur for treatment [24]. From the perspective of the influence of tourists' perceived value on behavior intentions in large-scale activities, Wang et al. did a comprehensive analysis of perceived value and behavioral characteristics of inbound tourists and local tourists [25]. Hussain et al. explored the satisfaction of foreign inbound tourists with the services provided by Chinese restaurants [26]. Abranches et al. think Guinea-Bissau's food and other products have brought happiness and security to immigrants from Portugal [27]. Chen et al. analyze the issue of whether happy inbound tourism destinations would bring happiness to tourists [28].

Research on inbound tourism has long been based on a macro perspective. In recent years, more studies on the micro-level of inbound tourism consumers have emerged, which indicates that the research on inbound tourism is more focused and closer to reality. However, other aspects such as inbound tourists' perceptions under the COVID-19 pandemic, still require further attention. After all, a deeper understanding of individuals at the micro-level is more conducive to the development of macro strategies.

4.4.7 Immigrants and Cross-border Tourists

Inbound tourism is a combination of cross-border tourism and transnational tourism. Immigrants also belong to the category of inbound tourists, so immigrants and cross-border tourists are also the research hotspots in global inbound tourism. Wong et al. investigate the motivation of British and Japanese retirees to regard Malaysia as their international second hometown [29]. Huang et al. take Chinese Americans as the research object and investigate the experiences of second-generation immigrants' transnational tourism and leisure [30]. Seetaram et al. explore the connection between immigration and international inbound tourism by explaining dummy variables such as income, real exchange rates, and airfare prices [31]. Balli et al. find in their research that inbound tourists from various countries are affected by the number of immigrants to the country [32]. The above studies show that scholars are interested in the links between immigrants and inbound tourism, as well as the impact of immigration.

4.5 *Relationships Among Research Hotspots*

Scholars discuss the phenomena existing in the field of inbound tourism from different perspectives, covering a wide range of themes such as:

- Consumption behavior and psychology of inbound tourists.
- Service and marketing of inbound tourism.
- Natural environment of inbound tourism destination.
- The influence of negative social factors on inbound tourism.
- Service and marketing of inbound tourism.
- Demand and forecast of inbound tourists.
- Consumption behavior and psychology of inbound tourists.
- Representatives of new inbound tourism formats such as 'inbound ecological and medical tourism'.

Since 'immigrants and cross-border tourists' refers to the flow between inbound tourists and inbound tourism destinations and is viewed as a bridge between them, so it belongs to the research field of either.

Figure 7 shows the various levels and connections among the research hotspots of inbound tourism, with the colors of circles from dark to light representing the levels from high to low. The outer circle is at the first level and contains all fields of inbound tourism studies. The two inner circles at the second level are 'inbound tourism destination' and 'inbound tourists', representing two mainstream directions of inbound tourism studies. The seven research hotspots are at the third level and are mainly discussed by scholars based on the two mainstream directions. Some of these research hotspots partially overlap with each other. For example, the intersection of 'natural environment of inbound tourism destination' and 'consumption behavior and psychology of inbound tourists' represents relevant studies on the perception and evaluation of inbound tourists to inbound tourism destination environment; the intersection of 'the influence of negative social factors on inbound tourism' and 'demand and forecast of inbound tourists' represents relevant studies on the influence of negative social factors on consumers' motivation and demand.

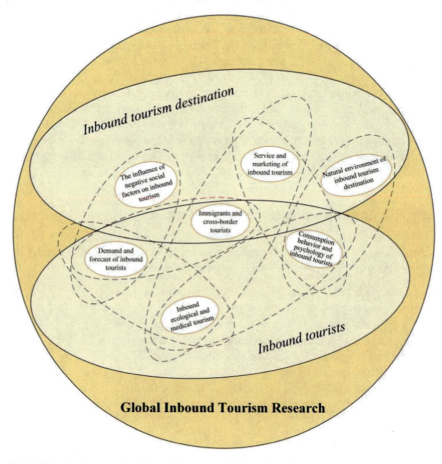

Fig. 7 Relational network of research hotspots on inbound tourism

In the future, scholars may still start from the two mainstream directions of inbound tourism destination and inbound tourists. However, more in-depth and detailed research around different fields or cross-fields may need to be carried out. The research topics may need to be continuously expanded so that to extend more branches and to make the research system of inbound tourism more diverse. In addition, these research areas may also have new theoretical and practical value in the context of the normalization of pandemic prevention and control. Making it very meaningful to discuss traditional hot topics based on the context of the new era.

5 Conclusion

It is apparent that cross-border tourism is still in a hard situation as some countries could not be open the border to foreigners to prevent the potential COVID-19 infection. But the research field is opposite for the quite bright future and new issues of inbound tourism. This study tries to visualize and analyze the basic characteristics of articles and research hotspots of inbound tourism.

Firstly, the research on global inbound tourism could be divided into three stages. The number of articles published in each new stage was a great leap, the average number of articles published between 2017 and 2020 is 152. In 2020, the number of publications reaches its highest level, with many excellent works related to the COVID-19 outbreak.

Secondly, the United States, England, China, and other countries with high international influence are the main forces of inbound tourism research, while other countries or regions are less involved in this field. Among research institutions or authors, only a partially centralized and overall decentralized cooperative network has been formed, indicating that their cooperative relationships are not close, and they tend to conduct independent research.

Finally, through cluster analysis, this paper summarizes 2 main directions and 7 hotspots of inbound tourism research. The results show that they are closely related to each other. At the same time, the relationship between the pandemic and inbound tourism research has been discussed. Among them, studies on the impact of the pandemic as a negative factor on inbound tourism are common. Few studies discuss the needs, marketing, and individual behaviors of inbound tourists during the pandemic. Therefore, to provide theoretical contribution and practical enlightenment for the development of inbound tourism, more reflections on these aspects may need to be made.

In terms of future research directions, the selection of databases and journals could not be limited to the scope of Web of Science and core journals. Master's and Doctoral thesis and related monographs may also be considered, which are conducive to improving the objectivity and scientific basis of data. Moreover, in the application of software functions in the future, scholars could try to apply more data processing software, to enrich the content of bibliometric analysis on inbound tourism. What's more, inbound tourism research could be compared with relevant conference topics and expert interviews, to analyze the correlation between theoretical research and practical topics.

Acknowledgements This paper was supported by the funds of:
 1. Study on measurement of development level of beautiful China and the influence on quality and quantity change of inbound tourism flow, the National Social Science Fund of China, No. 19BJY207;
 2. Study on International Tourism Attraction of National Image of Beautiful China, the Major Cultivation Project of Central Universities, South China University of Technology, No. 2020ZDPY16;
 3. Study on the International Tourism Attraction of the City Image of Guangdong-Hong Kong-Macao Greater Bay Area, the Double First-class University Project, South China University of Technology, No. K5201100;
 4. Graduate Education Innovation Program "Exploring Research on the Teaching Reform of International Education for Graduate Students Majoring in Tourism Management", Department of Education of Guangdong Province, China, No. 2017JGXM-ZD03;
 5. The project of Guangzhou City University of technology, Guangdong Provincial first-class major in Business Administration, the project of Guangdong Provincial Excellent Professional Program of Business Administration;
 6. The projects of Guangzhou City University of Technology, No. 57-CQ190050, No. 57JY200305.
 7. Research on International Education Cooperation of Tourism Management Major in Double First-class Universities, Recruit Program of Foreign Experts, Department of Science and Technology of Guangdong Province (Social Science), No. 2020A1414010017

References

1. Wang, C.: Research progress of China's inbound tourism since 2000—based on the visual analysis of knowledge graph. J. Hubei Univ. Arts Sci. **40**(11), 20–24+43 (2019)
2. You, Y., Liu, H.: Research on hot spot and development of inbound tourism based on CiteSpace. Xinjiang Finance **05**, 41–49 (2018)
3. Yao, X., Xu, C., Li, J., et al.: Establishing the user base of core candidate authors of a sci-tech journal based on Price Law and Pareto' s Law and online submission system. Acta Editologica **29**(01), 64–66 (2017)
4. Pintassilgo, P., Rossello, J., Santana-Gallego, M., et al.: The economic dimension of climate change impacts on tourism: the case of Portugal. Sustainability **22**(4), 685–769 (2016)
5. Yang, Y., Chen, G.: In search of fresher air: The influence of relative air quality on vacationers' perceptions of destinations' restorative qualities. Int. J. Tour. Res. (2020)
6. Zhou, X., Jiménez, Y., Rodríguez, J., et al.: Air pollution and tourism demand: A case study of Beijing, China. Int. J. Tour. Res. **21**(6) (2019)
7. Dong, D., Xu, X., Wong, Y.: Estimating the impact of air pollution on inbound tourism in China: An analysis based on regression discontinuity design. Sustainability **11**(6), 1–18 (2019)
8. Tang, J., Yuan, X., Ramos, V., et al.: Does air pollution decrease inbound tourist arrivals? The case of Beijing. Asia Pac. J. Tour. Res. **24**(6) (2019)
9. Ruan, W., Kang, S., Song, H.: Applying protection motivation theory to understand international tourists' behavioural intentions under the threat of air pollution: A case of Beijing, China. Curr. Issues Tour. **23**(16)(2020)
10. Drakos, K.: Regional effects of terrorism on tourism in three mediterranean countries. J. Conflict Resolut. **47**(5), 621–641 (2003)

11. Saha, S., Yap, G.: The moderation effects of political instability and terrorism on tourism development. J. Travel Res. **53**(4), 509–521 (2014)
12. Shi, W., Li, K.: Impact of unexpected events on inbound tourism demand modeling: evidence of Middle East Respiratory Syndrome outbreak in South Korea. Asia Pac. J. Tour. Res. **22**(3) (2017)
13. Johan, F., Jaume, R., María, S.: Fatal attraction: how security threats hurt tourism. J. Travel Res. **59**(2), 209–219 (2020)
14. Zhang, L., Yang, H., Wang, K., et al. Measuring imported case risk of COVID-19 from inbound international flights—a case study on China. J. Air Transp. Manag. **89** (2020)
15. Sun, Z., He, G., Huang, N, et al.: Impact of the inflow population from outbreak areas on the COVID-19 Epidemic in Yunnan province and the recommended control measures: a preliminary study. Frontiers in Public Health (2020)
16. Seetanah, B., Durbarry, R., Ragodoo, J.: Using the panel cointegration approach to analyse the determinants of tourism demand in South Africa. Tour. Econ. **16**(3), 715–729 (2010)
17. Claveria, O., Monte, E., Torra, S.: Common trends in international tourism demand: are they useful to improve tourism predictions? Tour. Manag. Perspect. **16** (2015)
18. Kim, J., Lee, C.: Role of tourism price in attracting international tourists: the case of Japanese inbound tourism from South Korea. J. Destin. Mark. Manag. **6**(1), 76–83 (2016)
19. Song, H., Li, G.: Tourism demand modelling and forecasting—a review of recent research. Tour. Manag. **29**(2) (2007)
20. Peng, B., Song, H., Crouch, G.: A meta-analysis of international tourism demand forecasting and implications for practice. Tour. Manag. **45** (2014)
21. Kim, H., Lee, T.: Brand equity of a tourist destination. Sustainability **10**(2) (2018)
22. Chen, H., Weiler, B., Young, M.: Examining service shortfalls—a case study of Chinese group package tours to Australia. J. Vacat. Mark. **24**(4), 371–386 (2018)
23. Shapoval, V., Wang, M., Hara, T., et al.: Data mining in tourism data analysis: inbound visitors to Japan. J. Travel Res. **57**(3), 310–323 (2018)
24. Musa, G., Doshi, D., Wong, K., et al.: How satisfied are inbound medical tourists in Malaysia? A study on private hospitals in Kuala Lumpur. J. Travel. Tour. Mark. **29**(7) (2012)
25. Wang, C., Lu, L., Xia, Q.: Impact of tourists' perceived value on behavioralintention for mega events: analysis of inbound and domestic tourists at Shanghai World Expo. Chin. Geogra. Sci. **22**(06), 742–754 (2012)
26. Hussain, K., Jing, F., Parveen, K.: How do foreigners perceive? Exploring foreign diners' satisfaction with service quality of Chinese restaurants. Asia Pac. J. Tour. Res. **23**(6) (2018)
27. Abranches, M.: Remitting wealth, reciprocating health? The "travel" of the land from Guinea-Bissau to Portugal. Am. Ethnol. **41**(2) (2014)
28. Chen, Y., Li, X.: Does a happy destination bring you happiness? Evidence from Swiss inbound tourism. Tour. Manag. **65** (2018)
29. Wong, K., Musa, G.: International second home retirement motives in Malaysia: comparing British and Japanese Retirees. Asia Pac. J. Tour. Res. **20**(9) (2015)
30. Huang, W., William, N., Gregory, R., et al.: Transnational leisure experience of second-generation immigrants: the case of Chinese-Americans. J. Leis. Res. **47**(1), 6179–6179 (2015)
31. Seetaram, N.: Immigration and international inbound tourism: Empirical evidence from Australia. Tour. Manag. **33**(6) (2012)
32. Balli, F., Balli, H., Louis, R.: The impacts of immigrants and institutions on bilateral tourism flows. Tour. Manag. **52** (2016)

Printed in the United States
by Baker & Taylor Publisher Services